GOD CARRIED ME
THROUGH
—THE—
STORMS

GOD CARRIED ME
THROUGH
—THE—
STORMS

Alice M. Jackson

Note: All scripture quotations are taken from the King James Version translation.

Original idea concerning spiritual storms in a persons' life was inspired by a teaching by Christina Patterson, and in reflection of author's life became the book, *God Carried Me Through the Storms*.

God Carried Me Through The Storms
A Memoir

©2024 Alice M. Jackson
Printed in the United States
ISBN: 978-1-958923-33-7

Author picture on cover by Lanasia Diehl

Dedication

*I dedicate this book to the two
most important women in my life.*

To my loving mother, Mrs. Jearldine Johnson (Deceased), whom God called home on September 13, 2021. You left a legacy for your children by the Godly character you lived before us and how you exemplified your love for God. You were a mother who loved her children and the generations after them. You taught us about God, you were trustworthy, and had integrity. Although you didn't live to see this book to completion, I dedicate it to you! God blessed Mama to live ninety-three years. As far back as I can remember, she was a Proverb 31 woman. She took her children to church and taught us respect,

My Mother

values, and a good work ethic. She was an excellent mother, wife, and a hard worker. Her children still call her blessed.

To my mother-in-law, Mrs. Blanche L. Jackson (Deceased), whom we affectionately call "Mommy." She left a legacy of excellence and love. She was the friendliness person I ever met, and everyone she met loved her. Mommy loved her family and raised her children in the admonition of the Lord. She took me under her wings as a young adult after marrying her son and was like a mother to me. She treated me like her daughter, and people called us Naomi and Ruth, like the mother and daughter-in-law in the bible, because we were together so often. God called her home on June 12, 2017. She was a beacon of light wherever she went. Most people knew her from always sharing and encouraging others to live out her favorite scripture, Galatians 5:22-23 The Fruit of the Spirit. She faithfully tried her best to live all nine fruits each day until she departed this earth.

My Mother-In-Law

Table of Contents

Preface

We will all face storms in our lives. During our storms, you and I have the same God with us that the disciples had with them in the boat. Sometimes we call on people instead of God when we are going through storms. But we must be careful who we share our storms with. Someone in our life that we used to care about may be toxic and harmful. They lurk in our inner circles, and they endanger our inner serenity. The secret to personal growth is to recognize them and disconnect poisonous people from our path. Invest in dependable people. I call them Anchored Philanthropists.

"Anchored Philanthropist." They are good-hearted people who care about others. They encourage, support, and give hope. They are people who are selfless, empathetic, considerate, giving, kind, and gentle human beings who will be there in the good times as well as the bad times.

"Be not deceived evil companionships corrupt good morals" 1 Corinthians 15:33.

Three People to Be Aware Of: The Loquacious, The Inquisitive, and The Data Processor.

"The Loquacious" are people who talk nonstop. Instead of helping you through your storm, they will burden you with their problems and make you feel worse. They will wear out their visit while you are in the hospital with constant chitchat but will never offer a prayer or share a scripture.

"The Inquisitive" are people who are curious about others' affairs and will pry into the person's situation , then sit around and gossip to others about you.

"The Data Processor" The Data Processor is the worst. They will hug you while having a knife in your back, then smile in your face. They pretend to like you, but they are backstabbers. They will come bearing gifts when you are sick as if they are concerned about you, but underneath the façade, they only come to collect and capture information in their database so they can transfer and spread negative information and rejoice in your iniquity. Much worse, they will have you in the grave while you are still alive.

These are people who we should stay clear of, especially during times of storms. God will provide a hedge of protection from our enemies and a shield from their weapons. He will even cause our enemies to bless us.

When God inspired me to write this book, I didn't know where to begin because I had never written a book before. God let me know I was well equipped because I had the credentials for the job. My credentials would be my testimonies because I have personally experienced the storms. The stories in this book are about storms that I've gone through from my childhood and throughout my adult life. Why God inspired me to write this book the same day as I was to have a stem cell transplant is beyond me.

Why would He tell me to write "How He Carried Me Through the Storms" at such a time as that? I would soon understand after He performed a miracle after raising me from my bed of affliction after having stage three Cancer. God would demonstrate that His healing power in the 21st century still works. This would be the perfect time to look back and see how God brought me through my storms, so that I might encourage others to never give up while going through their storms.

As you read, it might seem as though storm clouds hung over most of my life, but I thank God that all of my good days outweighed my bad days. I've been a Christian for more than fifty years, but living a consecrated life in Jesus Christ will not exempt us from calamity and hardship. It could be a medical issue, family problems, marital problems, legal problems, abuse, or it could be the loss of a loved one or much more. It could be a spiritual, emotional, or physical storm.

Some immediately associate storms with being out of the will of God. It may be at times, but not always. The Parable in Luke 15:11-32 KJV tells us of the prodigal son who strayed from God. His sinfulness cost him a lot. He experienced storms while being out of the will of God, fulfilling his lust for the flesh in the world, but God was right there waiting to receive him back once he turned back to him. What about innocent children who have experienced storms of sexual, mental, or spiritual abuse? These are storms that can damage a child forever. Some storms just don't seem fair.

We will all be put to the test at some point in life. One of the worst storms we will all face is the death of a love one. Some storms come to test our faith. Job was a good man, but God allowed Satan to test his faith. It was a hard and painful test, but Job passed with flying colors. He lost everything he had. His health, wealth, and children, but he never lost his faith. Although his wife told him to curse God and die, he remained strong in his faith. Job 2:10 KJV—But he said unto her, Thou speakest as one of the foolish women speakest. What? Shall we receive good at the hand of God, and shall we not receive evil? In all this did not Job sin with his lips. God healed Job and blessed him with more than he had before his storms.

God allows storms to get our attention and to grow us spiritually, to build us, and to get glory out of us. There may have been many times that Job wanted to give up, but he held on and trusted God through the Tsunami of storms he faced. There were times in my life when the physical storms became so unbearable, I almost gave up. I was at a point where I prayed letting God know that if He was ready to take me home to heaven, I was ready to go. I had no fear of death because I knew I had a beautiful Inheritance waiting for me. I would have a new body that wouldn't be subject to sickness or death. But then I remembered Job.

I began repeating over and over Psalms 118:17 "I shall not die, but live, and declare the works of the Lord." God assured me that I would live and not die and finish the course that He predestined. With that assurance, I drew strength and remained steadfast during my pain and suffering. If I hadn't gone through storms, I wouldn't have a reason to write this book because I wouldn't have the testimonies to share and encourage others.

God extended Hezekiah's life and added 15 years after he prayed in Isaiah 38:1-5. I prayed a similar prayer when I was in distress, and I'm grateful that God turned back the hands of time, letting me live too. Whatever time God gives me on this earth, I'm going to live to please him and spread the gospel of Christ. Although God allows us to experience storms,

He promises to never leave nor forsake us; He is right there with us, demonstrating his love for each of us.

Some non-believers will conclude that God does not exist because if He did, why would He allow so much suffering in the world? God does exist, and He's kind and loving. But because we live in a fallen world, all creation suffers as a result of sin.

I thank God that my life has been filled with more joyful and prosperous years rather than the storms I've endured. It was during my darkest times that I drew closer to God. The storms in my life gave me the purpose to write this book that it might encourage someone while on their journey through life. I personally found out that I could take comfort in knowing that God controls my storms and His mighty power and unfailing love govern whatever comes my way.

Acknowledgements

There are several people who I would like to acknowledge.

First and foremost, I would like to acknowledge and give my deepest thanks to my Father God almighty, who inspired me to write this book. You directed my every step. You have carried me through many storms throughout my life and have never forsaken me.

There are many people who have made a difference in my life whom I would like to acknowledge. While writing this book, many supported, prayed, and encouraged me.

My love and gratitude to my soul mate, Morrow Jackson, who has stood beside me through thick and thin, through good times and bad, through joys and sorrows. Your prayers have encouraged and strengthened me throughout our marriage. Thank you for your listening ears and support during my writing of this book.

Thank you to my children Tyrone, Steven, Suhdeena, and daughter-in-law Teresa. Thanks also to my grandchildren Lanasia, Xaria, Jaylan, and Samiah, who sat and listened attentively as my sounding boards as I read story after story to you.

My gratitude and love to my siblings, Janice, Mike, Linda, Eddie, Ricky, and Cindy, who are a great component of the stories in this book and helped bring clarity to some of the stories. I love each of you, and I'm forever grateful to you all for being there when I needed you the most.

Thank you to my cherished friends Patricia Moore, Sandra Crudup, Bettye Edwards, Carolyn Gordon, and Cynthia Willie (deceased). You have truly been loyal friends.

Thank you to my church family for your prayers, support, and investment in assignments God has called me to.

My gratitude and love to Julia Buchanan, whom I met in the admissions office at the hospital. God appointed us to meet so we could support and encourage each other through the storms we both would face.

My gratitude and thanks to Cynthia Crayton for your compassion, support and concern. God chose you to walk by my side step by step through my transplant journey.

My gratitude and thanks to Dr. Brown at Moffit Hospital, my neurosurgeon, my oncologist, the Transplant Team, and my beloved Transplant nurse Vania Alabata who was compassionate and tirelessly labored during my Transplant. Also, thanks to the entire staff at Advent Health Hospital for their compassion and professionalism.

My gratitude and appreciation to Legacy Book Publishing, who tirelessly labored to enhance this project with insight and creativity. Legacy's professionalism and development of this book were significant components of my assignment to get this book out to the people who need it most.

Introduction

While writing this book, there were times when tears streamed down my face, and I had to stop writing because of the fleeting memories that flooded my mind. God won't always carry us over our storms, but he will be right there holding our hands while carrying us through them. He is there to fight against any demonic spirit or any circumstance that would try to intimidate, discourage, depress, or even try to kill us.

On my life's journey, I have endured many things that could have left me on a downward spiral or even killed me, but God had a plan for my life. God knew me before I was born. He gifted me to perform a special mission that I alone was created to do. He knew every trial I would face in life, and he knew my trials would push me into my destiny.

Some people have committed suicide because they couldn't rise above the hurt and pain they endured in life. Although I had caring, loving parents, there were some things that they couldn't protect me from when I was a child; only God could. As an adult, no matter how hard I fasted and prayed, testing times would come, but I knew God would never leave nor forsake me.

Part of our inheritance as believers is to be secure and know who we are in Christ and to have a feeling of righteousness or rightness with God. God lets us know that we have worth and value by the fact that he sent his son Jesus to die for us. Isaiah 54:17 tells us that no weapon formed against us shall prosper. Knowing this alone should give us hope that God will carry us through whatever storm we face in life.

Psalms 46:1-3, "God is our refuge and strength, a very present help in trouble" (NKJV), was one of the scriptures that strengthened and gave me hope during my worst storm. Deuteronomy 31:8, "And the Lord, he it is that doth go before thee; he will be with thee, he will not fail thee, neither forsake thee: fear not, neither be dismayed,"(KJV).

We should be bold and share our testimonies when the holy spirit leads us because our testimonies not only help us heal, but our story can be the catalyst for healing in others.

I pray that my stories will give you hope and deliver you from unbelief, un-forgiveness, defeat, condemnation, fear, inadequacy, distrust, insecurities, and whatever else you need to be healed, delivered, and set free from. I pray that you will begin to experience hope and healing and just know that you are never alone. If God carried me through my storms, He can do the same for you and give you ultimate triumph over your circumstances.

CHAPTER ONE

Early Beginnings

The year was 1955. I was born in a quaint town named Yuma, Arizona, on a cold Valentine's Day. Mama said I came so fast she couldn't make it to the hospital, so daddy ran up the street to get a lady who was a midwife to deliver me. I am the third child born of mama and daddy's nine children. Before meeting and marrying mama, daddy married a beautiful young lady and fathered four children. A boy name Eddie, and three girls named Juanita, Evelyn, and Louise. Sadly, daddy's first marriage didn't last but he loved all of his twelve children and we all became one big happy family. I was a vivacious, curious, and happy little girl in my early years. My parents were the best parents ever. Daddy was very protective of his children and worked hard to provide for his family. Daddy was a construction worker for almost forty years. He was also a skilled mechanic who repaired vehicles as a side job when construction work was slow.

Mama stayed home with her nine children while daddy worked. Sadly, by the time her fourth child, named JC, was

The Nunn Family

seven months old, he died from pneumonia. Years passed, but Mama grieved over JC for decades. Mama now had eight children, and she loved us. She regretted having to leave us to go to work when my baby sister Cindy was less than a year old, but construction work had gotten very slow for Daddy, and she felt the need to help Daddy provide for us children, so mama took on a house cleaning job. Mama worked while we older children were in school during the day, and she made sure the two younger siblings were in good hands at her friend Mrs. Hazel's home, who lived on the next block while she worked.

We never felt neglected because mama was home by the time we got home from school. Mama did domestic work during the day and to make extra money she brought her boss's laundry home and ironed it at night after we went to bed. Back then spray starch was unheard of; Mama used Faultless powdered starch and she would boil the powdered faultless starch and then let it cool for fifteen minutes. Then she would sprinkle the starch onto the clothes with her fingers, ball the clothes up, and put them in a pillow case and store them in the refrigerator overnight. The next evening, she would stay up late and iron the laundry. The clothes looked as though they had just come off the rack from a clothing store. A Cleaners couldn't have done a better job.

Mama was such a loving and caring mother. Although she worked hard, she cooked a hot breakfast each morning and a full meal at dinner time for her family. We had family fun times together every Friday night when Daddy came home from working out of town on his construction job. Daddy was a comedian in his own right. We would sit around the fireplace and Daddy would tell us funny stories. The stories were so funny we would fall on the floor laughing. Daddy also loved to sing and blow his harmonica. He sang in a quartet group when he was a young adult. The group traveled from state-to-state singing gospel songs.

We would end the night singing and praising God. Mama loved singing too. Her signature song was "You Got to Move." She would sing the lead while we children were her background singers, and Daddy blew his harmonica. Then Daddy would break out into the signature song that he blew on his harmonica called the "Night Train." Daddy would hold a water glass underneath his harmonica while blowing because the glass made the harmonica have a different sound. He would blow from the pit of his belly until the sound from his harmonica sounded as though a real train was coming right through our living room. We children would jump up and down dancing all around the room. I had so much fun with my family when I was a little girl.

I'll never forget that exciting day when I was four years old when Mama took me with her down town to pay for a layaway at Kress Department Store. As we walked in front of the big glass window outside of the store, there stood a tall pink doll standing in the display case. The doll was as tall as I was. She was a Patti PayPal walking doll with long blonde hair. If her hand was held, she would walk alongside you. Whenever she was laid down, her eyes would close as if she was asleep. In the 1960s, we had never seen a black doll before in our small hometown stores. I didn't care what color she was, I just wanted Mama to buy the doll. I was so excited, I jumped up and down begging and pleading for Mama to buy the doll for me.

She said not today but maybe another time. I was sad because I wanted the doll so much. I had never had a doll before. Since I couldn't have the doll, I asked Mama if she could buy me the piano that I saw on the shelf not knowing it was a Magnum Organ which was popular in the sixties. Mama's answer was the same; she said maybe another time. I was sad but had hopes that mama would one day buy me the blonde-haired, tall, and pink doll in the window. After seeing that doll's long hair that day I knew I wanted to become a hairdresser. This doll was already in God's plan for my future.

In the 1960s there was an income gap between races. Living wage earnings were low, and most black families lived at the poverty level, primarily because of their education level. Black men's jobs dropped sharply, and times were hard for most black families in my hometown, but surprisingly many black families were homeowners. We moved quite a bit because many times, Daddy would get laid off from his construction job for months at a time, but he would find a way to provide for his family. Daddy didn't have a great education because he was born during the great depression, but he had common sense and skills. No job was too small or hard for him as long as it was legal.

Daddy was a self-taught mechanic. He could fix a car just as good as, or better than, a professional skilled mechanic. He worked on people's cars as his side job to helped support his family. Daddy even collected and sold scrap metal. Those jobs help pay the bills when daddy was laid off from his construction jobs. Layaway back then was the thing that helped most black families be able to purchase household items, clothes, and buy gifts at Christmas time. Mama would put items on layaway, and it would take her the entire year to pay for them. By the time she paid off the Christmas layaway, she would turn around and put our school clothes on layaway for the following school year. By the time school started, she would have the layaway paid off.

Two years had gone by since I saw the doll in the window. I'm six years old and now getting ready to start school. The consensus in my home state in 1961 when I started school was that high-quality early childhood education can improve a child's economic and social outcome over the long term. But there were no funds allocated for early kindergarten. Therefore, all students had to begin school in first grade. I was excited about starting school. Mama was now doing housekeeping work for a lady who owned a clothing store in downtown Yuma. She was kind enough to let Mama choose five outfits each for Janice and me for school and allowed her to pay weekly until she paid off the bill. Mama had also gotten our shoes out of layaway from Kress Department Store. She bought all of her children who were in school a pair of school shoes and a pair of church shoes which had to last the entire year.

We had our choice of a pair of Oxfords or Penny Loafer shoes; I chose the Oxfords. Daddy would threaten to put cardboard in the bottom of our shoes if we wore the soles out before the year was over. Without having layaways back then, it would have been hard for some families to manage. My older sister Janice and I were sixteen months apart. Mama must have wanted twins because she always dressed us alike, although we didn't resemble each other. The Saturday before school started, Mama shampooed and pressed our hair to make sure we looked nice on the first day of school.

Monday had come, and the first day of school was finally here. Mama styled our hair alike in two ponytails and a bang. She made sure she took her children to school on the first day. My sister Janice and I looked so pretty in our new dresses and Oxford shoes. Mama had bought us five dresses for each day of the school week. She told us to make sure we changed out of our school clothes and put on play clothes when we came home from school.

Mama walked me into my classroom and introduced me to the teacher, then gave me a hug and left. I was excited to meet other children and was so happy when I saw one of my cousins in my class. Mrs. Clark introduced herself to her students and then called each student's name from her roll sheet. When she called our names, we had to answer "Here". In the 1960s there was still a lot of racism in my quaint hometown. I can remember, as I got older, the signs posted on some businesses saying "Whites only." I remember two places in particular. A movie theatre downtown allowed Blacks to come in, but they segregated the Whites from the Blacks. There was a sign inside the theatre that said "Whites only" that pointed to the main floor.

There was another sign with an arrow that pointed upstairs to the balcony that said "Colored's Only." I also remember a restaurant where black people could only order at the back door in the rear of the building through a window. A sign was posted on the door that said "Colored's Served Here." There were also restaurants who wouldn't serve Blacks.

Mrs. Clark was Caucasian but she never showed any prejudice towards any of her students. She was such a loving, kind, and caring teacher. She treated all of her students the same. I learned how to read and write in her class. My first-grade experience was great and I was promoted to second grade. I would miss Mrs. Clark and the friends I had made in first grade, but I was looking forward to going to the second grade.

CHAPTER TWO

Tormented By A Bully

The year was now 1962. I was seven years old. I was excited about starting second grade, and was looking forward to meeting my teacher and new friends until Mama sat me down two weeks before school started to have a talk with me. She told me that my second-grade teacher would be Mrs. Dailey, and she wasn't very nice to my older brother when he was in her class. She said she didn't want me to be afraid but wanted me to let her know if Mrs. Dailey ever treated me mean. At that moment, I became afraid and didn't want to go to second grade. The excitement I had was now gone.

My life was about to change drastically. This would be the beginning of a nightmare and the first storm that God would carry me through. The second grade would be one of the worst and most unforgettable years of my life. The vivacious, curious, and happy little girl that I was in first grade would soon be no more. I would become depressed and an introvert. Although I was young, the look on Mama's face as she talked to me let me know that she was displeased with me being in Mrs. Dailey's class. The day before school started Mama gave me a reminder. I'm sure Mama dreaded having to tell me such a thing as this, and surely, she didn't want to frighten me, but she just wanted to make sure I would be safe.

I didn't know what Mrs. Dailey had done to my brother because Mama didn't tell me, but from the moment Mama told me Mrs. Daily was mean to my brother, I became very afraid. I would soon find out the significance of Mama's warning. In our quaint school back then, there was one teacher for each grade, so it was inevitable that every child had to pass through Mrs. Dailey's classroom. Sadly, I was one of her students who did not escape her wrath.

On the first day of school, Mama prayed then walked me to my classroom. She made sure I was nicely dressed, wearing the clothes and shoes she had gotten off layaway, and my hair was neatly combed. We walked into the classroom, and

Mama said good morning to Mrs. Dailey, but she didn't respond back. She ignored Mama and then turned away as we stood there. I guess when she saw Mama's face, it reminded her of what happened when my brother was in her class. I sensed something was wrong and began to cry.

I ran out the door back to my first-grade class. Mrs. Clark was standing at her desk, and I ran into her arms. She grabbed me and gave me a big hug. Mama ran behind me, and both of them began comforting me, telling me that everything would be all right. Mrs. Clark assumed that I wanted to return to her classroom instead of going to second grade.

She hugged me and assured me that I would like my second-grade teacher. If only she knew what was really going on in that classroom. I didn't want Mama to leave me, but she told me to be a big girl and to remember what she told me. She walked me back to Mrs. Dailey's class while I was clinging onto her leg. She gave me a hug and guided me through the door. Mama stood there and watched until Mrs. Dailey told me where to sit, then she left. I sat there shaking like a leaf on a tree on a windy day while the teacher looked at me in disgust.

Mrs. Dailey treated some of the children differently. She made assumptions just by observing how the children were dressed on the first day of school to determine where they would be seated. If children were dressed nicely, she felt as though they were upper class and intelligent. She sat those children on the left side of the classroom near the chalkboard.

The children who were not so well dressed, she felt as though they were dim-wit indigents. She sat those children on the right side of the room. Although I was dressed nicely, she sat me on the right side of the classroom not knowing anything about me. I would soon find out it was because she wanted to have easy access to take her revenge on me for what happened in the past with my brother.

It's amazing how bullying can affect children. I had been in Mrs. Dailey's class for about two months, and she basically ignored me. One day I didn't understand my classwork and raised my hand several times, but she ignored me. I remember my parents telling us children that if we didn't understand our schoolwork to ask the teacher. I nervously stood up and began walking towards her desk; she stood up and met me halfway down the row. She grabbed me by my ear, twisting it really hard while digging her nails into my arm until I began to bleed. She pulled me down the row by my ear back to my desk, then slammed me down in my seat. I cried out loud while the other children watched in fear. She told me to shut up and then called me dumb. Back then, the word "bully" was unheard of in my quaint town. But now I know I was being abused and bullied by an adult and a teacher at that.

My teacher was supposed to help form the early stages of my life by nurturing, teaching, and helping me to grow into a confident child. Instead, she insulted, threatened, and treated me cruelly in an aggressive way. She harmed me physically, emotionally, and mentally. Each day before I left school, Mrs. Daily would always threaten me by telling me that if I told my parents or anyone else, she would retain me. If I was retained, I would have to repeat her class another year.

I remember what Mama had told me. I wanted to tell her so badly and show her the bruises on my arm, but I knew what the consequences would be. I didn't want to repeat Mrs. Dailey's class again, and I sure didn't want Mama to get in trouble, not knowing what her reaction would be if she knew what my teacher had done to me.

Daddy worked out of town during the week, but he was always home on weekends. Daddy loved his children and didn't play when it came to his girls. If he knew what had happened to me, there was no telling what he would have done. I stayed quiet and hid the marks on my arm because I didn't want to cause any trouble for my parents.

Mama and Daddy taught us to respect our elders. Back then, many parents believed the adults to be right over the children. Many times, adults would lie on children. I was thankful that my parents listened to us children whenever we had a problem and got to the bottom of the matter.

Mrs. Dailey was heavy and tall in stature. As an adult looking back, she looked to be more than six feet tall and weighed about three hundred pounds. She towered over my little body like a giant. Every time I would see her coming, I would close my eyes because I knew she was going to pinch me for no reason as she passed by my desk. I wouldn't say a word; I just sat there with tears running down my face.

Although she didn't give the children whom she deemed as dim-wits as much attention with their school work as she did the children who she thought were smarter, she did allow them to play at recess, all except me. I had to sit on the hot ground until recess was over. I was just a little girl and couldn't understand why Mrs. Dailey was so mean to me because I was a good girl and never defied her in any way.

That year, I went from being that vivacious, curious, happy little girl to a quiet, insecure, depressed, introverted child. I had endured name-calling, physical abuse, and being tormented the entire year by this teacher. I had become reclusive and frightened, but I made sure my schoolwork was completed each day because I did not want to repeat Mrs. Dailey's class. It seemed like the year would never end, but finally, it was the last day of school, and I was overjoyed. Back then, we were not allowed to look at our report cards. I couldn't wait to get home so Mama could read it and tell me if I was promoted to third grade.

Thank God I was promoted! I was extremely happy to be out of Mrs. Dailey's class. If I had to repeat her class, I probably would have had a nervous breakdown. Whenever I would see her from time to time during the next three years while in elementary school, I would turn and go in the opposite direction. More than forty years later, as I visited my mother one summer, I shared with her what happened to me when I was in Mrs. Daily's second-grade class. After hearing the horror story, it was as if I was still Mama's little girl. Mama was sad and told me she was sorry I went through the same thing as my brother did while in Mrs. Daily's class. Then she became upset and asked me why I didn't tell her.

I told Mama about the threats Mrs. Dailey made towards me and how afraid I was. Mama began telling me the story of how Mrs. Dailey abused my older brother when he was in her class. She said she confronted her about the abuse, and it angered her, plus she denied it. Mama said the teacher had to be an evil person to harm a child.

Mama began telling me the story of the day my brother came home crying hysterically, with blood streaming down his arm onto his shirt. He could no longer keep the secret of his teacher abusing him, so he told Mama what Mrs. Daily was doing to him. He said Mrs. Dailey dismissed the class that day and told him to stay seated. After all the children had left and he was alone in the classroom with her, she began tormenting him by calling him names such as ugly, stupid, and dumb and told him he would never amount to anything in life.

Then she began pinching him on his shoulder and then warned him that if he told anyone, he would have to repeat her class the following year. I wondered why she hated my brother so much. They say hurt people hurt people. Maybe she was physically abused as a child and took it out on other children. It's really sad that a person can hold a grudge for years against a person they dislike and then take out their revenge by harming someone close to them.

I was treated badly because Mrs. Dailey didn't like my brother years before I was in her class, but it sounded as though my brother was treated much worse than I was. Mama said when my brother walked through the door with blood on his shirt and explained what happened to him, she didn't waste any time. Mama couldn't drive, but she said she put on her shoes, grabbed Herman by the hand, and ran to the schoolhouse to catch Mrs. Dailey before she went home. Mama said she went straight to the office to speak with the principal. The principal came out of his office, and Mama told my brother to explain what Mrs. Dailey had done to him.

Mama said my poor brother was clinging to her skirt in fear as tears rolled down his eyes. He tried to the best of his ability to explain to the principal while shaking with fear what Mrs. Dailey had done to him. The Principal immediately came to his teacher's defense and said Mrs. Dailey would never hurt a child because she was one of his best teachers. Mama demanded that the principal call Mrs. Dailey to the office. She was still in her class when the principal called her over the intercom. Eventually, she walked into the principal's office, and when she saw my brother standing next to Mama with blood on his shirt and Mama looking like a raging bull ready to attack. Mama said she looked like she had seen a ghost.

My brother was so afraid. He held on to Mama's skirt even tighter while his teacher stared at him with her evil eyes. The principal asked Mrs. Dailey if she did this to this innocent child, and immediately she said no. She explained how she loved all of her students and would never do anything to hurt a child. She denied ever touching my brother or any other student. Of course, the principal believed her over a child. He said maybe my brother got in a fight on the way home from school and didn't want to get in trouble.

Mama said she was so mad at that point she could have wrung the principal and teacher's neck off. In Mama's anger, she used wisdom not to wring anyone's neck off, but she said she did give the teacher a piece of her mind before she left because she wanted to assure her son that he would never be hurt again by that teacher. Mama couldn't remember exactly what she told Mrs. Dailey that day, but whatever she told her must have put fear in her because she never touched my brother again, and she promoted him to third grade.

Years ago, I use to hear some Church folks say 'If you mess with my child I will lay down my religion, whip your behind then pick it back up again and be on my way.' That reminded me of the religious crowd who celebrated Jesus as the Messiah earlier in the week, by Friday there may have been some from the same crowd who shouted and crucified Him. They laid down their religion. Even in Mama's anger, she did not sin. I would hate to be the reason for a person to never reach their highest potential in life. My brother never graduated, he dropped out of school in the eleventh grade and at one point his life took a bad turn.

Who's to say it wasn't because of how he was treated from his early childhood by this teacher's abuse? Psalms 17:22 says, "A merry heart doeth good like a medicine: but a broken spirit drieth the bones. KJV." Being bullied takes away a person's self-esteem, joy, and beliefs in who God created them to be. It also crushes their dreams. It emotionally tears a person down to the point where their personality changes to someone who has no hope.

I always wondered what kind of childhood Mrs. Daily had that made her extremely dislike some children so much. Oh! With all the prejudice that took place in my home town, I failed to mention this teacher was an "African American" who was prejudice against, and tormented her own race. She mentally and physically abused her own race of innocent children who couldn't defend themselves. There were only a few Black teachers in our quaint town and I would think she would be proud to help all students, especially those of her race who she assumed were impoverished.

Every Black person in our quaint town knew each other because in the 1960s, blacks we were only allowed to live between First Street and Eight Avenue, which was about a five mile radius of each other in every direction, but Mama said no one seemed to know much about Mrs. Daily. She wasn't from our town and none of the Blacks knew where she lived, or where she migrated from. I say to all parents, "Be conscious of changes in your child's behavior, demeanor, and attitude when they are exposed to new people, places, or things." I was just a child back then, but this was the first and would be one of the biggest storms God would carry me through during my childhood because it affected me throughout my life.

I forgave Mrs. Daily years ago, but it saddens me to this day to think that she never took the time to know some of her students. Instead, she favored some and crushed others. Many times, those who abuse others have been victimized themselves. I was tormented by a bully who was my teacher and it affected me both mentally and physically. It would be years before I would recover from this storm horrific effects.

I pray that Mrs. Daily repented and got her life right with God. "Hebrews 8:12 KJV" says, "For I will be merciful to their unrighteousness and their sin and their iniquity will I remember no more." This was a terrible storm for a six year old child to experience but I thank God for carrying me through the storm.

CHAPTER THREE

Bullied By Five Brutish Boys

Summer was over and now it was time for me to begin third grade. I wasn't looking forward to going back to school because I didn't want to see Mrs. Dailey, and I didn't know if my third grade teacher would be mean to me like she was. Mrs. Martin was just the opposite. She was the only other African American teacher at the school and she demonstrated devotion and kindness to all of her students. I began third grade frightened and an introvert. Mrs. Martin recognized my insecurities at the beginning of the school year and began encouraging and pushing me to my highest potential.

She soon recognized that spelling was my strong point, so she encouraged me to be in the school National Spelling Bee Contest. I told her I was afraid, and she told me not to be afraid because she would prepare me for the contest. I said I would try since she was going to help me. She asked my mother if she could tutor me after school to prepare me for the contest and Mama said yes. Mrs. Martin lived three doors on the opposite side of the street from us so I walked to her home after school to be tutored.

I became Mrs. Martin's best student in spelling, but I would get nervous and begin trembling whenever she would call me to the front of the class to spell a word. I had so many insecurities from the abuse I experienced from my second grade teacher. Third grade started out great! My favorite cousin who was in my first grade class was in my class, and every day we sat together in the cafeteria. About three weeks after school started, my cousin and I were sitting at the lunch table when the fourth and fifth graders came in to eat.

A group of five brutish boys passed by our table and began teasing and calling us ugly names. Oh No! What is this? Do I have a sign on my forehead that says BULLY ME? I don't understand. I asked myself why this continued to happen to me. These brutish boys bullied us the entire school year. I was just a little girl who didn't bother anyone, so I didn't understand why people were so mean to me. When the third graders were out for recess on the playground, these boys would leave the older children play area and sneak over to the younger children playground to harass and call us ugly names.

The brutish boys were cunning; the teachers never caught on to their mischief. They would repeatedly threaten to beat us up after school if we told anyone. All my cousin and I could do was sit there and cry. Surely we weren't going to tell because of the threats these mean boys had made towards us. I was so afraid I couldn't eat my lunch, and my stomach would hurt every day. The abuse affected me not only at school, but at home too.

I began sleep walking and having nightmares. One night Daddy came in my room to check on me and I wasn't in my bed. He searched the house and I was nowhere to be found. He went outside and spotted me a half block away from our home nearing a busy road. He ran to my rescue and brought me home. The next morning, I couldn't recall ever getting out of my bed.

This bullying continued for the remainder of my third grade. By the end of the year, I had almost shut completely down. It was as though I went into a cave and never wanted to come out. Mrs. Martin always observed my personality. She knew whenever I was happy or sad. The little joy that I felt when I was around her had gone. She began asking me what was wrong so she could help me, but I couldn't tell her because of the threats the brutish boys had made.

The National spelling bee contest was nearing, but I was no longer interested in being a part of it. Mrs. Martin began encouraging me to cheer up. She began inspiring me by telling me I was a winner. She motivated me so much that I soon became excited again and was determined to win the contest. On the day of the contest, there were students competing from other counties, and although I was nervous, I was ready to compete because of Mrs. Martins encouragement. She had prepared me to be a winner.

I spelled every word correctly until it was two of us left in the competition. The last word to be spelled was "Faucet." I went first and spelled it "Faucett," with two t's. The boy spelled

Faucet correctly and won. Although I lost, Mrs. Martin made me feel like I was a winner because I didn't give up; I hung in there until the end. My self esteem rose to the top that day only to be brought down the next day by the five brutish boys.

I had become very withdrawn at times, even with my own parents. I remember swallowing a penny and thought I was going to die but I was too afraid to tell my parents. I also became rebellious and combative. When my parents went to work they left my older sister Janice in charge of the younger children. When my sister would tell me to do my chores, I would tell her she's not my Mama, so don't tell me what to do. I felt that she wasn't much older than me, so why should I have to do what she says?

At that point I was so tired of being treated badly by those who tormented me that I put up a shield and lashed out at the wrong people, who were my family. Thank God the end of the school year had finally come. All of those brutish boys will move on to middle school and I won't have to face them again until High School. Hopefully by then they will have changed their mean ways.

The sleep walking stopped shortly after the school year ended. Children don't realize the damage bullying can cause other children. Bullying caused me depression, anxiety, sadness, loneliness, and it affected my sleep pattern. It also caused me to lose interest in activities I used to enjoy. I spent lots of time alone; that's where I felt safe.

Bullying can negatively impact mental health and well being. It can cause depression, substance use, school dropout, and some students become violent and retaliate, and some commit suicide. It's hard to believe that by the time I was seven years old, I had endured bullying from a teacher and five mischievous boys. Who would have ever thought bullying was so prevalent in the 1960's, especially in a small town where most people knew each other.

My cousin and I were not strangers to these five mischievous boys. We were young, but we knew these boys' families and where they lived. They knew us, and we knew them. The leader of the pack was known for being a trouble maker. I guess the brutish boys made a unanimous decision to follow him and bully someone whom they scouted out to be their prey. My cousin and I would be their bully of choice for the school year. I wondered how many other children had they bullied. Bullying is even worse today, being that children have access to computers.

The United States is one of the three countries where Social media cyber bullying is the most prevalent. Today, mental health counseling is available for young people who are affected from being bullied, but in 1960's mental health was unheard of. I hope my story will encourage parents to talk to their children about bullying. Children should be told why it's important not to bully, and how bullying can affect others. Today's family structure is much different from years back when families would sit around the dinner table and parents would ask their children how their day was at school.

This gave parents and children an opportunity to talk and share with one another how their day went. It's also very important that parents let their children know how important it is to let them know if they are being bullied. Sometimes children are too afraid to let their parents know like I was if they are threatened by their bullies. Back then, I had no idea those horrific life storms would help push me into my destiny. God was with me along my journey and He carried me through this traumatizing storm that would also affect my life for many years. Romans 8:28 says, "and all things work together for good to them that love God, to them who are called according to his purpose."

CHAPTER FOUR

Dreams Do Come True

Summer had come and I graduated to fourth grade. I thank God for carrying me through that horrifying storm that made me feel like running into a cave and never coming out. God kept me, and I was overjoyed that the end of the school year had finally come and those brutish boys had moved on to middle school. That summer we moved to a new neighborhood in a big house right next door to my mom's mother. My siblings and I loved living next door to grandma. We loved helping her feed her chickens and working in her garden that summer. She had all kinds of vegetables that she shared with us. We had a great summer, but now it was time for school to start.

My fourth grade teacher was a Spanish male named Mr. Garcia. He was a nice teacher and I met many classmates who I'm still acquainted with to this day. How great it was not to be bullied. Although I still had my guard up, I began to flourish and trust people a little. I had become confident enough to make friends. I would see Mrs. Martin often and give her a big hug, but whenever I would see Mrs. Dailey I would turn and go the opposite direction.

Christmas season was fast approaching and it was grandma's tradition to bake homemade cookies for all of her grandchildren. She also gave us fruits and nuts in a brown paper bag every Christmas. I was excited that in a few weeks Christmas would be here. I never forgot the tall pink doll with the blonde hair in the window at Kress Department Store. It had been five years since Mama told me not today, but maybe one day. I never gave up hope.

One of the ladies that Mama worked for had given my sister Janice and I two Siamese cats. We didn't know the cat's gender or breed, but Janice named her cat Fluffy, and I named mine Puff. One day, as I rubbed through Puff's mane and discovered it was long enough to comb, I became my cat's personal hairdresser. I combed Puff's mane in different styles. One time, I put grease on it and styled it with the front going forward, so it would look like he had a bang. I also combed my baby Sister Cindy's hair too.

I didn't have bows to put in Cindy's hair, so I would rip an old sheet that Mama no longer used and made bows. By now, combing hair was all I wanted to do all day. I dreamt about having that tall doll so I could comb her hair too. Christmas Eve had finally come. Mama had cooked her entire Christmas dinner and she and daddy stayed up past midnight wrapping gifts. Our older brother Herman arranged a plan for us children to sneak a peek into one of our small gifts after Mama and Daddy went to bed.

He told us to be quiet as he led us down the hallway. We tiptoed with excitement and with our hands over our mouths to help us keep quiet. As we entered the living room, we saw all of the gifts that were beautifully wrapped under the Christmas tree. We could barely hold back our excitement of joy but we managed to keep quiet. Mama and Daddy worked very hard that year to be able to buy us eight children Christmas gifts. Herman told us children to find a small gift with our names on it then punch a small hole in it to take a peek.

The closer Christmas got, I began having dreams of playing with the tall pink doll and combing her hair. I saw two big boxes beautifully wrapped near the back of the tree. One had my name on it, and the other one had my sister Janice's name on it. We were obedient to our big brother and didn't touch the larger gifts, plus we wanted to be surprised when we opened the gifts around the fire place with Mama and Daddy on Christmas morning.

Years had passed since I asked Mama for the doll in the window, and I was a big girl now, but I was hoping that tall pink doll would be in that large box under the Christmas tree. On Christmas day December 25, 1964, my dreams came true! Christmas had come and we children were knocked out after staying up late peeking in our gifts. Whenever we would over sleep on Christmas mama would come in our rooms and wake us singing her traditional Christmas song "The Little Drummer Boy". The only words she knew were "Pa Rump Pa Pa Pum.. Me and My Drum". She would repeat it over and over again until we all woke up.

That was our signal to run to the tree and open our gifts. I ran to the Christmas tree and grabbed the two boxes that had my name on them. I opened the smaller box first and there was the Electric Magnus Organ that I had gotten a peek of on Christmas Eve. I knew Mama couldn't afford to buy both the organ and the doll, so I couldn't imagine what was in the big box. I ripped the paper off the box and to my surprise! There she stood. The tall, pink, blonde haired Patti Play Pal doll that I wanted so much.

I almost fainted because I was so happy. I screamed and gave Mama a big hug, then thanked her and Daddy for my gifts. I loved my doll so much! I combed her hair and took her for a walk every day. Then, I would lay her down just to see her eyes close. I no longer had time to comb puff's mane, or my baby sister Cindy's hair. I would sit and comb my doll's hair every opportunity I got in different styles. I was still very shy and somewhat withdrawn, but my doll helped me so much. I could tell her all of my problems, although she couldn't hear or answer me. This was the best Christmas I ever had. "Dreams Do Come True."

My Inspirations

The Christmas holiday had passed and we were back in school. Mama was back to her routine, pressing Janice and my hair on Saturday's. She decided to ask Mrs. Albright, who had been her hairdresser for years, if she could care for Janice's hair and my hair to help relieve her. Mrs. Albright agreed and we were so excited. Mama was relieved too. Now Mama would only have the two younger girls, Linda's and Cindy's, hair to care for. Mama still worked for the lady who owned the clothing store down town, and she also cleaned Mrs. Albright's home one day out of the week and took care of her laundry. Mama was a hard working woman.

Mama and Mrs. Albright must have worked out a deal because Mama didn't have extra money to splurge on beautifying our hair. Whatever she did, I'm sure it was a great sacrifice just so my sister and I could get our hair taken care of. She was such a great mother who gave her best to her children. I was glad Mrs. Albright was now my new hair dresser because I was tender headed, and every time Mama got near my ears with that straightening comb I would jump and scream then yank my head from Mama. I would even grab her hand if I felt she was getting to close to my ear. Mama would pop me on my shoulder with the comb and tell me to sit still. The many burns on my ears wasn't Mama's fault, it was mine because I just wouldn't sit still.

I loved going to Mrs. Albright's beauty salon. I felt like a big girl sitting in that big chair. The salon was always clean and cozy, and she was gentle while combing and pressing my hair. It wasn't funny then, but I find it to be hilarious now. July and August were the hottest months in my quaint town in Arizona. The summer weather would be 110 degrees or hotter. Janice and I had to walk home after Mrs. Albright pressed our hair. The hair grease would become heated by the hot sun and seep to our scalps. We had to run under shade trees to get relief.

I couldn't wait to get home to style my dolls hair just like Mrs. Albright styled mine. One day Mrs. Albright asked me what I want to be when I grew up. I told her I wanted to be a hairdresser and own a salon just like her. After that conversation, she began inspiring me to reach for the stars. She said I could become anything that I wanted to be if I believed in myself and worked hard to achieve it. She said I was destined for greatness. When I turned ten, Mrs. Albright asked if would like to help her in the salon on Saturday's if Mama agreed, and she would pay me. Mama said yes and I was ecstatic. This would be my first job. My responsibilities were washing combs and brushes, taking out the trash, and sweeping the floors. I enjoyed watching Mrs. Albright as she beautified the lady's hair.

Summer had come and Mrs. Albright's three grandchildren came to stay with her during their mother's illness. The children stayed in the salon with her while she worked. She kept them occupied by playing games and coloring. Her salon was attached to her home, so it was easy for her to go next door to feed her grandchildren lunch while her clients were under the dryer. She had a great rapport with all of her clients and they understood the situation with her grandchildren while their mother was sick. She would ask me to keep an eye on her clients while she fed her grandchildren lunch and told me to come get her if they needed her for any reason.

Mrs. Albright was such a professional lady. She had worked in the beauty industry for many years in our quaint town and her clients had much respect for her. After the first week of leaving her clients under the dryer to go feed her grandchildren lunch, Mrs. Albright felt this was unprofessional, so she trusted me enough to ask me if I would be willing to sit with her three grandchildren while she worked if it was alright with Mama.

She said she was just steps away and would check on us periodically. I told her I would if it was alright with Mama. I was just a child myself but I knew I could do it. Mama said yes. She knew I was a responsible ten year old girl. I had experience from helping care for my younger siblings, and doing chores around the house. I was so happy Mrs. Albright entrusted me to babysit for her grandchildren when I wasn't much older than they were. I no longer worked in the salon that summer, but I would start back working again once summer was over and her grandchildren returned home. I couldn't wait!

Mrs. Albright had our lunches already prepared. All I had to do was pass out the brown paper bags and wipe off the table after we finished eating. After eating we watched cartoons, played games, colored in coloring books and I read the children stories. Mrs. Albright paid me double from what I made in the salon. After summer was over and her grandchildren went home, I began working in the salon again on Saturdays. I missed the children but I was glad to be back working and observing Mrs. Albright in the salon.

I worked for Mrs. Albright an entire year and I learned so much before having to stop. My deepest fulfillment came from watching how she made her clients feel right at home, and how she took such good care of their hair. I appreciated the money and the skills I learned from her, but mostly I loved the encouragement she gave me. She told me to dream big. I just knew one day my dream of becoming a hair dresser would come true just like my dream of having a Patty Play Pal Doll. Mrs. Albright was my inspiration to dream big and work hard for what I wanted to achieve in life.

Two years had passed since Mama bought my Patty Play Pal doll. I had to retire her after combing her head almost completely bald. My older brother, Herman, was now seventeen and he also had an interest in doing hair. Herman was a big inspiration and really had an impact on me wanting to become a hairdresser. One hot Saturday afternoon, my siblings and I gathered on the front lawn under the big shaded tree as spectators to watch our brother conk his cousin TJ'S hair in Mama's silver wash tub. We watched as if we were watching a movie at a drive in theatre. I was enthused watching him conk his cousin TJ'S hair.

TJ sat in one of our kitchen chairs while Herman applied the toxic lye on his hair. He smoothed it out with a comb until it got bone straight, then rinsed the chemical out with the water hose as he leaned over Mama's silver wash tub. Herman kept reminding TJ to keep his eyes closed tight as he shampooed his hair. After shampooing, Herman slicked the sides of TJ'S hair down with gel and styled the top in a pompadour style which looked nice. He never charged his friends for his services, and thank God he never blinded anyone with the toxic chemical.

From the 1920's through 1960's, the conk style was very popular among Black musicians in the beginning and middle of the 20th Century with likes of Cab Calloway, Chuck Berry, Little Richard, and James Brown. Members of the Temptations and the Miracles sported the style. It could be worn in different ways. Some wore it slick on the sides and high on the top in a pompadour style, and some wore it all slicked back. Conking was popular with men back then.

My brother Herman wore his hair like his idle. It was conked with a high pompadour on top and slicked back on the sides. He was well dressed, cool, and could dance doing the famous split like his idle Mr. Dynamite James Brown. My sister Janice and I were going to children's camp that summer for a week and we wanted Herman to straighten our hair with the conk so it would be easy to manage. Mrs. Albright was still pressing our hair, but we were excited when Mama allowed Herman to conk our hair. It would be easier for us to manage when we got out of the pool.

I will always remember the great time we had at camp that year. The games we played helped me build my self-esteem, and taught me to trust others by relying on teammates to work together to succeed in winning games. God was still carrying me through my storms that I had endured at an early age. He chose Mrs. Albright, my brother Herman, and summer camp to help me along my journey.

CHAPTER SIX

Near Death Experience

That summer, shortly after returning home from camp, Daddy wanted to take us older children deer hunting for the first time. Mama and the younger children would stay home while Daddy and the older children went for the weekend. Daddy had a truck with a camper on the back that slept five. We were excited and all packed up ready to go. My siblings went ahead to get in the truck but I waited for Daddy. We had a gas heater that was inside of the fire place that warmed the front of the house. Daddy reached down to turn the flames down in the heater, and as he leaned down his pistol fell out of his pants pocket and fired.

I was standing right next to him when the gun fired and the bullet rick-a-shade off the fire place and went right between my legs. Daddy grabbed me and asked if I was alright. I was so afraid I was shaking like a leaf after the bullet had just barely missed hitting me. I fell limp into Daddy's arms and couldn't say a word for a few minutes. I told Daddy I was alright but I no longer wanted to go hunting. I couldn't bare hearing gun shots again. After consoling me Daddy said I could stay home. He apologized telling me how sorry he was. Daddy and my siblings went on the trip and I stayed home with Mama and the younger siblings. I was young and didn't understand why all of these bad things were happening to me. I would realize later that there's a purpose for every storm. I could have lost my life that day but God directed that bullet away from me. I thank God for carrying me through another storm that could have killed me.

That winter, another terrible incident happened at that same fire place. The same gas heater that Daddy reached down to lower the heat when his gun fell out of his pocket would be the same heater that I would be burned by. I used to watch Daddy light the heater. He would turn the knob, then strike a match and put it on the pilot light. The fire would ignite and the flames would soon warm the room. One night we went to bed with the house being warm, but we woke up to a cold winter morning. Mama had gone to work and Daddy was out of town working. It was cold in the house so I thought I could light the heater after watching daddy light it numerous times. I would soon find out that I didn't fully know as much as I needed to know about lighting a gas heater.

My older sister Janice was in charge when Mama and Daddy were at work, but I took it upon myself that day to warm the house. I turned the gas heater on then went to look for a match. I didn't realize that gas was escaping while I was looking for a match. A few minutes later I returned with the match then put my head inside of the fire place and struck the match. All I heard was a big boom and saw a blaze of fire. I was on fire; my hair and eye brows were singed. I screamed to the top of my lungs.

I was eleven years old, and Janice was only fifteen months older than me. Janice ran to my rescue and grabbed me from behind under my arms and ran backwards, dragging me to the kitchen sink. She held my head over the sink and ran the water over my entire head and face as I was screaming. I thought she was going to drown me. Water flooded the kitchen floor, and I was soaked by the time she put the fire out. I smelled like burnt chicken feathers. My eyebrows and hair were singed. My eyebrows never grew back the same but I thank God my hair grew back.

God protected my body because I didn't have a scar on my face. I appreciate my older sister Janice, who God had in place that day to rescue me. The bullet could have lodged into a part of my body and killed me, and the heater could have exploded and burned the house down with me and my siblings in it. I realize that parents have to work and sometimes can't afford to pay someone to watch their children, but parents should always give their children instructions and make sure they are safe before leaving them alone. These were near death experiences. Praises be to God! Once again, God carried me through a blazing fire storm.

Isaiah 43:2 KJV, "When Thou passes through the waters, I will be with thee, and through the rivers, they shall not overflow thee: when thou walks through the fire, thou shalt not be burned neither shall the flame kindle upon thee."

CHAPTER SEVEN

An Imposter

By the time I turned twelve years old I had become more trusting of people. But just when I began to let my guard down, something else would push me right back into my cave. The cave was the battle in my mind. The mind is the devil's playground and he tried his best to take me out before I had reached my destiny. It seemed as though the enemy's favorite time to attack me was during the summer months when I was a child.

That summer, Mama's church had a week's revival. A flamboyant evangelist who preaches redemption while traveling from town to town was the guest revivalist for an entire week. He was one of those preachers who the Saints say could really preach. I remember him holding his ear and dropping down to the floor on one knee like the famous James Brown saying, "I heard... I heard ... I heard a voice from Heaven ... And It Sounds like Jesus." The Saints would jump up and down and some ran around the church shouting. The church enjoyed his preaching so much that the Pastor invited the revivalist to preach another week. The man seemed friendly and had warmed up to a few members during his visit.

One night after service, the preacher approached Mama in a friendly way and expressed to her how well-mannered her children were. In those days it was normal for church members to invite guest to their homes for Sunday dinner, especially the Pastor and his wife. Mama was such a thoughtful and friendly person; she thought nothing of it when she invited the preacher over for Sunday dinner the last weekend before he left town.

What a mistake that would end up being. Mama took it upon herself to invite this preacher over for dinner without asking Daddy. And never mind this preacher said he was a single man. Mama introduced Daddy to the preacher and Daddy was cordial, but didn't have much to say at the dinner table. In a cunning way, the preacher asked enough questions to know Daddy and Mama's work schedules. Shortly after we finished eating, he thanked my parents for the meal and left.

Daddy was so angry at Mama. He wasn't a Christian at the time, and I could only remember him going to church twice during my entire childhood. He went one Easter to hear us children recite our Easter speeches, and the other time was when he attended one night at our church revival. I'll never forget the mothers of the church calling Daddy to the altar to kneel at the mourner's bench so he could be saved. They told him to call on the name of Jesus over and over again. After Daddy said "Jesus" at least one hundred times and nothing happened, he got up off of his knees and walked out the front church door.

Thank God! Years later, Daddy did give his life to Christ and was instrumental to the church that he attended by using his gifts and talents to the ministry, blowing his harmonica and singing. After the preacher left that day, I can remember Daddy telling Mama that she better not ever invite another preacher to put his feet under his table to eat his food ever again. He said he worked hard to feed ten mouths, and he sure wasn't going to feed a grown man. He told Mama all those preachers want is your money anyway. Poor Mama was only trying to do a good deed.

I can remember the time when we children were playing in the front yard when a strange lady and a little girl with a tube hanging from her neck walked in our front yard. We ran in the house and told Mama. We were afraid because we had never seen a tube hanging from someone's neck before. We were peeking through the curtains when the lady knocked on our front door. Mama opened the door and said, "Hello, may I help you?" The lady told Mama that she and her daughter had nowhere to live. She asked Mama if she had a room that she could rent for one month until she could find a place.

Mama stood there in awe as she watched the lady wipe mucus that was flowing from the tube on the little girl's neck. Finally, Mama asked the lady what was wrong with her daughter. She explained that the little girl had to have a tracheotomy. She told Mama that the doctors had to cut an incision in her daughter's throat and place the tube into her windpipe so she could breathe.

Mama felt sorry for the lady and her daughter. She told the lady she didn't have an extra room, but she welcomed them to stay on the front porch which was screened in and had a bed. The lady was so happy; she cried and thanked Mama. Daddy was working out of town but Mama didn't wait around until he came home to ask him if it was alright for them to stay on the porch. Mama had a big heart, and whenever she saw a need she would help. That's the person she was. So when she invited the preacher over for dinner, that was just another good deed from her heart.

I guess that preacher scouted me out from amongst all of Mama's children that night at the revival while talking to Mama, telling her how well-behaved her children were, because a day later, he would remember me by name. That Monday after the revival ended, my siblings and I were playing inside when we heard a knock on the door. Mama trusted us older children to look after the younger ones during the summer while she worked. Mama was also able to save money because Mrs. Hazel Cunningham wouldn't have to baby sit my two youngest siblings.

From an early age, mama taught Janice, Linda, and me how to change diapers, cook, clean, and care for our younger siblings. We were told to never let anyone in the house while our parents were at work, but that day, as we ran to look out the curtains, there stood the preacher whom Mama invited over for dinner. Daddy had left that Sunday night to work on a construction job in California, and Mama was still at work. We wondered what the preacher wanted, and why would he come back to our home after the look Daddy gave him at the dinner table. As I said earlier, children were taught to respect their elders. The elders were always right in most adults' eyes back then. We opened the door and told the preacher that Mama and Daddy weren't home.

He said he was getting ready to leave town and stopped by to thank my parents for being so kind to invite him over for dinner. He knew Daddy and Mama would not be home from the questions he had asked at the dinner table. Again, we told him our parents weren't home, but he asked if he could come in for a few minutes. If he only knew how Daddy felt about him, it would have been best for him to leave town as soon as possible. We felt that he was a nice man so we let him in. He came in and made himself comfortable on the couch. After being friendly and talking to us children for a little while, he asked us if there was a store nearby. We said yes and he said he wanted to buy us some candy before he left town since we were such good children.

My younger siblings got so excited. The preacher gave my older sister money and told her to take all of my siblings to the store and buy whatever candy they wanted, and bring me some back too. He insisted on me staying home with my baby sister once he found out she was asleep in our parent's bedroom. As soon as my siblings left, the preacher told me to come to him. I was afraid and just stood there. He kept telling me it was alright. He got up and pulled me onto his lap. I sat there trembling because Daddy had warned us about dirty men touching little girls.

I became confused. I didn't know why this man of God would ask me to sit on his lap. I was so afraid and didn't know what to do. He began assaulting me by rubbing my thighs and kissing my neck. I immediately jumped up and ran out the front door, forgetting my baby sister was asleep in my parent's bed. I ran six blocks without stopping until I reached the store where my siblings were. I was frantic. When I ran into the store, Janice couldn't understand why I left my baby sister alone with this man. I couldn't say a word. She paid for the candy and we ran back home.

I was horrified! I would have hated to know what Daddy would have done to this man if he knew what he did to his precious daughter because he didn't play about his children, especially his daughters. When we returned home, the preacher's car was gone but I was still afraid to walk back into the house. Thank God my baby sister was not harmed. She was still asleep in her crib when we went to check on her. The imposter preacher had left. I believe this man had every intention of raping me if I had not run.

Although he didn't get a chance to rape me, it caused great trauma. It caused me to run right back into my cave again. I can't imagine how children who have been raped must feel; I pray for those victims. When I had children, I was never an advocate of them spending a night with their friends or some family members because we never know if there's a child molester in the homes until something bad happens to our children. I'm sixty- seven years old now and can still remember this incident as if it were yesterday. Even other children molest children.

I never told anyone what had happened to me until about fifteen years ago. When I told Mama, she was about seventy-nine years old. Mama looked upset and thought awhile, then she remembered the flamboyant preacher. Her eyes filled with tears after hearing what he had done to me as a child. She felt bad and blamed herself for inviting this Imposter over for dinner. Then she became furious and wanted him prosecuted for what he had done to me. I told Mama the man is probably dead by now because it had been more than fifty years since that incident happened. He had to be at least in his late nineties if he were living. I let mama know that I had forgiven and released him to God a long time ago, although I never forgot what he did to me. I told her that I just hoped he repented for his dreadful sins.

While writing this book, I saw a movie about a man pretending to be a preacher, who rode into a small town selling healing oil out of his stage coach for one dollar a bottle. The people in the small town flocked to his stage coach to purchase a bottle of the fake oil. I thought about that evangelist who came through our quaint town. Instead of selling fake healing oil, he was selling a lie, pretending to be a man of God ripping off of the Saints. A true man of God would not take advantage of the church, and surely wouldn't try to molest an innocent child. He was a conman who had no fear of God. He was an "Imposter." There's no telling how many innocent children this pedophile assaulted while leaving his trail through small towns. I never knew what happened to this Imposter, but one day he will have to answer to God, if he hasn't already. That was a terrible storm that no child should have to ever face. I thank God for watching over me, protecting me, giving me a way of escape, and carrying me through this horrifying storm. Proverbs 18:10 KJV says, "The name of the Lord is a strong tower; the righteous run into it and is safe."

CHAPTER EIGHT

Good Times

I was now a freshman in high school. I was praying that I wouldn't meet up with those bullies from elementary school who were now sophomores. I had managed to dodge them until now. I was about to come face to face with the ring leader of the pack. The one who called me all of the ugly names and threatened me. I was at my locker getting my science book for my next class when I looked up and saw the ring leader walking down the hall coming towards me.

Me in 9th grade

I felt like putting my head in my locker or running in the opposite direction, but he was too close. I had come a long way from being the shy little girl in elementary school, but the minute he approached me, all the bad memories of him bullying me surfaced. My stomach balled up in knots and I felt like a third grader again. I was trembling and afraid as he walked up to me and said, "Hello." I was shaking like a leaf but I managed to say hello back. He told me that I had grown into a beautiful young lady. I told him thank you.

He then began apologizing, telling me what a jerk he was when he was a boy. He said he was seeking attention. But now, being a young man, he felt such guilt for how he bullied my cousin and me when we were children. I told him how much he hurt me and how the bullying affected me. He sincerely began telling me how sorry he was for hurting me and asked me to forgive him. He told me he was no longer a boy, but a man now and wanted to make amends with all the people he hurt. I told him I forgive him, but I had to get to class. As I walked away he walked beside me and continued talking. He told me he was going to join the Army as soon as he graduated.

By that time, I had made it to my class just seconds before the bell rang. As I walked into my classroom, I said goodbye, and he whispered, "Can I take you on a date?" I ignored him and kept walking to my desk. After that day, he would sometimes be waiting at my locker between classes so that he could ask me for a date, but I turned him down every time. I told him I was too young to date. Just the thought of going on a date with this guy who tormented me sickened me, although it had been years prior.

This guy tried his best for two years straight to date me, but I turned him down. He left and joined the US Army shortly after graduation. Finally, I thought I had gotten him out of my life forever. Shortly after he got settled at the military base where he was stationed, he began sending me letters and pictures of himself in his army fatigue standing in the barrack. I must admit, he looked handsome in his uniform. He must have driven by my house before leaving to get my address. I did not respond to any of his letters, but that didn't stop him from continuing sending more letters.

I had forgiven him, but what he did to me would not be forgotten overnight. I didn't respond to any of his letters, but I did read them. After reading his sincere letters for several months, I felt he was sincere and had matured, but I still didn't want to have anything to do with him. A year later, when I was a sophomore, I heard a knock on the door and opened it. There stood this handsome guy dressed in his army fatigue. It was the guy who bullied me. I couldn't believe my eyes; this guy had not yet given up on a date with me.

I was surprised to see him and was a bit shaken, but invited him to sit on the front porch. He explained that he was home on leave for fifteen days because his grandmother who raised him had passed. He began telling me his experiences in the army and how much he loved it because it had made a man out of him. Eventually, he asked me why I hadn't responded to any of his letters. I told him I was busy with work and school. He asked if he could take me out on just one date while he was home. After reading his letters, I began to look at him differently, more as a person than a monster, so I told him to wait there while I asked Daddy.

Daddy came outside and the guy stood up and shook his hand. My dad knew his grandfather who raised him, but he asked him his name and where was it that he wanted to take me on a date. A brand new restaurant that everyone was raving about named Kentucky Fried Chicken had opened on Fourth Avenue, so that's where he wanted to take me. In the late 60's and early 70's, there were still some restaurants where blacks could not patronize in my quaint town. Daddy said yes, but sternly ordered what time to bring me back. I told the guy to wait on the porch while I got ready. I quickly showered and got dressed to go on a date with the man who once bullied me. If Daddy had known what he had done to me in the past, I was sure I wouldn't be going on a date with this guy.

We had a nice date, and he was a gentleman while he talked and we ate our chicken, but the feelings weren't mutual. I could barely eat because as I looked into his eyes, I had flashbacks of sitting at the cafeteria table in the third grade, crying while my stomach hurt as the brutish boys bullied us. As he talked, I didn't hear a word he said until he told me the next time he came home, he would like to take me on a real, fancy date. I thanked him for the date, but I didn't want to give him any hopes of thinking we could be boy and girl friend, so I told him we could be friends, but my interest wasn't the same as his.

He had tried so hard to get this date, but now I guess he felt defeated. He looked sad and didn't say much after that. He took me home; we shook hands and said our goodbyes. He seemed really emotional as he walked away, then he drove off. Years later, after I had my daughter, I realized that when some boys like a girl, they don't know how to approach her, so they will do silly or hurtful things to get her attention. This guy probably had a crush on me since third grade but was young and dumb, and didn't know how to say I like you, so he used his posse to help get my attention in the wrong way. I felt it still bothered him and he wanted to make up for the hurt he caused me. That would be my last time seeing him.

He continued writing me letters, but I didn't want to lead him on, so I never answered and soon he stopped writing. Years later I was told he left the army and had become a Radical Christian. While he was sharing the gospel of Christ to an unbeliever, he was murdered because the person didn't want to hear anything about God's word. I was sad to hear such devastating news, but I was glad to know he had given his life to Christ.

Some things that we experience in life is not about us. It's to help someone else who is lost or is strengthened by observing our strength. I'll never forget a lady who was much older than me, whom I looked up to, told me that she was drawing strength from me while we were going through the same storm. I wondered if I had given up, would she have given up? We never know who's watching us.

Even through our weary times when we don't see a way out, we can trust God. Instead of falling back into that cave where we feel secure when trouble arises, we should fall into the security of Jesus' everlasting arms. Maybe, by this guy being a bully at such a young age, it caused him to repent and give his life to Christ in his adult years. I thank God he allowed this young man and I to reunite so we both would have the opportunity to forgive and mend our differences. This was a devastating storm that I endured with the brutish boys while in elementary school, but if it caused one of the boys to repent and give his life to Christ in his adulthood, it was worth going through the torment. I thanked God for carrying me through another childhood storm. Luke 23:34 – KJV says, "Then said Jesus, Father, forgive them; for they know not what they do."

It's was now 1971 and I was in the eleventh grade. I had blossomed into a young lady and had begun enjoying my teenage life. My self-esteem had flourished, and God had increased my trust in people. I had met three girls and one became my best friend. Carolyn Robinson and I had a lot in common. We both came from big families, were in the eleventh grade, and were involved in almost every high school sport. Carolyn and I decided to enter the high school talent show. We decided that we would wear matching outfits. Carolyn was young, but she was an awesome seamstress. She designed and sewed our outfits on her sewing machine.

We wore lavender-colored knickers and a long matching vest paired with a black satin long-sleeved shirt. We also wore black knee-high boots, which were popular in the seventies. My hair was parted down the middle into two pony tails on the sides with two afro puffs attached. Carolyn combed her hair into one pony tail with an afro puff attached at the back of her head. Afros and Afro puff hairstyles were popular among the young people in the 70's. I lived around the block from Carolyn, so we rehearsed for an entire month at her house in her bedroom, perfecting our dance moves. A week before the talent show, I met this guy at our high school dance when he asked me to be in the dance contest with him. He was handsome, respectful, and smooth. I invited him to come watch our performance in the talent show.

The night of the talent show had finally come. Several students performed their acts ahead of us, so that gave us time to rehearse our dance moves behind stage. Finally, we knew we were going to be called out next to perform, so we calmed ourselves down. The teacher announced to the audience, "Next to the stage is Alice Nunn and Carolyn Robinson, performing the song 'Want Ads' By the Honey Cone." The song was the number-one pop song on the Billboard in 1971.

There was this black guy who was the smoothest guy on campus because he had a voice that sounded exactly like the great Smokey Robinson. He was a true performer, but that didn't matter because we were determined to win the talent show that night. We had practiced our dance steps and learned the song so we would be able to lip sync it perfectly. We were finally called out to perform, and we were ready. We walked out with our matching outfits on and our puffy hair puffs. We stood center stage with our knee-high boots on with a newspaper in our hands until the music started. Once the music began, we opened the newspaper to the "want ads" section and held it up high, and began our dance while lip-syncing to the song "Want Ads." We didn't miss a beat. After we finished our act, everyone stood up screaming and applauding. We just knew we had won.

Next up, the teacher called the guy that sounded like Smokey Robinson to the stage. He walked out from behind the curtain dressed in black attire with a stool in his hand.

He placed the stool front and center stage, then stood in front of the stool with his head down. Carolyn and I were behind the curtains watching. When I was in fifth grade, I had a crush on this guy, but he never knew because I was always so shy. My feelings for him had subsided by the time I reached middle school, and he was now dating one of the girls who became my friend. He stood there a few seconds with the microphone in his hand and then walked off stage. Everyone thought he had chickened out.

He came back stage and grabbed me by the hand. He ushered me to the stage and helped me sit on the stool. The music began to play, and he put the microphone to his mouth and began singing one of Smokey Robinson's most popular songs, "Ooo Baby Baby" to me. The girls went wild as he began to sing and I sat there like a stiff turkey. I was in shock! I felt like Smokey Robinson was singing to me. I also felt embarrassed because I had invited a young man named Morrow Jackson, who I had met at our high school dance a week before, to come see us perform, and he was in the audience. Plus, his girlfriend was in the audience.

The girls were jumping up and down screaming as if this guy was Smokey himself. He serenaded me, then walked to the edge of the stage and sang to the girls in the audience with his smooth Smokey Robinson sounding voice. The girls went wild; not only the Black girls, but the Caucasians, Indians, and Mexican girls did too. After he finished singing he took my hand, picked up his stool, and we walked off the stage. The girls were still screaming and I almost fainted. I think he knew I had a crush on him years ago and decided at the last minute to make me a part of his act. I later apologized to my friend and she said, "Girl, he would have done just about anything to win that contest."

Best friend Carolyn

It sounded like we were at a concert, but we were in Snyder Hall our high school auditorium. We knew by the screams and applauses that this Smokey Impersonator had won first place. Everyone began chanting his name over and over again.!"

Several teachers came onto the stage as one announced the winners. The teacher announced, "The third-place winners are... Alice Nunn and Carolyn Robinson!" Everyone was surprised and upset, including Carolyn and myself. We couldn't believe we placed third place after we had worked so hard. We should have at least won second place.

The teacher then announced, "The second place winner was the smooth guy who sounded like Smokey Robinson." I thought the students were going to stampede the teachers on the stage. Everyone disagreed and began booing because everyone knew he should have won first place, but instead, they chose a girl playing a boring song on the piano. Our quaint town still had some racism in the 1970's. We didn't win first place, but we had a great time entertaining the crowd.

Finally, the storms in my life had subsided and God had brought me out of my cave. I was enjoying my teen years and experiencing good times. I was once again becoming that vibrant, vivacious, loving and caring young lady, like I was when I was that little three year old girl. I was becoming the person God created me to be.

The 1970's were my best years, and I was enjoying being a teenager. I had left the Conkalene straight hair styles and was now sporting Afro wigs and hair puffs, which was the style in the 70's. This was the era of "SAY IT LOUD – I'M BLACK AND I'M PROUD." I was now dating the young man who I met at our high school dance. I can't recall why our school dance was held at another school in their gymnasium instead of our high school cafeteria, where it was normally held. And I'm not sure how or why these two college guys were allowed to attend a high school dance, but I guess it was predestined so we could meet.

His name was Morrow Jackson. As I mentioned, he was polite and respectful. He was also handsome, smooth, and well-dressed. He was a sophomore at Arizona Western College, and I was a junior in high school. I met him shortly after the guy who bullied me stopped writing me letters. The night we met, Morrow and a friend walked into the gymnasium and stood against the wall; it was time for the big dance contest. A friend and I were standing, waiting to see who would enter

Morrow and Me 1971

the contest and I saw this guy with his eyes focused on me from across the room.

He smoothly walked over to me and asked me if I would like to enter the contest with him. I was very shy but a good dancer, so I said yes, not knowing that this guy needed to brush up on his dancing skills. The music began playing and all of my shyness left. I was focused on winning the contest. We ended up winning first place by accident. I would soon find out that this guy wasn't the best dancer, but he gave it his best. He made a dance move that caused his feet to get tangled up and trip him. As he fell to the floor it looked as though he did a split. He then choreographed a smooth move as he slowly got up and continued dancing.

The judges were applauding because they thought he had done the James Brown split, so they declared us the winners. I learned since that time that if a man really wants a woman, he will come after her by any means necessary. I guess that's why the other guy kept coming back. This guy knew he wasn't a good dancer, but he wanted to win the prize that night and he did, which was me. My entire life changed after meeting Morrow.

I told my parents about him and my dad wanted to meet him. Mama invited him over for dinner and what a great time we all had. He was funny and was such a nice and respectful young man. My parents learned that he was a Christian and had moved to our quaint town to attend college. After talking to him, my parents found him to be an honorable young man and allowed me to date him.

Daddy paid close attention to him and was impressed at how independent he was. Not only was he a full time college student, but he worked at the Mesa Drive Inn Theatre at night, and Sir Georges restaurant on Saturday evenings. All of his friends lived on campus twelve miles from town, but he lived off-campus in town, in a nice little one-bedroom trailer that he rented and paid for from the money he earned from his jobs. He also owned a 1962 Alpha Romeo. Most college students lived on campus and didn't own a car. This guy was so independent.

We didn't see each other during the week because of school and work, but we looked forward to seeing each other on Saturdays to watch "Soul Train" together. Morrow would come over my house and we would gather in the living room with all of my little siblings to watch the dancers on the show. All of us would stand in front of the television and learn all of the new dances that the dancers were doing. A few times, I watched soul train at Morrow's tiny trailer house, along with six of his college buddies. We were crammed in his trailer like a can of sardines, but it didn't bother them. They were appreciative to Morrow for letting them come over to watch Soul Train because they didn't have televisions in their dorms.

Those were some fun times! God had brought me out of my cave. Morrow and I were young and full of fun. We both had big afros and wore the latest fashions. We had so much in common. We were both raised in Christian homes and had the same morals. We both wanted to date someone who didn't smoke, curse, or drink. Most importantly, we both wanted to date someone who was a Christian. What attracted me to Morrow was his funny way of making me laugh. I could also let my guard down because I felt safe with him.

Mama and Daddy really liked Morrow because he was such a respectful young man. Mama always invited Morrow to attend church with our family on Sundays and then have dinner afterward. Morrow loved eating Mama's home cooked meals because all he knew how to cook for dinner were hot dogs, apple sauce, and pork and beans. Daddy didn't roll his eyes at Morrow when he was eating Mama's good ole fried chicken like he did with the Imposter preacher. Morrow ate all the fried chicken he wanted.

My parents knew Morrow was thousands of miles from his family, so Mama and Daddy made him feel welcome, and Mama was happy to fatten up this skinny college young man. Two things that Morrow and I had in common were our sense of humor, and we both loved candy. We made each other laugh and we spent many hours sitting on the hood of his car talking, eating penny candies, and laughing. To this day, he still has a sweet tooth and makes me laugh. He stashes his candy in different places in the house for easy access.

Arizona Western College was a junior college, and time was drawing near for Morrow to graduate. His plans were to move to Florida where his family lived, so he could continue his education at a four-year University. This should have been a happy time, knowing the importance of him continuing his education, but instead, as time drew nearer to him leaving, it became sad and heartbreaking for both of us because we didn't want to part. We had fallen in love.

Before I met Morrow, I had talked to Mama about joining the U.S. Military. I really didn't want to join the army, but my parents couldn't afford for me to attend college and there were not many good job opportunities in my quaint home town, so this was my next choice. Morrow and I were young and hadn't known each other quite a year yet, but the love we had for each other in just eleven months was more than just puppy love. We knew we would miss each other tremendously. Finally, the time had come when Morrow graduated; now it was time for him to leave.

I remember the day he left like it was yesterday. As we stood on the front porch, he held my hands as we talked and said our goodbyes. I was standing there crying when my parents and siblings came outside to say their goodbyes. We were all sad to see him leave because he was such a great guy. Before he left Mama prayed for him, then we all hugged him and bided him farewell as he got in his little Alfa Romeo sports car and drove off. I thought we would never see each other again because of the distance between us.

We agreed to keep in touch regularly by letter because we didn't have a house phone. There was a pay phone a block from my job, so every Friday after I left work, I would walk to the phone booth and call Morrow. He was loved by everyone that he came in contact with. My Grandma Lula, who was my father's mother, was from the old school. When she spoke, we moved. She was the one who would say to my father, "Eddie, why are you allowing your daughter to date a boy in college when she is in high school?" Grandma Lula never said that about Morrow. She loved him, too, and expressed her love toward him.

After Morrow left, I continued immersing myself into my school work, sports, and my after school job at the Neighborhood Youth Corp where I worked as an assistant secretary since the tenth grade. I was hired because of my typing skills. I've typed ninety-five words per minute ever since I was in ninth grade, and I knew how to file. My responsibilities were typing, filing, and answering the phone. During the summer, when my boss wasn't in the office, she allowed me to hire young people for the summer job program. Working that job really helped me mature and come out of my shell even more because I had to face the public.

Morrow was living with his parents and had settled in college at FTU (Florida Tech University). Daddy finally got a phone for the house, and Morrow would call me once a week. I was always excited to hear from him. I was also happy that I no longer had to stand in the hot phone booth in 110-degree weather that summer to talk to him. I had decided not to join the Army, but continued working at the Neighborhood Youth Corp until I married and moved from my quaint home town to a big city.

After getting married, Daddy told me to call home collect once a month and let him know how we were doing. Back then, there was an extra charge for long-distance phone calls, and Daddy knew we were a young couple just starting out, so he agreed to pay for the calls. I was so happy being married to my prince charming; he made me feel like his Cinderella.

I know that by now, you are wondering what happened to Morrow, the one I loved in high school. Well, let me tell you my fairy tale story. Morrow and I kept in touch once a week for a long time, and then one day, he called and gave me the surprise of my life. After talking on the phone for a while, out of the blue he said four words that almost caused me to go in shock. "Will You Marry Me?" Thank God I was sitting down because I almost fainted. I literally sat there and couldn't say a word. He continued talking, letting me know that he tried to move on with his life, but loved me so much that he wanted me to be his wife. He said he knew we were young, but felt God chose me to be his soul mate. He wanted to fly back to Arizona and marry me as soon as possible. After the shock wore off, before I knew it, I said "YES."

I was still young and living in Daddy's house, so I told Morrow he needed to ask Daddy for my hand in marriage. Although I was young, I was mature for my age and felt I would be a good wife. Mama was a good example of how to be a good wife, and she taught me well. And I knew how to manage my money from my after school job. Morrow wanted to ask Daddy in person to marry me, but he was thousands of miles away, so he would have to ask him over the phone. He said he would call the following day to ask the big question.

CHAPTER NINE

Young and Married

Morrow and me sitting on car

Morrow had become like another son to my parents, and they loved him. They watched how respectful, mature, and responsible he was, and they had gotten to know him well. I was hoping Daddy would give us his blessing. Late the following evening, after daddy had gotten relaxed after a hard day's work, the phone rang. I knew it was Morrow because I told him what time to call. I answered the phone and told Daddy it was Morrow and he wanted to talk to him. I was so nervous because I didn't know what Daddy's answer would be, being that I was so young and how protective he was of his daughters.

While they were talking, I sat there listening like a pointy-eared Chihuahua while pretending to look at the television. Daddy and Morrow talked for quite some time, then I heard Daddy say, "Son, you've proved yourself to be a responsible young man, so YES, I give you and Alice my blessing because I trust you. You are both young, but I believe your marriage will work out." Then daddy said, "If you guys ever need Mama or myself, we will come on the fastest freight train." Florida was too far for Daddy to drive, and he sure wasn't getting on an airplane. I sat there wanting to scream.

Daddy talked to Mama and she gave her blessing. Morrow assured Daddy that he wouldn't have to worry about anything, and that he would make sure I continued my education. After hanging up, Daddy had a long talk with me, then he told me that he prayed our marriage would work out, but just know that his doors are always open if I need to come home. Our love for each other had triumphed over all the obstacles that had kept us apart. A month later, Morrow flew back to my quaint home town and we got married at Lutes Chapel, which still stands in the same place some fifty years later. Many famous people such as Betty Davis, Charlie Chaplin, Joe Louise, and many Hollywood stars married there. Mama and Daddy were our witnesses.

After we married, I teased Daddy, telling him he now had one less mouth to feed. After the wedding, Morrow and I sat in the back seat of Daddy's car while he drove through town, dragging cans from the fender of his car while blowing the horn. This was a common thing to do in the 1970's. Daddy drove by just about everyone's house he knew, including Grandma Lula and Aunt Leora's house. People ran outside to see who got married. My dear friend Carolyn Robinson gave me a bridal shower after I told her I was getting married. I would miss my dear friends and my family very much, but now I was married and on my way to Florida. That night we stayed at a local hotel, and early the next morning, we got up to begin the long journey to Orlando, Florida. I was looking forward to starting a new life with my prince charming, but as we drove further away from my hometown fear set in.

I felt like telling my husband to turn around and take me back home. I was going to the unknown and would be so far from my family. I trusted Morrow to keep the promise he made to Daddy, but it was frightening coming from a small town going to a big city, leaving my family behind, but I knew I would be safe with Morrow. As we drove, many questions began circling in my mind. I wondered if his family would like me or if they would be nice to me; I had not met them yet. I had only talked to his mom once on the phone. I would soon find out that my mother and father in law would be the most caring and loving people I would ever meet.

They treated me like I was their own daughter. My mother-in-law encouraged me and supported me in every endeavor I set out to do. Some people called us Naomi and Ruth, like the mother and daughter-in-law in the Bible, because we were together so much. She encouraged me to strive for the best in life, and to follow the path that God had set before me. She was my greatest cheerleader and such a positive role model for me to follow as a young adult. She taught me so much and I loved my new family. I had become a member of a large family like mine. I had gained a mother and father-in-law, a sister-in-law, and five brothers in-laws.

Years later, Morrow was now out of college and working two jobs. I was a stay at home mom to our two sons until my first son turned five. My mother-in-law encouraged me to continue my education, which I was determined to do. Since I was a fast typist, I began taking classes at Mid Florida Technical School to brush up on my typing skills to become a court stenographer. I had not given up on my dreams of becoming a hairdresser like my childhood mentor, Mrs. Albright. I believed my dream would come true one day, just like it did when Mama finally bought me my Patty Play Pal doll from Kress Department store. I also held on to my hopes of one day owning my own salon.

We joined Tangelo Baptist Church, where my husband's parents attended in our community. I became active in Sunday school and sang in the choir. In later years, I taught Sunday school, was Youth choir director, and the Youth director of the Youth department. I also worked with the media department and I'm still a member of WMU, "Woman's Missionary Union." Deacon James Moten was my favorite Sunday school teacher. He was a studious man and allowed the class to chime in on the lesson. He recently passed while in his nineties, but he taught the Adult Sunday School class until the Covid 19 outbreak in 2020. I was one of his students for almost fifty years. I loved my new place of worship and looked forward to going each week. The word of God taught in Sunday school instilled in me who I am in Christ, how to forgive, and move forward with life.

My husband has loved motorcycles since his early childhood. He bought his first scooter at fifteen; it was a Lambretta Scooter. In 1976, he bought a 350 Honda motorcycle. He's had many motorcycles throughout the years; he built a chopper, had a 500 Honda, a 750 Honda, a Magnum V-65, and lastly, a 1500 three-wheel Gold Wing Trike that we still ride. We were in our twenties when riding motorcycles became our hobby. We enjoyed getting away and spending time to ourselves riding in the wind, attending Bike Week in Daytona Beach and other surrounding cities.

My in-laws are a close-knit family, and they loved spending time together at the beach. Daytona Beach was our favorite spot. I was young and energetic and was looking forward to something I had never experienced before, not knowing that this would be my first storm since I moved to Florida. My husband wasn't fond of the ocean, but I was, along with one of my younger brothers-in-laws. He and I loved to go as far out into the ocean water as we could on our floats. After riding the waves for about an hour, my brother-in-law decided to go back to shore with the family, but I decided to continue riding the waves on my float.

All of a sudden, a big wave knocked me off of my float, and my foot got caught in the rope on the side of the float. No matter how hard I tried, I couldn't lift myself on top of the float. I was a great swimmer in high school, so my PE teacher got me a lifeguard job at the swimming pool across the street from our high school. I was a skinny little ninth grader when I jumped into twelve feet of water to save a big guy twice my size from drowning. But that day at the beach, no matter how well I could swim, I couldn't save myself. I was underneath the float drowning, and all I could do was pray within my heart. I cried out to the Lord to save me, and He heard my cry because another big wave came and pushed me to shore. My family was nearby when I was on the float, but no one noticed I had disappeared under water and was drowning.

I don't know how long I was underwater, but I laid there on the wet dirt for a few minutes, gasping for breath before I could untangle my foot from the rope. I began thanking God for saving me. I then stood up looking for my family and realized the waves had pushed me far away from them. I was still shaken while I walked back to where they were and told them what happened. It had been years since I experienced a storm. I could have died that day and left my sons motherless and my husband a widow in his twenties, but the hand of God was upon me. He wouldn't allow me to drown because he had a purpose for my life. You would think I would have learned my lesson that day and stayed close to the shore whenever I got in the ocean, but I loved the sea and enjoyed going out in the deep waters.

When our family returned to the beach the following summer, it was as though I had forgotten about the almost drowning the year before. I ventured out into the deep until I came upon a mound of dirt that I was excited to climb upon. I would later find out it was a "Sand Bar." A sandbar is built up by currents and can disappear with a change in tide or current. A few minutes after climbing on top of the sand bar, the water ripped through the sand and I began to tumble like cloths in a dryer. I had never heard of a sand bar or rip current before.

After the sand was washed away by the current, the ocean waters pulled me further out into the deep. Fear overshadowed me and I fought hard to swim out of the current. I thought I was going to die, but suddenly I heard the voice of God saying, "Be Still and Know That I Am God." At that moment, I received God's peace. I felt calm and my body went limp. After what seemed to be an eternity, I felt the hand of God carry me out of the deep waters.

A few weeks later, it was reported on the news that a college student died after being caught in a rip current. It was advised that if this should happen to you, don't fight the current but swim parallel to the shore and you will be able to swim out of the rip current. I don't know what direction I was facing that day, but I do know it was God who carried me to shore. I had only swam in swimming pools and didn't know the great danger and power of the ocean. My family was stunned when I told them what had happened. To this day, I have a great respect for the ocean, and you couldn't pay me a million dollars to go in the deep waters. I'm content in the shallow waters.

Some parents sit in their lounge chair while allowing their children to go in the ocean alone as they watch from afar. Things can happen suddenly and the parent may not get to the child in time. A wave can sweep over them and pull them under in a second. Our neighbor's son got stung by a jelly fish that was lying on the sand when he went to the beach with us. When my two older granddaughters were young, they wanted to go in the water at the beach. I held their hands and took them in the shallow waters. Suddenly, my younger granddaughter's foot went into a deep hole. The waves came over her head and she lost her balance and went underwater.

If I had not been there holding her hand, she may have drowned. Many children have died right before their parents' eyes because they allowed them to go in the ocean alone. The ocean is a fun place for families to visit, especially during the summer, but it has many dangers that could hurt or kill you, even in the shallow water. There are rip currents, big waves, sandbars, sharks, jelly fish, and even vehicles on the beach that can run over a child while they run to the water.

Although I was oblivious to God's grace and mercy when I was young, God rescued me twice from drowning in the treacherous waters at Daytona Beach. Since that time, I've repented because it seemed as though I was ungrateful to God for rescuing me, because I turned around and went into the deep waters again. I thank God for His grace and mercy and for watching over me when I was young and unaware of the great dangers in the ocean. I thank God for rescuing me from what I call two Tsunami ocean storms during those hot summers. Psalms 46:1 KJV – "God is our refuge and strength, a very present help in trouble."

CHAPTER TEN

Reaching My Goals

I completed my typing class at Mid Florida Tech, but I never applied for the court stenographer job. I worked several jobs before I had the opportunity to begin reaching my goals. July 1980 I became a student at Wilfred's Beauty Academy. I had the idea that cosmetology school only taught students how to shampoo, cut, color, and style hair. I thought the clients who were being serviced were our guinea pigs since they were paying a cheaper price at a school rather than a salon.

I had a rude awakening on the first day of school. The beginner students would not be allowed to step foot on the main floor until we had received three months of theory upstairs on the second floor. Only trained students were allowed to service clients on the main floor. Although the customers paid a cheaper price at a beauty school rather than an established salon, we had to give them our best service and treat them with the upmost respect. The requirements in school would be much more extensive than just the four services I thought we were going to be taught.

The theory class consisted of anatomy, chemistry, hair cutting, hair coloring, nail care, facials, makeup, salon management, and the state board laws. There were thirty two students in my class during the first month of school. A month later, half of the students dropped out. It wasn't as easy as we all had thought. The twelve hundred hour course to become a cosmetologist normally takes a year to complete, but I completed the course in ten months. I took the state board test a few weeks after graduating and was now waiting on my results from DPR (Department of Professional Regulations). I worked hard night and day while in school so I felt good about passing my state board test. I had a student license which allowed me to work as an apprentice. While I waited on my license, I decided to get my first job. I had previously met Mrs. Sarah who was a female barber at a hair convention.

She owned a barber shop near downtown Orlando in the black community. I had never met a female barber before, but I remember her telling me that if I ever needed a place to work she would be happy to have me work in her shop. I called Mrs. Sarah and explained that I had graduated and had my student license, and was looking for a place to work as an apprentice temporary until I received my license. She welcomed me to assist her in the barber shop and pay me commission. I never gave thought to ever working in a barber shop but it gave me the opportunity to assist Mrs. Sarah in hair coloring, shampooing, and keeping the salon clean. Working in her small barber shop reminded me of when I worked in Mrs. Albright salon when I was ten years old. Mrs. Sarah was kind and she always told me I did a great job.

All of Mrs. Sarah's clients were male and they were very respectful, all except for one. One day as I shampooed the cold black color out of one of the men's hairs while he laid back in the shampoo bowl, the fresh man winked his eye at me and smiled. It was such a shock because I had shampooed his hair before and he was a gentleman. I got nervous and the hose suddenly slipped out of my hand. I tried to retrieve it, but it was like a snake on the run. The water went in this man's eyes and nose, and wet his entire body. He jumped out of the chair and all the guys had a good laugh, even Mrs. Sarah. I finally was able to grab the hose and I apologized. The man stood there drenched. He looked at himself then began laughing along with everyone else. I mopped the water up while Mrs. Sarah finished shampooing the man's hair.

The next time the man came in the shop for a shampoo, I didn't get a wink out of him because he laid back in the shampoo bowl with his teeth quenched together and his eyes shut tighter than a lid on a jar of jelly. Mrs. Sarah was so kind. I asked her if I could purchase a manicure table and offer her clients manicures on our slow days. She thought that was the funniest thing ever, being that most of her clients were hard-working men with rough hands. Some were construction workers and others were painters. I told her they probably would appreciate a manicure.

She agreed and even purchased the manicure table for me. She told me I could keep all of the money that I made from the manicures instead of giving her a commission. I was grateful to her for that because it would help me with gas. I made more money doing manicures than assisting her. The men were respectful and happy to have their nails and hands looking nice. After working at Mrs. Sarah's shop for three months, I received my license. I was so excited that day! I jumped and shouted, then screamed for my sons to share the good news but they were down the street playing. I began thanking God for what he had done, and for those people He chose to help me along my journey.

Mama, who bought me the tall doll in the window, Mrs. Albright, my brother Herman, and Mrs. Sarah, also my instructors at Wilfred Beauty Academy who were all in God's plan for my journey. I was told that I scored the highest of everyone in my class. My instructor told me that out of all the students, only two of us passed the state board test the first time. I knew that God had predestined my steps and now I was getting ready to walk into my destiny and reach my goals. I still had some fears and insecurities but God was getting ready to take me down the path He predestined for my life. God was going to deliver me from myself, stir my gifts and talents, and allow me to minister all while working behind the salon chair.

I had previously told Mrs. Sarah that I would work at her shop until I received my license because my goal was to work in a beauty salon. Now it was time to give her my two-week notice and move on. During the three months working with Mrs. Sarah, we had become close and she was such a great mentor to me. I felt bad having to leave after such a short time, but it was time for me to step into my purpose that God predestined. I thanked Mrs. Sarah for giving me the opportunity to work in her shop. I was now ready to pursue my lifelong dream of being a cosmetologist and salon owner. Mrs. Sarah was the only person working in her salon and she told me she was going to miss my company and my help. She said it was such a pleasure working with me but she understood and was happy for me.

After leaving, I would periodically visit her until she retired. I was sad when I heard she had passed. I was excited to begin my journey in the beauty Industry. The first salon I worked at as an independent contractor was Mademoiselle Beauty Salon. The salon owner was my hairstylists when I moved to Florida. She was such a nice Christian woman. God began blessing me with a large clientele right away with mostly my church family and friends. I was doing well in my business although it was frightening starting out being my own boss. Most people right out of beauty school began working on commission assisting salon owners, but I stepped out on faith and became an entrepreneur. God had brought me from a dark place into the light.

I would soon love being my own boss, but being an entrepreneur was a big responsibility and would require working long hours, which led to me working late nights. Most days I worked fifteen hours to accommodate my client's. My husband was supportive of my business but he didn't like me working late nights, he felt it wasn't safe. It also impeded upon our family time together. I told my husband I would work on adjusting my evening clients to come in on Saturdays.

I was still a bit shy and quiet when it came to talking to people, but I learned fast that in the Beauty Industry I had to communicate and build a rapport with my clients if I wanted to keep them. I asked God to help me work out my schedule so it wouldn't interfere with my family and home, and to take away fear and help me to be bold. Soon, God began to give me such boldness it shocked me. I began relating to my clients and before long I had built a rapport with each client. It also led to a great camaraderie with a few clients.

I thanked God for blessing me with a large clientele in such a short time, and I felt bad having to lose a few clients after having to adjust my work schedule but my family was my first priority. God was working things out for my good. I had become close to some of my clients and we would have helpful or encouraging conversations. Two of my clients shared how their child was being bullied. It was as though a beam went off in my head. This would be my first opportunity to share my stories about how I was bullied as a child. After hearing what their child was going through, I shared my story and encouraged them not to take bullying lightly.

I let them know how bullying affected me, and told them to encourage their children to tell them if they are being threatened by the bully because bullying can be detrimental to a child. I shared how I was afraid to tell my parents because of the threats made towards me by my bullies. I encouraged them by letting them know that if God carried me through my storms, He can and will do the same for their child.

God is amazing! He showed me that what I went through was not in vain, because now I can encourage someone who may be going through the same thing as I did. I had the best clients ever, and although I was tired at the end of the day, I gave my last client the same professional care as I gave my first client. God directed me how to build my clientele by giving my clients incentives. Whenever a client referred someone to me for a chemical service, I gave them a free chemical service in return. In less than two years my clientele grew vastly. I was totally booked every day and couldn't take on anymore clients. God blessed my business abundantly! After the second year in business, I never had to pass another business card out in the thirty six years that I was in business.

I thank God for that pink doll in the window that inspired me to want to become a hair designer which we now called it. I was predestined for this job because God knew this would be my way of escape from the dark cave that I had been entrenched in, and had me bound for years. It would also give me the opportunity to witness, encourage, and help others while working behind the salon chair.

It took years, but God healed my wounded heart and lifted my spirit from the inside out, and taught me how to trust people because I didn't know what trust really looked like accept through my parents, Mrs. Martin, Mrs. Albright, my mother and father in law, and my husband. It felt so good to be able to trust someone outside of the people in my close circle. Glory to God! He had given me a joy and hope that lets me know that "I can do all things through Christ who strengthened me." Philippians 4:13 KJV.

CHAPTER ELEVEN

Stepping Out On Faith

I was enjoying my job and was enthused about learning more about the hair Industry so I began entering hair shows in 1981. I had entered a student hair competition when I was in school but now I was about to enter my first local competition at a hair show given by Revlon. The category I entered was the Up Do Hair Style category. I was excited when I won first place and was awarded a big trophy, and a one hundred dollar bill. This built my confidence even more. When I returned home my family saw my big trophy that read "First Place". My husband and sons congratulated me then my sons began jumping up and down cheering for me.

I attended many hairs shows after that day to help sharpen my skills. I even became a trend setter in the Orlando area with my specialty asymmetrical stacked bob hair cut on permanent wave Jheri curls. I was no longer an introvert, and most of my fears had gone. Many of my clients and I had become so close we were like family. We attended birthday parties, family weddings, funerals, graduations, family reunions, and much more in support of each other. I worked at three salons before deciding to step out on faith to own my own business. God had blessed me with a large clientele in just five years of being in the hair industry. I felt confident, and I was financially secure enough to open my own salon.

On July 1, 1986 I opened Classic Impressions Beauty Salon. We opened with a big grand opening. My Pastor Rev. Herman Brandon prayed for my business to be a success, and he prayed for my family. My family, clients, and friends were there to support me. We had a joyous time. Many stylists were interested in renting a booth in my salon, but I decided to work alone until God sent the right people to work with me after witnessing such unprofessionalism in some salons where I had worked.

Once the people saw the new salon in the community, I began to get lots of walk in customers who I had to turn away because I couldn't take on anymore clients. So, I hired two exceptional young ladies who had just graduated cosmetology school to assist me. They reminded me of when I worked at Mrs. Sarah's barber shop as an apprentice. They worked on commission and they were great assistants. Their help made my work load easier and my work hours shorter. Things were going great until I allowed an ex-coworker join our team. I knew her to be a nice lady from working with her in the past so I made her feel like a part of our team. A few days after she began working in my salon, she asked me if four of her ex- co-workers could rent a booth because the salon where they worked suddenly closed. I told her no, because I had heard appalling things about the character of the stylists and I didn't want that stigma brought to my business. I ran a peaceful and respectful salon where the clients felt comfortable.

Before coming to work at my salon, my ex-coworker was the manager at the salon where the four stylists worked. She gave me such sob stories as to why they needed to work, and she assured me that I wouldn't have any problems with the stylists if I allowed them to work in my salon. Being a salon owner was new to me but I had done my homework about rules and regulations for independent contractors who rented booths. After praying, I scheduled individual interviews with each stylists. After they all agreed to comply with the states rules and regulations, also abide by my salons rules and contract I gave them an opportunity to join our team.

I gave them each a copy of the contract in case they needed a reminder because some Independent contractors do not like to comply with salon rules. It only took a couple of weeks before I began to have problems with three of the stylists. My salon was small but immaculate inside and out and was ran professionally. The male stylist was a smoker who began leaving his cigarette butts in front of the entry door and down the sidewalk daily. I swept the cigarette butts off the sidewalk for a couple of weeks without saying anything until one day I became frustrated. I waited until he wasn't busy and asked him if I could talk to him outside and he said yes. I didn't know this guy so I tried to be gentle and kind although I was aggravated with him. I kindly asked him if he would not throw his cigarette butts on the sidewalk in front of the businesses. He immediately got an attitude and responded with harsh words, then said he was a grown man and no woman tells him what to do. He said if I didn't like it, the rest was an explicit language with a threat behind it. The rumors I had heard about this crew were true, but what this guy didn't know was God was using him to strengthen and make me bold for my journey. God gave me boldness that I had never felt before.

I looked the guy in his eyes and told him, "Your threats don't scare me, and because of the threat you just made towards me, you need to pack your belongings and leave my business immediately." God had brought me out! I was a bold soldier from that day on. I would never again allow anyone to intimidate me and drive me back into a cave. He told me he wasn't going anywhere. I told him I would call the police and have him arrested for making threats against me. You might have guessed, he quickly got out of dodge never to be seen again. I would later witness while working in other salons Christians who were persecuted just because they were Christians.

These stylists had only been working in my salon a month when the two female stylists began offering excuses why they couldn't pay their booth rent on time. Booth rent was due every Saturday. At the end of the day, they would leave pretending they would be back after going out to get dinner, but I wouldn't see them again until Tuesday the following week. Then they would have to work a couple of days before they could make enough money to pay for the past week' booth rent. This went on for two weeks and was quickly becoming a cycle so I knew I had to nip this in the bud quickly. That Tuesday I scheduled a mandatory salon meeting for Friday morning at 9:00 am.

Everyone attended including my two assistants who felt uncomfortable working with this crew. I prayed, then told the stylists I was sorry I needed to address this topic when everyone was given a contract but changes had to be made. I then reviewed the contract with the stylist again and reminded them when their booth rent was due. I told them that I understood that they were independent contractors but they agreed to pay their rent on the day specified on the contract. I told them I had a problem with them working all week and not paying their booth rent on time. I gave them an example, "If you rent an apartment you must pay your rent on the specific day that you agreed on the contract." I said it wasn't fair for them to use my electricity, water, and salon furniture on a daily basis but don't want to pay their rent at the end of the week.

I let them know that because some had violated their contracts, stipulations had to be put in place. Booth rent had to be paid by 1:00 pm each Saturday. If their rent wasn't paid by the specified time, they would have to pack their belongings and vacate the premises. I supplied envelopes for them to put their booth rent in, and place it in a designated safe place by 1:00 pm. These stylists had such a bad reputation in Orlando. I received phone calls from salon owners in disbelief that I allowed the stylist to work in my salon. The salon owners in the black community had heard about the kind of people these stylists were. I'm sure the stylists knew it would be hard for them to find another work place in the black community so they had no problem paying their booth rent on time after that meeting but they still continued to cause trouble.

God was teaching me hard lessons. I was learning how to stand strong when dealing with difficult people, how to be bold, and how to run a business. With much regret, I had to begin working long hours again because I didn't trust the stylists with a key to my salon. One stylist was defiant and ignored the opening and closing hours in the contract from 8:00 am to 9:00 pm. Numerous times, she worked past 10:00 pm and I had to wait until she finished working before I could go home. I reminded her that couldn't continue to happen. During that time, as long as the stylists had access to working the salon hours, it wasn't mandatory that they have a key to the salon. The stylists couldn't complain about not having a key because I was there from opening to closing hours. Once again, my husband did not like me working long hours and then coming home stressed and tired, but mostly he felt it was dangerous working late nights. He wasn't happy that our family time together was affected also by me working long hours. By now I had a four year old daughter and it hurt me to the core to come home at night to find her asleep. I would drop her off at the day care and wouldn't see her again until the next morning.

I missed our story time together, saying prayers with her and kissing her good night. My husband said money isn't everything. I told him it wasn't about the money; I was just sharing my compassion with fellow hairstylists and got bamboozled. He insisted that I make some changes soon. Things had gotten worse in the salon. I had prayed and did all I could to get alone with the stylists so everyone could have a pleasant atmosphere to work, but these stylists were disorderly. The stylists would sit on the hoods of their cars with their clients, while smoking and cursing, with music blasting while chemical was processing on their client's hair.

Yes they were independent contractors, but my name was attached to the name on the marquee. I wasn't going to allow anyone to disgrace my good name and ruin my business in the community. Proverbs 22: 1 KJV says, "A good name is more desirable than great riches." I told the stylists what they were doing was unprofessional conduct and unsafe. I also let them know that the businesses beside us might be affected by the loud music and the hanging out. One of the stylists said won't you mind your business. As I walked away, she said "Mrs. Holy Roller better watch her back when she leaves tonight." She and the clients began laughing but I let the name calling roll right off my back because I refused to be tormented ever again in life by bullies.

What broke the camel's back was I had to go to home on an emergency trip. I didn't have a salon manager and I didn't want to close the salon due to salon regulations. So, I asked the stylist who ask if this crew could work in my salon if she would manage the salon for four days until I came back. I told her I would compensate her and she agreed. When I returned and walked in my salon I stood in one place in disbelief. As I stood there, I looked around to see the blinds on the floor in the waiting area and the carpet looked as though someone threw black hair color on it.

The back splash had black color all over it, foot prints were on the wall as if someone sat in the styling chair and kicked the wall, a styling chair was broken, and it was a foul smell in the salon. I opened the bathroom door to find the toilet clogged and had overflowed. The salon was filled with clients but you could hear a pin drop it was so quiet. Everyone starred at me in anticipation of waiting to see what I was going to do. No one seemed bothered by the stench in the salon. I didn't say a word; I walked out of the front door and went home.

I was heartbroken after seeing something that I had worked so hard for intentionally destroyed by evil people who I tried to help. It's sad how people will persecute you for being a Christian. That evening I called the stylist who I left in charge and asked her what happened in my salon. She said she became ill the same day I left so she gave the key to one of the stylists so they could get in the salon to work. She said the same day I came back, was when she returned to work, and no one gave an explanation as to what happened.

CHAPTER TWELVE

A Change Is Coming

After much discussion with my husband, we felt it was best that I closed the salon. Owning my first business was a short lived venture and it wasn't easy, but it was an amazing two year experience, a blessing, and an answered prayer. I knew this was the path God chose for me. It was a lesson that I would later need for my journey. Being an entrepreneur taught me how to deal with people, be a leader, how to stand up in boldness, and how to run a business. Mostly, it taught me that all things are possible to those who love God, and I'm able to do immeasurably more than all I ask or imagine. God used all of this to make me strong and to teach me how to face life's difficulties so I can reach my purpose which He predestined.

The following day I went back to my salon in boldness after much prayer. The Holy Spirit led me in how to handle the situation with these violent stylists. I let the Lord fight my battles. I was there earlier than usual, and as each stylist walked in the salon I didn't say a word, I just handed them a letter that read: "Dear Tenant: This is a notice to let you know you must vacate the premises immediately. The Federal Law entitles the stylist a safe place to work but due to unsafe conditions in the salon cause by workers, it is unsafe to occupy the business. Secondly, you violated the contract when you destroyed my salon. If you do not vacate the premises immediately I will call the law and be forced to pursue legal action for damages to my property."

These ladies began trying to explain, telling me the kids kicked the wall, and someone in the restaurant next door clogged the toilet. They suddenly offered many excuses when before, no one said a word. I told them to please pack their belongings and leave. Of course, they couldn't leave without persecuting me. I was quiet and they soon got out of dodge just as fast as they came. I couldn't fire them because they were not my employees, but once they violated the contract by destroying my property, I had the right to ask them to vacate my business, but it's usually done through the courts. Thank God they left without me having to call the law or take further actions. I never saw any of those stylists again.

God will use your enemies to bless you. Although I had never encountered grown folks like that before, I was on the path right where God wanted me. He used these people to stretch me, grow me, and taught me how to let Him fight my battles. So, I say thank you Lord for allowing those people to cross my path. You used my enemies to bless me, although this was a treacherous storm that you carried me through.

2 Corinthians 4:9, "Persecuted, but not forsaken, cast down, but not destroyed."

We had the salon renovated, and I worked until my lease was up before closing my business. I was appreciative of my assistants but one had left due to fear of the stylists, and the other stylist found another salon to work at after I closed my business. I prayed asking God to direct me where to work. I didn't want to work in a salon that wasn't run professionally. I thought it would be hard to work in someone else's salon after being a salon owner, but I found it to be just the opposite at the salon where I would end up working. I was lead to call a friend who I met in beauty school named Patricia Moore. Pat and I had worked together in a salon where she was manager for two years until she stepped out on faith and became a salon owner. I told her my dilemma and she welcomed me to come work with her and Sandra. Sandra had worked with us also and we knew each other well.

A change is coming! This was the best decision I could have ever made. The stress of being a salon owner subsided, and I felt such a relief. The three of us developed a strong sisterhood. I enjoyed working with these ladies again. This turned out to be the best salon I ever worked in. Pat was a young Christian who was not ashamed of the gospel of Jesus Christ. We watched Christian television, and the atmosphere in the salon was pleasant filled with the Spirit of God. Our clientele looked forward to patronizing the salon, and no one was ever offended by the Christian atmosphere, they loved it. They also loved the fellowship and camaraderie we had with each other. Many lives were changed over the years in

Salon Dimensions, and several clients gave their lives to Christ right there in the salon.

Every year at Christmas time we would express our gratitude to our clients by having a big Christmas party for them in the salon. We had many good times in that salon. Pat was one of the kindest, confident, and savvy business women in Orlando. She would later become one of my closest friends and prayer warrior to this day. Pat salon was closed on Saturday's and that was alright with me, because it meant I would have three days off. I had decided to cut back in my schedule and work Tuesday through Friday.

Crime was on the rise in Orlando with beauty salons being robbed. One of my clients referred a co-worker to me and the lady asked if I could schedule her after work at 6:00 pm, but said she couldn't arrive until 6:30. I was hesitant because the Reconstructive Care Free Curl would take at least three hours to finish but I agreed because of my faithful client who referred her. Although it meant losing some clients whose work schedule I could no longer accommodate when I moved to Salon Dimensions, I felt a big relief. I had completely changed my schedule and was only working four days a week. I told the lady I would do her hair this one time, but couldn't continue unless she could come in earlier.

I was enjoying spending time with my family and helping my daughter with her homework, and I wasn't about to go back to my old schedule. I waited, and waited on this client. It was almost seven o'clock before the client arrived. I was steaming but I kept my composure since she was a new client. My regular clients knew that if they were twenty minutes late, they had to reschedule. This lady didn't give an apology, she just flopped down in my chair, opened her chicken box and said let's get started. I introduced myself and told her the importance of being on time. She responded by saying she knew that she would be here late so she had to stop and get something to eat. It was 10:00 pm before I finished her hair.

As I was finishing up trimming her hair, I asked her if she could wait five minutes until I swept the hair up so we could walk out together. Without hesitation she answered, "NO." She said it was late and her husband was going to be upset that she had been in the salon so late. I wanted to say,

"Lady, I did you a favor." I walked her to the door and made sure she got in her car safely. This ungrateful lady did not even give me a tip, but that was alright because she would never sit in my chair again.

While standing in the door as she got in her car, I noticed a car parked in the church parking lot across the street. Even though it was after 10:00 pm, I didn't think it was unusual because sometimes cars would be left there overnight. She left and I finished cleaning up my area. Before setting the alarm, I took another look out the window to make sure the coast was clear before walking out. As I put the key in my car door, the car at the church sped off very fast and came in the parking lot where I was. I nervously rushed to get in my car and put the key in the ignition. Before I could back out, the car drove up behind my car and blocked me in.

Four tall guys got out of the car and approached my car. By then, I knew they had been waiting for me to come out of the salon so they could rob me. Many robberies had taken place in nearby salons during that time. I couldn't go forward because the building was in front of me, and I couldn't go backward because their car was behind me. All I could do was pray. Psalms 50:15 KJV says, "And call upon me in the day of trouble; I will deliver thee and thou shall glorify me." I called as loud as I could, HELP ME JESUS. At that moment the owner of the Laundromat and his employee came rushing down the sidewalk towards the guys. Thank God the Laundromat stayed open late hours. The four guys jumped in their car and sped off. I was shaking like a leaf when the two guys from the Laundromat asked if I was alright.

I said yes, and thanked them for coming to my rescue. I sat there glorifying and thanking God until I calmed down. The two men at the Laundromat always looked out for us stylists, even during the day. Those tall guys could have easily over powered those two small guys. But God! He's never late, but always on time. As I left the salon that night, I noticed several cars at the far end of the shopping center where another salon was located. I was praying that their salon door were locked in case the crooks returned. The next morning as I was explaining to my co-workers what had happened, the salon owner from the other salon came to tell us they were robbed last night by four tall guys who had guns.

She began telling us that someone forgot to lock the door and the robbers came in. She said the robbers made everyone get on the floor as they held guns to their heads, and robbed everyone in the place. She told us one client had his young son lying beside him and he refused to give up his wallet, because he had just cashed his check that he worked hard all week for. She said one of the robbers put the gun to the man's head and threatened to shoot him and his son if he didn't give up his wallet. The client gave up his wallet to save their lives. After hearing this, I began to shudder. If God had not sent those guys from the Laundromat I could have been forced to open my car door and been robbed, raped, or kidnapped.

I never knew that being a hairstylist would bring so many problems, but I knew this was what I was predestined to do because God would use me working from behind the chair as a tool for many other things in my life that would bless many. Everything was working for my good, because even now I'm more conscience of my surroundings. This was frightening mental and emotional storm that God carried me through that late night. That storm shook me to the core whenever I thought about what could have happened. It took months to get over the fear. Even in the daytime whenever I had to leave the salon, I would look across the street at the church parking lot to make sure that car wasn't there to follow me. Soon, I was able to bring my thoughts back to God, instead of concentrating on the fear of the past. The next time the client called for an appointment, I told her I wouldn't be able to accommodate her because of my work schedule.

I never worked late again after that night. I worked ten blessed years at this amazing salon with those two wonderful ladies, Sandra and Pat. Sandra has since passed on but Pat and I are still treasured friends today after thirty three years. It was a sad time when my friend announced she was retiring. The three of us were like sisters and we were sad that we had to part, but we knew that nothing last forever but only for a season. After leaving Salon Dimensions, I worked in several salons but I never found the camaraderie that Pat, Sandra, and I had.

Two years later, while working in another salon I was rolling my client's hair when God gave me a vision of a play that I could plainly see. It was as though the script was rolled out on a scroll before me. I had written a couple of skits for the Youth Department at my church when I was Youth Director, but I had never thought about writing a play. I didn't understand why God would inspire me to write a play in the middle of rolling my clients hair, and one on a level which I had never written. But as soon as I put my client under the dryer, I went in the break room and jotted down what God inspired me to write.

God only let me see the beginning and ending of the play at that time. It took months before he gave me the entire message of play. The title He gave me was "A Mother's Prayer". God waited until I was forty five years old to stir my gift to become a playwright. God can use anyone at any age, and at any time to do His will if they are willing. Before I could complete the first play, God inspired me to write a second play titled "Deception."

At times, I felt overwhelmed after working all day then writing plays in my spare time, but I wanted to be obedient to the assignments God had given me, knowing that He would not give me more than I could bare. I wrote at work between clients and late nights, but mostly I penned what God spoke early in the morning before going to work. Mornings were quiet and I wouldn't be easily distracted, God would have my full attention. Most assignments God gave me would not be easy but its purpose would outweigh my sacrifices.

On June 25, 2005 both plays were performed at my church. The church was filled to its capacity with members, friends, and the community. The church members and friends who took on the role as cast member interacted well together. The crowd responded with laughter, tears, and rejoicing. Some got so caught up in the play, one lady shouted, "Don't Do It," at one of the actors who played a college girl desperate to find a man. What she didn't know was this older guy she met was married and had ten children from different women, and was taking advantage of church girls from Florida, to New York to pay his child support for his ten children, and all of his expensive wants such as fine jewelry and expensive shoes.

He invited her out to dinner then lied when it was time to pay, pretending he forgot his wallet on the dresser. The college girl willingly said she would pay. The reaction from the crowd was incredible. People began applauding in the middle of scenes during the play Deception. Most importantly, a young man was reunited with his family, and one lady rededicated her life back to God. Many people came to the altar for prayer at the end of the production. If I had decided to stay in my cave when God wanted to deliver me from my fears, those people wouldn't have had that opportunity to receive that blessing.

When I was a child I loved combing my dolls hair. And as a teenager, I loved writing letters to friends and family, but mostly I loved writing stories that I had to read in front of the class. As I read, I would sometimes get nervous, but the students always chose my stories as the best story. It's amazing how God would later intertwine "Hair and writing," the two things I loved doing the most and use them to inspire, motivate, and give others hope.

God had brought me out of my cave of reclusiveness, insecurity, hopelessness, and depression, and equipped me for my journey in life at middle age. Fear can block our blessings, keep us in bondage, and block the flow of Gods strength into a person. Some people can never rise above their fear. I had an aunt that was bound to fear all of her life. I don't know what happened that made her so fearful but it must have been tragic.

The last time I saw her she was about eighty years old and she was still fearful. She was very quiet, and I can remember from my early childhood how she held her head down most of the time, and would never look a person in their eyes when they talked to her. When we spend time with God, we are transformed by the renewing of our minds. The more I stayed in the presence of God, the stronger I got. If I had gotten stuck like my aunt did and stayed in my cave, I would have never had the opportunity to become a hair stylist or playwright, and many people wouldn't have had the opportunity to receive the blessings God had for them through me, and the ministries He called me to.

Sometimes we are our worse enemy and need to be delivered from ourselves. The battles that goes on in our minds have us trapped in our own cave, and most times we can't get out on our own. There may be times when we feel safe in our caves and don't won't to come out because we don't want to face the world. I thank God for rescuing and delivering me from my cave. Most people who know me now would never believe this is my story because now I'm a happy, vivacious senior citizen who is filled with laughter and joy.

In early 2012, God enlarged my territory. He inspired me to step out on faith to birth my own business "Kingdom Builder Productions." God gave me the opportunity to write, produce, and direct seven Gospel stage plays. I also had the opportunity to write plays and skits for Women's Day Programs, Children's Programs, and a Literacy program. I took time to invest in classes that helped me receive professional knowledge to sharpen my skills in writing, directing, and producing. But no matter how much I learned from instructors, I always allowed God to orchestrate each play.

CHAPTER THIRTEEN

I Will Carry You Through the Storms

June 9th, 2012 is a day I will never forget. The gospel stage play "Order in the House" was going to be presented that night at a church in Orlando that seated eight hundred people. We had sold more than four hundred tickets in advance and was expecting to sale tickets at the door. My eighty four year old mother at the time had flown in from Arizona to support me, and to take on a non-speaking role as the church mother in the play. In the seventeen years of me presenting plays, mama only missed being in one play. She was my greatest supporters and she insisted that I include her in all the plays and said I should give her a speaking role, we laughed. But in every play I added a character named mother Johnson in honor of my mother whose last name is Johnson.

Mama and I had left Costco early that afternoon and were on our way to the church after buying food for the cast. I had planned to arrive at the church two hours before the cast to have the food table set up for them. As we headed to the church that afternoon, the weather was sunny and nice. Mama and I were singing good old gospel song as we rode along, when all of a sudden it began to drizzle light rain. In a matter of seconds, out of the blue while the sun was still shinning it began to pour down torrential rain. I had never seen such heavy rain in the forty plus years I've lived in Florida. The rain came down so fast and hard, I thought I was going to collide in the back of the car in front of me because I couldn't see anything, not even brake lights. I was familiar with the road because I traveled it daily to work.

I wanted to go in the median of the highway and sit there until the rain stopped, but there were trees in the median and I didn't want to hit a tree. If I had stopped, I knew that would be tragic because the person behind me would collide into the back of my car, so I continued driving as slow as possible not being able to see anything. Every time I would hit the curb I would ease my way back onto the road. Mama and I began to pray. I began calling the name of Jesus repeatedly. Mama was praying to God, but I can recall Mama saying, "Father God, I ask you to take hold of the steering wheel and keep everyone on this highway safe and get us to the church house on time. In Jesus' name I pray." When Mama finished praying that powerful prayer, God answered.

Suddenly, the rain let up enough where I could see the lights of the car in front of me and we made it to the church safely. My dear mother and I sat in the church parking lot hugging and giving God thanks, because we knew we could have lost our lives that day, but it was as though the Holy Spirit directed the traffic that day. God was truly in control because we didn't hear any cars crash. This was truly Gods amazing grace, because thousands of people travel John Young Parkway every day. We thanked God for protecting everyone who was on that busy highway. God carried us through a violent torrential rain storm that sunny afternoon.

The rain had lifted some, but an hour before the play started the heavens opened up again and it began raining even harder. Thank God the entire cast had arrived at the church safely before the rain started. One requirement I had for the cast was to arrive three hours prior to the curtains opening. Although we had sold more than four hundred tickets in advance, I wondered if people would come out in the dangerous weather to see a play. Would they drive through the dangerous traffic? This would be my first production under my business name "Kingdom Builder Productions" and I was quite concerned if there would be an audience after the cast worked three long months rehearsing for this big night.

I had rented a U-Haul, furniture, bought props, paid for the venue, videographer, and so much more. I wondered if all of this would be a great loss. To my amazement, people began pouring into the church. People even bought tickets at the door. A couple who were in the play invited their family and friends from Titusville, Florida to come witness them in their debut appearance in their first stage play. While the last scene was going on, I was in the lobby as a couple walked into the lobby headed towards the exit door. I asked them if they enjoyed the play. They said they loved to be entertained by plays and "Order in the House" was one of the best plays they've ever witnessed.

They expressed that they regretted having to leave before the play ended, but it was getting late and they had to travel back to Miami which would take them three and a half hours to get home. I told them I was the writer of the play, and I shared the ending with them. They said what a great ending. I thanked them for traveling all the way from Miami to see the play. Only two people who bought tickets in advance didn't attend the play. I was amazed to see how many people purchase tickets at the door and didn't allow the rain to stop them from attending the play.

The last scene of the play was amazing. A well know choir, who was a part of the play, brought the audience to their feet as they sang one of their recordings "Get Your House In Order". I invited local Pastors and their wives to be a part of the last scenes. The scene depicted a big celebration for the Pastors retirement. The scene was so uplifting. The cast members got caught up in the spirit along with the audience, and forgot they were in a play when Mother Wanda Cobb, a senior citizen and mother of her church, came to the microphone and blew her signature song "Walk with Me Lord" on her saxophone. The cast were on their feet cheering mother Wand Cobb on and praising the Lord. She blew to the glory of God! The play was a great success, and to this day people still ask about one of the actors who played the character role of sister Panky. She stole the show portraying a nosey church usher!

I learned that day that whenever God gives me an assignment not to fret, nor fear because when He calls me to it, He will provide everything I need and will see me through it. I've also learned that Satan will try to stop Gods assignment because he knows it's going to bless someone. He will even try to kill us before we can complete the assignment. He doesn't want Christians to share the Gospel of Christ because he wants lost souls in hell with him. No matter what comes against you when you are called to an assignment by God, don't get discourage. God is always there and He promised to never leave nor forsake you.

I knew that if the people could witness that play they would receive a blessing. The play mostly spoke to pastors. It depicts a Pastor who was so busy taking care of his flock, and jumping through hoops to help his comrades in the gospel, he neglected his own family. His wife had an affair with the Co-Pastor whose wife was nine months pregnant, and his daughter got pregnant by her boyfriend, when the Pastor and wife didn't know she had a boyfriend. I received phone calls from Pastors thanking me and telling me that this play was a wakeup call for them, and a reminder of Gods Order in their homes.

Yes, that was a bad thunder storm that evening but God carried mama and I safely through the storm, and I am forever grateful.

November 2, 2016 was one of the worst days of my adult life, and would change my life forever. I was still working in the beauty industry and writing plays when I was forced to retire from both jobs. I had worked in the beauty Industry thirty six years, and was a playwright for thirteen years when I had to suddenly retire. I'll never forget that dreadful Friday. Thank God He had answered my childhood dream. I was now working in my own salon again that was attached to my home just like Mrs. Albright's salon where I worked as a child. Thank God I was working at home instead of someone else salon when this dreadful thing happened to me.

That morning one of my faithful clients arrived at her usual 9:00 o'clock appointment. I was shampooing her hair when I heard my back pop. Immediately I began experiencing severe pain and could barely stand. I mentioned it to my client and she was extremely concerned. I managed to stand long enough to finish shampooing and get her under the hair dryer before I began having excruciating pain in my back and down my right leg. I knew something was seriously wrong so I went to my bedroom to lie down until my client's hair dried. I managed to walk back to the salon and finish my client's hair. Thank God my husband was retired and was at home that day.

I made him aware of what was going on, and told him I wanted to go see my acupuncture doctor as soon as my client left. This doctor had been treating my sciatic nerve problem for at least ten years, but I had never experienced anything like this before. One doctor had told me years before that I might need surgery due to the sciatic problem. Instead, I chose acupuncture over surgery because I felt it was natural and safer.

I called to see if the doctor could see me right away and the receptionist said yes. As soon as my client left, my husband took me to see the doctor. They called me to the back as soon as I walked through the door. The pain was so severe I could barely get on the examining table. The doctor inserted the thin needles at strategic points of my body like he always did.

He saw how much pain I was experiencing, so he thought it would be best to turn the device that stimulated the needles up higher. It was almost unbearable, but I endured the discomfort because I thought it would alleviate the pain. In the past, the acupuncture treatments always helped with the sciatic pain, but this time would be different.

After my treatment, we arrived home and I went straight to bed. My husband asked if I would be alright by myself while he went to Costco which was fifteen minutes from our home. I said yes, and told him I was going to try to go to sleep.

Ten minutes after he left, my legs went completely numb and I couldn't walk. I had become temporarily paralyzed. I called my husband and was screaming to the top of my lungs for him to come back right now. My husband must have been speeding because he made it back in five minutes. He tried picking me up to take me to the hospital, but I couldn't stand for him to touch me because of the pain. He called an ambulance, and the EMS tried picking me up to carry me out of my bedroom to the ambulance, but I was in too much pain for them to touch me. Two of the guys stood in my bed with their shoes on, then picked me up in my bed sheet and brought me out of my bedroom to a waiting stretcher outside.

They took me to the closest hospital where I did not want to go because they were known for having a bad reputation. People complained about them giving poor health care, and being negligent to the patients. There was a saying about that hospital "You check in and you won't check out". The ride in the ambulance was horrendous. Seem like the driver hit every pot hole in the road.

When I arrived at the hospital, they assessed my health and gave me Percocet for the excruciating pain. The medication was so strong I regurgitated ten minutes after taking it. They took more tests then sometime later, a doctor walked in my room and introduced himself and told me he was an orthopedic doctor. He bluntly told me that he had looked at all of the test taken and I needed to have emergency back surgery.

He told me that if I didn't have a Laminectomy and Spinal Fusion Surgery that day, I would be permanently paralyzed. He even told me it was a chance that I could die on the operating table during the surgery. I understand that the physicians are required to provide potential risk information to the patient before surgery, but this doctor was nonchalant, blunt, and had no empathy. When he told me I could die on the operating table that was it for me. He said it in a way that he could care less if I did. He had no compassion and gave me little hope.

I was in so much pain I wanted something to be done immediately, but after his negative behavior, I told him I wanted to get a second opinion. He rudely said have it your way and walked out of the room. Whenever I have the feeling that something isn't right, it's the Holy Spirit warning me. It's almost like a flashing yellow warning light. God knew just how to orchestrate things and He's always on time. My sister Janice became a nurse, and had retired after her career in nursing for more than thirty years and moved to Florida. She lived only an hour from me. I had not seen her in ten years but God sent her to my rescue once again when I needed her most.

Janice was the sister who rescued me from the burning fire when I struck the match trying to light the heater that cold winter morning when I was eleven years old. I called her and she said she would be here first thing tomorrow morning. The hospital said there was nothing else they could do so they discharged me because I denied the back surgery. A portion of the numbness in my leg and foot had subsided and I had feeling once again. I was able to move and stand with someone helping me. The hospital sent me home in excruciating pain with a different pain medicine, but I continued to regurgitate shortly after taking it.

That night when I came home was awful. I cried all night because the pain was horrendous. I took an Ibuprofen 800 mg since the drugs made me sick but it gave me no relief.

Coming home gave me the opportunity to be able to search my Insurance booklet to try and find another doctor. I got up early the following morning after being up all night in pain. My husband borrowed our neighbor's wheel chair and managed to get me to the bathroom to shower, then he helped me get dressed. He pushed me to my computer and I began googling information about Laminectomy and Spinal Fusion Surgery while waiting on Janice to arrive. Soon my sister arrived and we were ecstatic to see each other. She was sad to see me in so much pain.

There had been several people in our church who had back surgeries that were unsuccessful, so I wanted to check out several doctors so I could choose the best doctor possible. I took another Ibuprofen 800 mg but it gave me no relief. Although I was in pain, it gave me comfort just knowing that my sister was who is an excellent nurse would be by my side. We talked a few minutes, and then we didn't waste any time. Janice began searching through my insurance booklet for a doctor. I wasn't sure what type of doctor I needed for back surgery, but since the doctor at the hospital told me he was an orthopedic doctor we searched for that same kind of doctor.

We prayed asking God for direction in choosing the best orthopedic doctor. I disliked having HMO Insurance at that time because we had to choose a doctor in the booklet and there were not many doctors to choose from. As we searched the booklet for a doctor I saw the name of the doctor who told me I needed to have back surgery.

Out of curiosity, I googled his name to get some background on him. I learned important things such as where he went to medical school, and where he worked previously. I also read the comments people posted and almost everyone said he had bad beside manners. I know sometime comments are exaggerated but I experienced the same, so I believed most of them to be true.

We kept searching and found another orthopedic doctor. We googled him and he had a five star rating, and excellent comments for doing back surgery. We read his college background and where he had worked. He was a young man who looked to be in his early thirties. He graduated from a prestigious college and had received additional training. We read he was also the orthopedic doctor for the Orlando Magic basketball team.

Although he was young, I was impressed by his education, the comments from his patients, and the prestigious places where he worked. Surely I thought I would have a top doctor since this doctor took care of the Orlando Magic players. After checking out every doctor in the booklet and discussing them with my sister, she totally left the choice up to me which doctor to choose. Because of all the positive things I read about this young doctor, I decided to choose him.

I called the doctor's office to see if he was accepting new patients. I was grateful he was. I was in so much pain I needed help as soon as possible. I was thankful that they got me in that same day. The receptionist told me I would need to bring with me the entire imaging test that was taken at the hospital. After spending a night and helping me confirm an appointment with the doctor, Janice left to go home. I was eternally grateful to her for coming at the last minute to see about me.

She told me to call her after my appointment and let her know what the doctor said, and if I had to have surgery she would come back to be by my side. It was comforting to know I would have my sister who was one of the best nurses I've ever known to be by my side in case I needed to have surgery. She has helped so many people in her lifetime, and still does in her retirement years. Janice was destined to become a nurse. I call her my "Nurse Doctor" because she has rescued me throughout my life. The knowledge she has as a nurse seems equal to some doctors, and sometimes seem to be better than some.

I called the hospital so they could have my records ready when my husband got there to pick them up. By the time he got back home it was time for me to go to my appointment. As I tried to get out of bed I could barely stand or walk. My husband is small in stature but he managed to get me in the car and drove ten miles to the doctor's office. Every bump in the road was agonizing.

The doctor was a tall young Indian doctor who seemed concerned but he didn't talk much. He looked at the MRI that had been taken at the hospital, then he examined me. He told me that I needed to have a Laminectomy and Spinal

Fusion surgery right away. This would be the same surgery the other doctor told me I needed to have. He told me this was serious, and I needed to go from his office straight to the hospital. I was praying that this doctor could do something other than surgery to eliminate my pain but that wasn't the case. I agreed to have the surgery because I needed some relief from the pain.

This doctor worked at two locations. One was located in a prestigious area named Celebration Florida where wealthy people lived. There was also a hospital near the office where I had my appointment. I assumed he would do the surgery at one of those hospitals. I was shocked when he told me that he would be doing my surgery at the same hospital that I had gone to the night before, the hospital with the bad reputation. I found out that I would be out of network if I went to the prestigious hospital, so I had to go to the hospital nearest me. The doctor called ahead so the hospital would be expecting me. He wanted me to check in that evening and said he would do the surgery early the following morning.

I dreaded going to that hospital again. I didn't know much about this doctor but I felt if he took good care of the Orlando Magic player's he would take good care of me. I had googled information about a spinal fusion and laminectomy surgery and found it to be risky. The laminectomy surgery would relieve pressure in the spinal cord and on the nerves, and the spinal fusion would stabilize the bones together by using screws and rods. This was scary but I was a bit relieved knowing that both doctors gave me the same diagnosis. I was hurting so much I could barely get off of the examining table. The doctor saw my pain and reminded my husband to take me straight to the hospital.

I was in excruciating pain but I was also hungry. I had not eaten in two days because of the pain. I knew that if I went straight to the hospital I probably wouldn't have anything to eat until after the surgery the following day. I asked my husband to stop by a local restaurant as we left the doctor office so I could get a takeout dinner. I came home and ate my dinner then went to the hospital. After getting me situated in my room, they nurse began giving me strong pain meds that the doctor had ordered. The food I had eaten was delicious and filling but it did not have time to digest before the medicine made me feel sick to my stomach.

My husband had gone to the family waiting area to call family members to let them know I would be having surgery tomorrow morning. Soon after he left I felt like I had to regurgitate. It was like Deja vu all over again. I pressed the call button for the nurse to help me to the bathroom. She handed me the bag that is normally given to patients when they fill sick, but I knew it wouldn't be large enough. So I asked the nurse to please help me to the bathroom and she did, but I couldn't make it to the toilet before my food began to come up and I had to regurgitate.

I regurgitated in the sink which was nearer. I felt like I was regurgitating my lungs out. The nurse stood there a minute then said she couldn't take it. She said I was making her sick to her stomach so she walked out of the room and never returned. As I stood there helplessly clinging to the sink, I thought about my sister Janice. She would have never treated her patients like that. The lady had no compassion and should have never become a nurse if her stomach was too weak to care for her patients properly. My husband returned right on time as I was trying to make it back to my bed. I was able to walk with some assistance but I was afraid to try and make it back to the bed by myself.

I refused to pull the string for help because I didn't want that same nurse to help me after she walked away when I needed her help. As I held onto the wall my husband, son, and daughter-in-law walked in the room and helped me in the bed. I told them what happened, and my husband told me to relax and not to worry myself about the small things, instead just try to keep calm before going in for surgery.

My husband always knows the right thing to say to keep me calm, although that was a big thing to me. He's one who does not like hospitals but he stayed until late that night. He prayed with me and assured me everything would be alright before leaving the hospital. He said he would be back early the next morning.

I endured pain all night because every medication I was given did not agree with my stomach. Thirty minutes after taking it I would regurgitate. I prayed and called on God all night. Early that next morning my husband, daughter, and sister were all there. The nurse came in and asked me to sign several papers before surgery. I was in so much pain my hand trembled while signing the papers. One paper I signed was giving the doctor consent to do the surgery, and another was giving the Anesthesiologist consent to give me anesthesia. After signing the papers the nurse told me someone would be coming to take me in for surgery.

While we were waiting, my husband asked us to join hands and he prayed. I was looking forward to the pain subsiding after the surgery. Finally, two wheel chair attendants came to take me to the operating room. My family kissed me and gave me positive sentiments. They told me that they would see me in a short while.

The attendees took me to the pre-operative holding area and helped me get onto the bed. There was a pre-operative nurse who greeted me. She told me she would take care of me until time for surgery. I asked her if I would see my doctor and anesthesiologist before surgery. She assured me that they would be in shortly, then she asked me to sign the same papers that I had just signed when the nurse came into my room.

I explained that a nurse had me sign the same papers right before I came down for surgery. She became very rude and told me I didn't have to sign the papers, but I wouldn't be receiving surgery today if I didn't. I looked over her rudeness, and agreed to sign the papers because I was trying to stay calm, and didn't want to get on this lady's bad side because she had the upper hand.

As I laid there waiting for the doctor and anesthesiologist to come in, I realized I had hair pins in my pinned up braids. I had been in so much pain my hair was the last thing on my mind. I remembered that usually during surgery they don't want any metal in the hair because it can interfere with the operation or surgical equipment. I began taking the pins out of my hair but needed something to put them in.

After the nurse's episode of rudeness, I was hesitant about asking her for something to put the hair pins in but I couldn't hold them in my hand. I told the nurse I forgot I had hair pins in my hair then kindly asked her if she had something that I could put the pins in. This lady must have gotten out of the wrong side of the bed because she was so rude it frightened me.

The nurse and I were the only ones in the room so I guess she felt comfortable talking to me rudely. She told me that people with common sense know to take metal out of their hair when they come to the hospital for surgery. I told her I was sorry and I just forgot they were in my hair. She gave me a bag to put the pins in and walked away. I thanked her but she did not respond back.

I laid there and began praying asking God to watch over me and protect me from all hurt, harm, and danger. A few minutes later, the nurse came towards me with a needle. I asked her what was she doing but she didn't say anything. She went to the Intravenous Line and began to inject the needle into it. I asked her if that was the anesthesia that she was putting in the bag and the next thing I knew I was out.

I never had the opportunity to see or talk to my doctor who I only met the day before. Nor did I get to see or talk to the anesthesiologist. I was put to sleep and taken into surgery without ever seeing either person who would be administering a serious surgery on me. I know that sometimes patients are given a sedative by the nurse prior to surgery to calm them, but I didn't need a sedative because I was calm and compliant.

I'm not sure what that nurse put into my veins that day, but I didn't wake up until nine hours later. My family was worried because the surgery was supposed to have lasted one hour and forty five minutes. Janice asked the nurses many times why I wasn't out of surgery. The nurses had no answer as to why I was in there so long. My sister insisted on an answer after a few more hours had passed.

My family was told that they had a dilemma with some equipment that they needed to perform the operation with, and the doctor had to wait until the problem with the equipment was solved. To this day, I wonder if they continued giving me anesthesia to keep me asleep during that long nine hour procedure. When I woke up in the recovery room I was in excruciating pain. I was on my knees banging on the wall crying out for Jesus to help me. I was in worse pain than before I had surgery. I no longer had pain on the right side, but now it had shifted to the left side from my hip to my toes, and the pain had tripled.

The nurse kept telling me to lie down. I knew that after having surgery it would take time for me to heal and I would experience some pain, but this pain was mind boggling. Soon they took me back to my room where my husband, daughter, and sister were waiting. My son and daughter in law soon arrived, and everyone was distressed when they saw me crying and shaking from the unbearable pain I was in.

My sister asked the nurse why was I in so much pain. The nurse said she would check to see if I could have some pain medicine. The nurse took my blood pressure while my sister stood there and watched. My blood pressure was 182 over 150. My sister insisted on them calling my doctor. It took the nurse a while to return with the pain medication. My sister asked her if she called the doctor.

The nurse said no they were giving me the medication that the doctor ordered on my chart. My sister told the nurse my blood pressure was extremely high because of the pain I was experiencing, and they needed to get my blood pressure down. The nurse seemed a bit upset with my sister demands, but my sister was not moved by her feelings she was only concerned about me. I had a headache that was so bad, I felt as though I would have a stroke or heart attack at any moment. The nurse took my pressure again and it had gone up to 230 over 180.

Although Janice was retired, she was still a licensed nurse because she kept her license current. Janice hurried to the nurses' station and explained to them that she was a licensed nurse, and demanded that they give her my doctor's phone number so she could call him herself because I was in a crisis. My sister was afraid I would have a stroke from my blood pressure being so high, and she felt the doctor needed to know how high it was.

One of the nurses called my doctor and he spoke with my sister at 3:00 a.m. My sister told the doctor she was a nurse then explained to the doctor how high my blood pressure was. He listened and told her he would take care of it and see me first thing in the morning. The nurse came in soon after my sister talked to the doctor and gave me additional blood pressure medication that the doctor ordered. It allowed me to sleep a few hours before the pain returned.

I will always remember my loving sister Janice telling my family to go home and get some rest and she would stay right beside me. My husband didn't like hospitals and he hadn't gotten any sleep in days, but he didn't want to leave me. I insisted that he go home and get some rest. He felt a bit relieved knowing that he could go home and I would be in good hands with my sister watching after me.

There was a cot in the room right next to my bed that was not like a normal cot. It was so low it looked like my sister was sleeping on the floor, but Janice slept on it without complaining. Every time I woke up, she was awake watching over me. When we were kids growing up I felt as though my big sister acted like she was my mother. But over the years, I realized she was only looking out for my best interest just like she was now. My sister truly expressed her love towards me through her actions, and my love for her has deepened for an eternity and there's nothing I wouldn't do for her. I feel that if she had not been here for me through that surgery, I would have been one of those patients who checked in but didn't check out alive.

I thank God for sending Janice to be by my side during that horrific time. She was right beside me when I needed her the most. The doctor came in early the next morning and I asked him why was I in so much pain on the opposite side of my body when there was no pain there before. He said it could be nerve damage from the surgery. He also told me prior to the surgery that the scar would only be an inch and a half long. There was a big patch on my back and after removing the patch there was a four inches scar down my back.

I asked him if the surgery was successful and he said he can't be sure right now, he would be able to tell me more at my post-op appointment. After that visit he never came to my room again. After two days in the hospital, I was released to go home. I was still in pain but I was grateful that my sister was with me when I went home. My husband went to get my pain prescription while my sister and daughter made me comfortable in bed.

My sister had to go home the following day, but before leaving my daughter and her made sure our home was sparkling clean. They even cleaned my closet room and dusted all of my shoes. By the time my husband returned with my prescription I was in agonizing pain. I glimpsed the name of the medicine on the bottle before taking it and saw that it was Oxycodone. I had heard on the news that lots of young people were highly addicted to this drug. I was in so much pain I took a pill without asking Janice questions about it until after taking it.

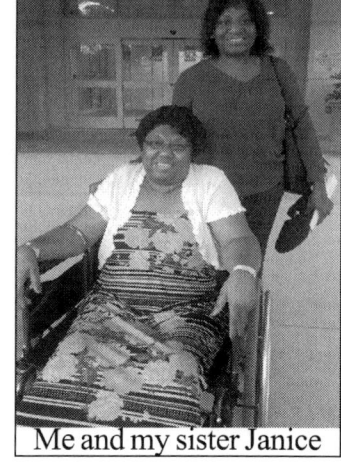

Me and my sister Janice

She said it would be alright to take it to ease my pain for a short time, but if I took it for a long period of time it could be highly addictive. Not long after taking the medication I regurgitated. It was a strong narcotic but it didn't take the pain away because I couldn't keep it down long enough. Before leaving, Janice called my doctor's office to let him know that I couldn't keep the medicine down so he changed the medication again.

It was now time for my sister to go home. Although I didn't want her to leave, I knew she had to go. We hugged, and she said she would keep in touch and would return if I needed her. My husband went to pick up the new prescription which was Hydrocodone. When he returned with the medicine I took it, and had the same reaction as I did with the other narcotics. By now, the doctor had prescribed so many narcotics that I couldn't keep down, I believe God wouldn't allow my body to accept the medications because I could have easily become addicted.

The next day, I called the doctor's office and explained that I was having the same problem with this medication as the others. He prescribed another medication named Tramadol. I could keep this medicine down and it took the pain away, but there were a few problems with this medicine too. Just minutes after taking it, it would knock me out for exactly two hours. When I woke up the pain would immediately return. I couldn't live like that. I wouldn't have any quality of life being drugged and sleeping all day. One morning I woke up and found myself sitting on the edge of the bed hitting at the air. I saw something that looked like a ghost floating in the air. It would enter my room and come near me until I would raise my hand to hit at it, then it would float down the hall but would return.

I'm not sure how long this went on, but God soon brought me to myself. I realized I was hallucinating and knew the enemy wanted me to fall off the bed so I would injure myself even worse. I called upon the name of the Lord and He rebuked Satan and made him flee. I watched that silhouette of the spirit float out of my bedroom down the hallway. God defeated the forces of evil, and that demonic spirit left my home to never return again.

Satan will sometimes come to attack us at our weakest moments, just like a lion after its prey, but God will lift up a standard against him and he will have to flee. God was right there with me all the time. I woke my husband up and told him what happened. He said it must be the medication that was causing the hallucination then he comforted me until I fell asleep.

I thanked God that I didn't fall off the high king-size bed because I could have been paralyzed if I had fallen. After sleeping a few hours, it was time to take the strong medication again. I had to take it as prescribed or else the pain would come back with a vengeance. The pain was so severe I could hardly wait for my next dose so I could fall asleep again. After taking the medicine for a week and sleeping most of the day, I felt like I was becoming addicted to it. I couldn't rely on this medication forever to sooth my pain, so I made up my mind I was going to go cold turkey with the help of God.

After waiting four hours the pain became unbearable. I had made up my mind that I would no longer take any more of those habit forming pills, so I took two of the 800 mg Tylenols instead, but the Tylenol didn't help at all. I tried going to sleep but that was hopeless. I could no longer take the pain so I went to the dresser and picked up the Tramadol once again. I was in so much pain I was trembling. I opened the bottle and poured a pill in my hand then put it to my mouth. Before putting the pill in my mouth, I threw it on the floor and began calling on the name of Jesus asking Him to help me. Psalms 50: 15 KJV tells us to "call upon me in the day of trouble: I will deliver thee, and thou shall glorify me."

Indeed, God delivered me that day and I gave Him all the glory. He helped me to be strong enough to endure the pain without taking those horrible pills. I even began to have compassion for people who are addicted to drugs. We must be careful when we judge other's because we don't know their story. The next day was my appointment to see the doctor. I was in so much pain but God was helping me to endure it.

My feet felt like they were on fire, I had to soak them in ice cold water to get some relief. I also had pain that felt like electric shocks going through my hip, down to my toes on the left side of my body. I could barely stand so my husband bought a walker from the pharmacy that had a seat on it to help me get around. My husband and son Steven took me to my post-op appointment. As we entered the doctor's office, there were at least twenty people in the waiting room. Some were patients, and others were family member who brought them to see the doctor. There were no seats available for us to sit.

Thank God I had the seat on my walker so I would have some where to sit because the wait was extremely long. My husband and son had to stand for quite a while before a seat became available. I thought it was appalling, having patients wait so long who were in such pain not long after surgery. I twisted and turned trying to find some comfort on the hard seat, I just wanted to lie down. I watched the receptionist send a patient home because he didn't have a twenty dollar co-payment. I thought to myself, what kind of place is this? Who would send a person home after having a serious surgery because he didn't have a twenty-dollar co-payment? She could have given him the option to mail in the payment later.

Finally, after waiting an hour they called my name. My husband pushed me to the back as I sat on the seat of my walker. I had not seen my doctor since he did the surgery. My doctor was standing talking to the radiologist and didn't see us as we passed by. I overheard him tell the radiologist that Mrs. Jackson has severe nerve damage, and I would like her to have an X-ray. As we entered the examining room I just wanted to lie down so I asked my husband to help me onto the table.

I tried to hold back the tears after over hearing what the doctor said, but I couldn't because I was in so much pain and in disbelief of what I had just heard. The doctor came into the room and didn't say much. I asked him why I was still experiencing so much pain after being out of the hospital for two weeks. I also asked him why there was pain on the left side of my body when there was no pain on that side before the surgery. He found it hard to answer and said he wanted me to have an X-ray taken. I knew then he was fishing for a way to break the bad news.

Shortly after taking the X-ray the doctor came back into the room and gave me the bad news. He told me that I had severe nerve damage. I told him I had done some research and an X-ray would not show nerve damage. I would need to have an MRI or a CAT scan. He already knew he had severely damaged my nerves during surgery because I overheard him tell the radiologist I had nerve damage. The X-ray was just a waste of time and money, and a way to make me think he had just discovered the problem. I felt he knew after the surgery that he had damaged my nerves because when I asked him why was I in so much pain he said it could be nerve damage.

This young doctor said, "It's nerve damage that you have." I was upset and disappointed because I thought I had chosen a competent doctor capable of doing my surgery, but I was wrong. I believe some doctors post false information online to attract patients, or have family and friends post positive comments about them. This doctor left me in worst pain than before I received surgery. He also left me with a four-inch scar on my back after telling me the scar would be an inch and a half. I asked him if the pain would cease in time and he assured me that it would.

I told him that I did not want to take any more narcotics because everything he ordered made me sick. I asked if he could prescribe a non-narcotic medication that would relieve my pain. He said he wanted me to try Gabapentin 100 mg. At this point, I felt like I was being used as a guinea pig. I felt he was experimenting with whatever medicine he could think of until something worked for me.

The pain was getting worse. There was sharp striking pain that went from my hip down to my toes and my feet. It felt like I was standing on hot coals every day, and all day. I continued soaking my feet in a tub of ice-cold water because that was the only thing that gave me relief from the burning. The Gabapentin agreed with my stomach but gave me little relief.

I had the back surgery on November 30, 2016. At the end of the year, I had to inform my Insurance Company if I was going to continue with the plan I had or choose a different plan. I decided to keep the plan I had for the following year so I could continue my care with this doctor until I could find another doctor who I felt comfortable with.

When I went back for my second appointment after the first of the year, the receptionist told me they were no longer accepting my insurance. I asked her why I wasn't informed at my last appointment. All she could say was I'm sorry. She said if I wanted to see the doctor without insurance I would have to pay out of pocket. That was like a slap in the face, but I ended up paying for that visit because I felt it would be for my best interest for the time being.

After leaving there that day I was determined not to return. I was disappointed and upset because I felt this doctor permanently damaged me, then wanted to get rid of me because he didn't want a law suit on his hand. Telling me they no longer accepted my insurance was their way of getting rid of me. This was the worst physical storm that I had ever encountered. I didn't know where to turn from here. 1 Peter: 5-7 says,"Casting all your cares upon him: for he cares for you." This scripture encouraged me by letting me know that if I stop worrying, God will carry me through every storm I would face.

CHAPTER FOURTEEN

Adjusting To Retirement

Sadly, four months after having back surgery I was still experiencing pain daily so I knew my time as a hair stylist was over. I was forced to suddenly retire from the hair industry after serving my clients for thirty six years. I could no longer bend over the shampoo bowl, or stand for long periods of time. I called each client and explained why I had to suddenly retire. My clients were devastated and sad for me but they understood. Most of the ladies began attempting to do their own hair while I was recuperating because they had been coming to me so long, they had a problem with someone else doing their hair.

I mentioned earlier that many of my clients had been coming to me for many years, they had become close acquaintances, and some became dear friends who are still my close friends to this day. We shared laughter and our utmost joys together. We attended graduations, weddings, birthdays, baby showers, family reunions, and so much more together. We supported each other during our deepest and saddest hours when a family member were sick, or on their death beds in the hospital. We have cried and leaned on each other at our most critical times. We were like family.

Many of my clients have supported me not only in the bad times, but the good times too and I appreciate them. It saddens me to this day having to close the salon. Two of my clients patronized my business the entire thirty six years of my career in the hair industry. I knew I would miss serving as their hair stylist, and having our inspiring conversations and those humorous laughs we had together. But Ecclesiastes 3: 1-8 KJV lets us know: "To everything there is a season, and a purpose under the heaven." I was experiencing verse six: "A time to get, and a time to lose, a time to keep, and a time to cast away."

Everyone will experience seasons in their lives just like the four seasons: Winter, Spring, Summer, and Fall. Like the changes in the four seasons, life's seasons brings about many changes also. My season in the hair industry regretfully was over and I would later experience many of these seasons. This was a devastating time for me and my clients, but I had to make sure my clients were not left without a hairstylist. I referred all of them to a beautiful Christian friend name Willie who I met shortly after graduating beauty school. We also worked together in a salon after Pat's salon closed. I knew Willie as a Christian woman, and felt she would do a great job and treat the ladies with the upmost respect. Some of the ladies are still patronizing Willie services to this day, seven years later. A few of my clients chose their own hair stylist.

It had been months since I had back surgery and a day didn't go by that I wasn't in pain. I cried out asking God to heal me, but if He didn't remove the pain I asked that He please give me the strength to endure it. I felt I needed closure

Retirement with Bettye and Sandra.

because every morning I would make my way to the salon in my home, and stand there in disbelief looking around the room. There were no longer clients or laughter; I missed my clients so much. My husband even missed talking to the ladies. My husband would sometimes pass through the salon, and some of the ladies who were widows would ask him questions about their ring door bells, home alarms, or the best cell phone or compute to purchase. We must seize every moment God gives us and make the best of it, because our lives can change in an instant.

Retirement with my husband

I told my husband and daughter I wanted to have a retirement banquet so I could have closure from the Beauty Industry. They agreed it would be a great idea. I then called two of my dear friends, Sandra and Bettye who I knew would help me with the plans. They didn't hesitate to say yes I would love to help. After my request to my family and close friends, a retirement banquet was planned. Family, friends, clients, and co-workers were invited.

Eight months after having back surgery, on July 22, 2017, at 5:00 p.m. a banquet was held in my honor. Adrian, another good friend of mine greeted the guess with a warm welcome at the guess table as they signed the guess book. My Pastor opened with a prayer, and a scripture was read by another Pastor. My son Steven and his wife Teresa gave a warm welcome. A special table was reserved for everyone. My clients, family, and close friends sat up front. Several of my clients were on the program to share memories of the many years I served as their hair stylist. It brought tears to my eyes to hear some of their annotations. It's important to treat people the way we want to be treated, and serve with our skills, gifts, and talents as though we are serving God. "A good name is chosen, rather than great riches, and loving favor rather than silver and gold." —Proverbs 22:1 KJV

That night would be a night to remember. We enjoyed a delicious catered meal. My daughter had a cake specially made with hair styling tools on top which was beautiful and delicious. We were entertained with a skit by my daughter and friends, Bettye and Sandra. My granddaughter's Lanasia and Xaria performed a skit, and danced a powerful praise dance. My daughter sang an anointing song, and my brother in law Mahlon played a beautiful rendition of the Lord's Prayer on the key board. The highlight of the evening was the fashion show. It was exciting to watch as family and friends graced the runway. I was blessed with monetary and beautiful gifts, but what moved me the most was seeing the support of my family, good friends, Co-workers, and Church members who came out to celebrate my retirement with me.

What a blessed time we had. My dear friend Carolyn Gordon who I met in beauty school thirty six years ago, traveled from Atlanta Georgia to support me. And my dear friend Patricia Moore who welcomed me to work in her salon after I closed mine was there with her husband Art. My dear ex-coworker Christine Dungie (Chris) attended. Chris would always fit me in her busy schedule whenever I needed my favorite updo hair style for special occasions. The retirement banquet was a grand occasion. It was now over and I thought I would have closure, but it wasn't so.

It took months before I could conceive that I could no longer work in the hair industry. Maybe if it hadn't been so sudden I could have accepted it better. It wasn't easy for me to sit down and do nothing after working most of my life. Eventually with God's help, I realized that I had to move on because I could never work in the salon again. Although I have moved on, to this day I miss my clients tremendously and I still call to check on many of the ladies, especially the elderly ones.

It was hard adjusting to retirement and not able to do all the things I use to do. I loved singing in the church choir and on the praise team, but I had to go on a sabbatical after singing in the choir for more than forty eight years because I could no longer stand for long periods of time. I also missed the fun times that I had with my grandchildren going to the park, library, shopping, and running around the yard playing with them. Although I was sixty one years old, I was still vivacious and had plenty of energy until having back surgery.

My youngest grandson was thirteen months old and I could no longer pick him up because of the pain. My husband and I loved riding his motorcycle. It had been our hobby for forty years but now I can no longer ride. For the next year and a half, I suffered muscle spasms and severe pain on a daily basis. I had visited numerous pain specialist doctors trying to find relief, but most of them wanted to prescribe strong drugs, or do surgery and I refuse. I felt like my life would never be the same as before.

I became very emotional and would sometimes cry myself to sleep. Self-pity is the worst thing you can experience when you are going through storms. Feeling sorry for yourself only makes matters worse. Self-pity brings on depression, doubt, loneliness, and it makes you want to give up. That's the point where I was. Then I thought about Jesus and how He suffered on the cross. His pain was so severe, mine couldn't compare. Jesus prayed on Mount Olive to the Father asking that "If thou be willing, remove this cup from me, nevertheless not my will, but Thy will be done." Luke 22:42-44 KJV. I began praying this prayer which gave me strength.

CHAPTER FIFTEEN

Hope Never Fails

I knew God wouldn't give me more than I could bear, and if He didn't remove the pain He would help me be able to bare it. God was helping me adjust to retirement and I knew He would carry me through this storm like he had done so many others, although this would be my first big physical storm. I held on to my faith and hope, and eventually self-pity and loneliness left. Sixteen months had passed since I had back surgery. One day I received a phone call from someone I knew who had recently had a successful back surgery. She had heard about my failed surgery and thought maybe her doctor could help me. She explained that she had recently had a successful back surgery from a renowned neurosurgeon who was one of the best in the world. She recommended that I talk to him about my condition and maybe he could help me. By now I didn't trust any doctor, but I did go online and do my research about him.

I read that he was one of the best neurosurgeons in the world but that didn't move me. It only reminded me of the doctor who said he was the Orlando Magic players' doctor who left me with nerve damage. I continued reading, and his reviews were great. Then I saw video testimonials of famous people who said their lives had been changed after he did their surgeries. Some said they had no quality of life until this renowned doctor fixed their problems. All of the comments said the doctor was patient and concerned about his patients. After reading about this doctor, I said maybe I will go in and talk to him but no more surgeries. I called and asked if they were accepting new patients. They said yes and accepted my insurance. Thank God!

The doctor was extremely busy so I couldn't get an appointment until a month later. I felt good about seeing him especially after knowing he did a successful back surgery on someone I knew. The day of my appointment was finally here. I brought all of my X-rays and other test that I had previous taken, but the doctor wanted new test in case there had been changes since those tests were taken.

I returned a week later with the results from the MRI I had taken. After reviewing them, the doctor told me gently that the MRI didn't look good. He said I might need to have another laminectomy and spinal fusion surgery to try and correct the problem, but he first wanted me to try steroid injections to see if it would alleviate the pain. My thoughts were, "Oh no." I didn't want anyone cutting my back again although everything I had read, or heard about this doctor was good. A pain specialist doctor worked with this doctor in the same building. This doctor also owned a surgical center near his office. I agreed to have the steroid injection. It was scheduled that same week. The pain specialist doctor would administer the steroid injection at the surgical center.

After having the steroid treatment twice without success, the doctor recommended moving forward with the surgery to try and relieve the pain. I had suffered for sixteen months and was desperate for some relief, so I agreed to have the surgery. The doctor advised me that it was a chance the surgery wouldn't be successful because the nerves were severely damaged from the first surgery. I agreed to have surgery once again but the horror of the failed surgery was etched in my mind. The doctor had such a pleasant personality and good bedside manners, and he made me feel that I could trust him but I had to pry my mind away from the last surgery. I put my total trust in the Lord because I knew He would protect me, and lead and guide the doctor through the surgery.

This doctor had an amazing team who would assist him during the surgery. The doctor explained that he would have to make a one and a half inch incision near the old scar because he didn't want to cut into the old incision because of the scar tissue that had formed. He said my recovery would take at least eight weeks. I agreed to have the second surgery because I was tired of living with the excruciating pain.

The surgery was performed March 3, 2017 at 7:00 am. My husband, daughter Suhdeena, and my youngest son Steven were there for support. The hospital was beautiful and clean, and the nurses were compassionate. The last thing I remembered before surgery was praying while the anesthesiologist administered medication to put me to sleep.

After the surgery I had minimum pain and my hospital stay was only three days.

Although the doctor did his best to correct the nerve damage, the surgery was unsuccessful. When I went home the pain was still there. At my post-op visit to see the doctor I told him I was still in pain. He was sincerely sorry, and said in time it may get somewhat better but it was just too much nerve damage done from the first surgery. He said there was nothing else he could do accept continue prescribing medication that would alleviate some of the pain.

In other words, he was saying I would have to live with the pain. I was devastated but I still had hope. I felt the doctor did his best to try and help me, but I know from working in the hair industry, that it's sometimes hard to try to fix something that someone else messed up. He prescribed Lyrica and the nurse called in the prescription to the pharmacy. After leaving the doctor's office, my husband took me home and went to pick up the prescription. The pharmacist told him that my portion to pay would be two hundred and fifty dollars. Unbelievable! She said the cost of one pill was five hundred dollars without insurance.

I had no choice but to stay on the Gabapentin, which was in the family of Lyrica, but was a generic brand. So now I was back at square one. I have submitted myself to God, and I'm a Christian who has strong faith, but that doesn't matter to Satan. If we do not serve Satan he becomes our enemy. He tried his best to discourage me and cause me to fall into depression again, and make me feel that I no longer had a purpose in life. He said I might as well give up and die because God no longer had need for me. He made me feel as though I would never have any quality of life. But then God's voice reigned above Satan's and told me, "I AM WITH YOU." These words kept me from falling into despair.

During my recovery, God began ministering to me, letting me know that He loved me and still had work for me to do. A short time after, He gave me another play to write titled "The Blind Barber and Five Hair Stylists." The last play I had presented was titled "Order in the House" on September 16, 2016. I believed God inspired me to write "The Blind Barber and Five Hair Stylists" to take my mind off of my pain.

I was still using my walker but I managed to make it to my computer to write what God had inspired. The first day I sat down to write, Satan showed up with one of his most dangerous tactics "FEAR." It normally takes me seven months to a year to write a play, but I completed this one hundred fifty page play in four months and wanted it performed as soon as possible because I didn't know what my future held.

Satan is the greatest deceiver of all. Just because you may be a religious person, don't think you can't be deceived. I wanted to complete the assignment God had given me, and I fell prey to Satan's deception that day. God had brought me through so much, and I loved and trusted God but I allowed Satan to bamboozle me like he did Eve in the Garden of Eden. Fear will cause you to do things unimaginable. Do not be deceived by the enemy through fear. I had never completed a play before in such short time, but because of fear I half-heartedly threw a script together and wanted it performed as soon as possible thinking I might die before completing it.

Yes, God had given me the assignment to write the play, but I presented Him with a half done job which was unacceptable to Him. I even added my two cents instead of staying on the path with the message that God inspired. When doing so, this changed the entire message God intended.

I even planned a time and date to have the play performed without acknowledging God. God had inspired me only to write the play, not to have it performed yet. In the past I had always prayed, asking God for direction when He gave me an assignment because Proverbs 3:6 KJV tells us: "In all thy ways acknowledge him, and he shall direct thy paths," but this time fear got the best of me. After completing the play, I planned a casting call for actors. I met with casting directors who were going to help me choose the cast. Lastly, I scheduled a table read on July 3, 2017 only four months after my back surgery. My plan was for the cast to learn the script in eight weeks then present the play shortly after. My timing was not Gods timing because it didn't happen.

I have always tried my best to stay in close communication with God, especially when He gives me an assignment. I learned a valuable lesson the hard way, that when we allow fear to overtake us, it's a trick of Satan's. Fear caused me to do things my way, instead of God's way. My dad used to say that you never get too old to learn. I learned that when God calls me to an assignment, I must trust Him and listen attentively to every detail and not just part of it. Satan came when I was weak and vulnerable to deceive me. I panicked and rushed because I didn't want to die without completing the assignment God had given. John 10:10 lets us know that, "The thief cometh not, but for to steal, and to kill, and destroy." I am come that they might have life, and that they might have it more abundantly. Satan's intent was to mislead me, and even kill me as I was rushing to do the play so soon after having back surgery, but God's grace prevailed. God's timing is not our timing.

I was feeling better and was glad to get out of the house and return to church. For more than twenty years my husband and I went out for dinner after church on Sunday. I was so happy to be back at church, and was looking forward to going to one of our favorite restaurants although I was still in pain from the second back surgery. Our grandson Jaylan, and granddaughter Samiah went to church with us after spending a night. As we left church on our way to dinner, a young man in our neighborhood was texting while driving and ran through the stop sign. He scarcely missed our car.

He would have hit the rear of our car where our grandchildren were sitting if my husband had not swerved and hit the curb, which landed us in someone's front yard. The guy kept going and never looked back as if nothing had happened. We checked to make sure our grandchildren were alright, then we sat there a minute in shock to calm ourselves. It happened so fast we couldn't get the tag number on the car. I wanted my husband to chase that joker down so we could get his tag number and report what had happened to the police, but my patient husband said no let's just thank God we are all alright.

By the time we got close to the restaurant, I began feeling radiating pain around my rib cage. I was able to walk in the restaurant and order my dinner, but minutes later the pain had become so bad I could barely sit up. It felt as though my chest had fallen into my stomach. I was praying that I had not reinjured my back. I told my husband we needed to leave so I could go home and lay down. He told the waitress to cancel our order as we had an emergency.

My daughter came to check on me, then took the grandchildren home so I could get some rest. We had chosen the cast for the upcoming play, and rehearsals were scheduled for the following Monday. I asked my daughter to call everyone and let them know the play had to be postponed until a later date. That night the pain got worse. I began praying asking God to take this unbearable pain away. We don't always understand why God allows us to go through things that seem so hard to bear, but I realized that all that I went through God was working it out for my good.

God knew that I had suffered severe pain from going through two back surgeries already, but He allowed me to go through this. What I didn't know was if that young man had not run through that stop sign that day I might not be here to write this book. As that night lingered, the pain became worse. It had only been four months since the last back surgery. As my husband helped me to the bathroom I had a sudden loss of bladder control.

I thank God for giving me a husband who has truly lived up to his wedding vows. It's easy to live out the health part of the vows, but what about the sickness part? My husband helped me shower then helped me back in bed. It was after midnight but he went to buy some women's incontinence underwear for me.

I never would have thought I would be wearing something like that, when just a few years prior I was vivacious and on the move for God, my family, and my business. By morning I could barely stand and was still losing control of my bladder. I could no longer make the few steps to the bathroom, so my husband brought in the portable toilet that we had in storage for my mother whenever she visited.

CHAPTER SIXTEEN

A Devastating Setback

My husband had called and left a message Sunday night to the neurologist office explaining what had happened. As soon as the doctor office opened Monday morning the nurse called and told my husband that the PA wanted me to come in immediately. Before leaving, my husband reclined the car seat and packed it with a blanket and pillows to make the ride as comfortable as possible.

He got my wheelchair out of the garage that I thought I would never have to use again, and managed to get me in the car. Every turn he made, and every bump he went over was so painful I could barely breathe. I panted and cried all the way to the doctor's office which was a twenty-five-minute ride to Ocoee, FL. The receptionist saw how much pain I was in, so she went to the back and told the PA. He came out and saw me bent over in my wheelchair crying loud, not caring if the other patients were looking on.

He told my husband I needed to go straight to the hospital, which was a few blocks away from the doctor's office. This was the same hospital I went to for the second back surgery. The receptionist had us wait until she called the hospital to make sure they had a room available. I was told that it would be at least four hours before a room would be available. I had the choice of going to the hospital and wait in the lobby for four hours, or ride twenty five minute back home and wait until the hospital called. I could not fathom sitting in that wheelchair for four hours, so my choice was to go home and wait for the phone call from the hospital.

I had to endure the painful ride home all over again. I asked my husband to help me to the couch instead of the bed, and then I took my medicine hoping I would get some relief but to no avail. The pain became worse by the minute, I couldn't eat nor sleep. Finally, about four o'clock that evening the hospital called. Once again we would have to go through the same process of my husband trying to make me comfortable enough to make it to the hospital. We could have called an ambulance, but the last time I was transported by ambulance the ride was atrocious. I felt every bump in the road so I preferred for my husband to drive me because he had more compassion than the EMT'S. Their job was to get me there safe, and as fast as possible.

After arriving at the hospital, they sent me to take an MRI that the doctor ordered. Later that evening my doctor came to my room and told me he did not like the results of the MRI. He told me that as much as he dreaded performing another surgery it was necessary, and he wanted to do it as soon as possible. I was in shock; I couldn't believe this couldn't be happening again. Three back surgeries in less than two years.

The last back surgery was just four months ago, and now the doctor's message would be the same as before, I would need surgery. But the news would be much worse than just surgery again. The doctor said he saw a spot on my spine that he was concerned about. I was so tired of suffering but the only thing I could do was continue trusting God. At this point I just wanted the pain to go away so I agreed to have surgery. I was hoping that whatever the spot was it wouldn't be anything serious, and the doctor would remove it during surgery. Early the next morning the surgery was performed. When I woke up I was in unbearable pain once again.

They administered the maximum dose of Tramadol which was that drug for chronic pain. This was the same drug that caused me to fall asleep minutes after taking it. I began having flash backs of all the medications I was prescribed after the first back surgery including Tramadol. Thank God I was able to keep the medication down but same as before, as soon as I took it I would fall asleep for two hours then the pain would return. Later that evening my doctor came to my room with a sad look on his face. I didn't think anything was wrong because I assumed the spot he had seen was nothing to worry about because he had removed it during surgery.

I thought the pain that I was still experiencing was from the surgery and I knew in time I would get better. The doctor began explaining that the surgery was more severe than he originally thought. He told me the spot that he saw on the

MRI was a tumor on my spine. He explained that my spine was weak due to the tumor deteriorating my bones, which caused the Thoracic Spine to fracture. The main function of the thoracic vertebrae (spine) is to hold the rib cage and protect the heart and lungs. This is why I felt all the weight from my chest bearing down on my stomach. My spine had fractured.

When the doctor went in to do the surgery, he wasn't sure what the spot on my spine was but he was hoping for the best. He told me it was a blessing that my husband jumped the curb that day because the tumor might have been detected too late. He didn't know how long the tumor had been growing on my spine, but he said if it had stayed there two more months I would have been permanently paralyzed.

I believe it was meant for the young man to run that stop sign just so I could live. I was walking around and had no idea a tumor was growing on my spine because I had no pain in my back. I was only experiencing the pain from the nerve damage. I thank God for working things out for my good, and for protecting my family from getting hurt.

The doctor had to remove an inch of my spine and do a bone graft. Bone grafting is beneficial in fixing bones that are damaged from trauma or problem joints. He had to use cement, a balloon, and titanium screws to stabilize my back. I also lost an inch of height. I was five feet six inches before the back surgery; I'm now five feet five inches. I must have been in shock after the doctor explained everything to me because I did not comprehend exactly what he was saying about the tumor. Before leaving my room he told me he was referring me to see an oncologist, but I still didn't put the two together.

Why would I need to see an oncologist if the doctor took the tumor off of my spine during the surgery? The next morning a tall Indian doctor came into my room. He introduced himself and gave me his business card. He said he was an oncologist doctor and told me I could call his office for an appointment. Later that afternoon, another oncologist came into my room telling me the same thing. I assumed my doctor referred these doctors. I still wasn't sure why my doctor wanted me to see an oncologist, but I chose the tall Indian doctor because his office was nearer to my home and I wouldn't have to go that far.

Weeks later, I saw a commercial on television from a well-known Law Firm in Orlando that said if a doctor comes into your hospital room whom you don't know, to call their firm and report it because it's against the law. I didn't know that at the time. To this day I'm not sure if my doctor referred these two doctors or not because neither said my doctor referred them. At this point I didn't trust any doctors. I wondered why the neurosurgeon didn't see the tumor when he did the surgery four months ago during surgery. I thought, wouldn't it have shown up on the MRI.

After I had surgery, I notice a difference in the nurse's behavior. One of my nurses was a male. He was a Christian and was always chipper and attentive. He took excellent care of me, but now he was standoffish. I even noticed a difference in the housekeepers. She had been so nice and was overjoyed talking to me about her upcoming vacation to the Bahamas. The nurses all seemed sad whenever they entered my room. Eventually I had new nurses and didn't see the two nurses I previously had anymore. I wondered did I do something to upset them. I had built a rapport with the nurses and the housekeeper, and I always try to be the best patient whenever I go to the hospital.

The housekeeper had told me she was going on vacation for two weeks so I knew I wouldn't see her anymore, but I didn't understand why the two nurses were no longer taking care of me. I asked another nurse what happened to the two nurses that I had come familiar with and she said they were working on another floor.

The day I was released to go home, I saw the male nurse standing at the nurse's station. When I first met him I was hesitant about having a male nurse, but after seeing how caring and professional he was, I was alright with him being my nurse. After having surgery I tossed and turned in pain all night because the mattress was so uncomfortable. I told my nurse, and right away he put in an order for a new mattress for me and it was delivered the next morning.

Every time he would come in my room we would talk about God's goodness. The nurses were all compassionate, so I guess whatever they read on my chart must have been devastating and to sad for them to face me knowing what they knew. I figured out later that they knew something that I didn't know.

It must have been hard for them to continue looking in my face with a smile with their hearts filled with empathy and sadness for me.

My husband pushed me in the wheelchair near the nurses' station and I said goodbye to the male nurse, and thanked him for taking such good care of me. He said it was his pleasure, and then told me he would be praying for me. The house keeper must have known something too. She told me she wouldn't see me anymore because she was going on vacation, but she told me not to worry and she would be praying for me. When I got home I was still in a lot of pain.

The following day after returning home, I called to schedule an appointment to see the oncologist like the doctor ordered. I still did not comprehend what my doctor had told me about the tumor he found on my spine. They scheduled me to come in right away. The day I saw the oncologist was a day that I will never forget.

It was like Deja Vu all over again. My husband pushed me in the office that day in my wheelchair, and everyone watched with pity when they heard me crying because of the pain I was experiencing, just like when I had the second back surgery. The receptionist asked me questions but I was in too much pain to answer. My husband had to answer and fill out the papers. The receptionist felt so bad for me and she kept saying, "I'm so sorry."

Finally, after waiting about twenty minutes, they called us to the back to see the doctor. There sat the tall dark hair Indian doctor that I had met in the hospital. He was soft spoken, friendly, and seemed concerned. He sat on his stool across from us, and the first thing he asked was did I know why I was referred to an oncologist. I said no but was just following my doctor's orders.

He then asked if my doctor told me the results from the tumor. I let him know that my doctor told me I had a tumor on my spine and I assumed it was benign and he removed it during the surgery. We were not ready for what was to come next. The oncologist said the doctor tried to perform the surgical procedure to remove the tumor but it was worse than he expected, so he had to leave it on my spine.

He said the tumor had fractured my spine because it was so deep into my spine, and it was cancerous. My husband

and I sat there in shock for at least five minutes without saying a word. It was as though time had stopped. The doctor gave us time to process the shocking news, then he explain that I would need to have radiation and chemo treatments to attack the cancer to save my life. I was like, is he talking about me? I felt as though I was dreaming. I could hear his voice way off into the distance as he sat right in front of me, but it took me some time to grasp, this was my life he was talking about. Tears streamed down both our faces, then we looked at each other and my husband held my hand tight, letting me know everything would be alright. Just the mention of the word "cancer" is bad news. I had a constant stream of bad news, but I wasn't going to give up without a fight, because one thing I knew was nothing was impossible with God.

The doctor went on to say the cancer I had was called Multiple Myeloma. He explained that it was a cancer of the plasma cells that weakens the bones. He said it was a very aggressive cancer. I never knew it was so many kinds of cancers, I thought cancer was just cancer. As the doctor continued to speak, I couldn't stop shaking because I was still in disbelief. We listened to everything the doctor said and I agreed to have the treatments the doctor suggested. The doctor said that normally patients start with chemo treatment first, then the radiation treatment to make sure the bad cancer cells are wiped out, but he was going to do the opposite for me.

He scheduled me to receive the radiation first so the aggressive cancer wouldn't spread, then the chemo afterwards. He said most of the pain I was experiencing was from the tumor on my spine and the radiation treatments would shrink the tumor, and the pain would subside. Finally, I asked him how bad it was. He said it was very aggressive and told me I had stage three cancer and had two years to live. This news almost knocked me off my feet but I just couldn't conceive that news. In my heart I began quoting Psalms 118:17-18 KJV, "I shall not die, but live and declare the works of the Lord," because I felt God still had work for me to do, and I knew He was in control of my life no matter what the doctors were saying.

Thank God I have already defied the odds of the life span he told me. I respect the knowledge of most doctors, but only God knows when we are going to be born and when we will die. Although it was devastating news, I wouldn't allow my mind to accept those results no matter what the doctor's report said. The doctor wanted me to start radiation treatments right away so I was scheduled to see a radiologist the following morning.

I went home and got in bed and a thousand memories flooded my mind. I always thought I was a strong person because I was always the shoulder to cry on for others, but sometimes no matter how strong you might think you are, it's good to have someone to lean on. I had gone through so much in such short time. If I didn't have God, my husband, family, and a few good friends, it would have been easy to give up. We need good people in our lives during good times, as well as bad times.

My adult children and daughter in law knew I was going to see the oncologist, and they were waiting on a call to hear what he had to say. I guess when I mentioned I had to see an oncologist, the word oncologist had them in a panic, when I hadn't given it much thought. I called and asked them to come over immediately because I needed to inform them of the doctor's report. I guess they assumed I had bad news to tell them from the sound of my voice. My daughter-in-law Teresa was the first to arrive. She ran into my bedroom while my husband sat in his office still in disbelief. Her eyes were filled with the look of fear. She looked at me and I couldn't hold back the tears.

She began consoling me. Then she said mom what's wrong, what's wrong. I cried telling her that I was diagnosed with cancer. She began to scream and ran down the hall shouting, "no no no." Then she began encouraging me telling me that everything would be alright. By that time my son Steven, and daughter Suhdeena and my grands arrived.

As I relayed the information to them everyone began to cry. No one spoke a word they just stood around my bed with the saddest looks I've ever seen crying. Then my son Steven came to my side and hugged me. He said, mom don't worry everything is going to be alright. My daughter Suhdeena couldn't hold back the tears. She hugged me but could barely whisper, "I love you mom, and it's going to be alright." All of the grands gave me a big hug while still crying. I told them all not to worry, God will see me through this.

It hurt so bad to see my family in such despair. They probably were thinking they would soon have to live without their mother and grandmother. Let me be real. I thought the same thing when the doctor gave me the diagnosis. It really tore me up inside to see my grandchildren crying. Jaylan and Samiah are my daughter's two younger children who were four and seven at the time. They didn't understand what cancer meant, but they knew something was terribly wrong with their granny when they saw everyone else crying, especially their mother. My family stayed awhile then told me to get some rest. I took my medicine and tried to go to sleep. I laid there thinking about what the doctor had said. God had healed me many times in the past, and I knew if He could raise Lazarus from the dead, He could heal me from this deadly disease.

As I laid there, the spirit of the Lord began to minister and show me many things. He let me know that even before I was born, my journey through life had already been written and carefully mapped out. He told me not to be dismayed of whatever storms I would face in life because He would hold my hand and carry me through the storms. Then He brought to mind that we needed to "GET OUR BUSINESS IN ORDER." I wondered, Lord are you getting ready to call me home? When He told Hezekiah in 2 Kings KJV 20 to set thine house in order, because he was going to die and not live. Thank God for hearing Hezekiah's prayer and added fifteen years to his life.

God made it plain that we needed to get our earthly (everyday) business in order. God knows the plans He has for our lives, but we should do some preparing. Many of us don't have anything in order if God were to call us home today. A Will, Trust, Beneficiary, Power of Attorney, Health Care Surrogate, and No Funeral arrangement set in order. So many people have life insurance but that's it. Most don't want to talk about death, make funeral arrangements in advance, or any of the above. These things are so important to discuss with spouses or a loved one, because it alleviates stress, arguments, and headaches from family members left behind when we are gone. And it's more of an assurance to you that things will likely go as you planned.

This earth is not our home, and it's sad when a person lives each day not giving any thought or concern of the responsibility that will fall on others when they die. I heard someone say, "I'm not worried about having insurance, because when I die my family will make sure I have a decent funeral." He died, and the burden fell upon his family to bury him. We should first have our spiritual house in order, and then make sure everything is in order in our homes. It will bring such peace even on our death beds knowing our family won't have to have a fish fry, car wash, or beg for money on a Go Fund Me Account to bury us.

I laid there still in the presence of God allowing Him to take control of my thoughts. God was letting me know that I would have many storms ahead, but he gave me the consolation in knowing I would live and not die, but to prepare because one day He would call my name. Romans 8:28 KJV, "And we all know that all things work together for good to them not that love God, to them who are called according to his purpose." After reading that scripture, I knew God was going to work things out and bring me through this for His purpose. But this was a warning for my husband and I to get our business in order because we don't know the minute, day, or hour the Lord will call us home.

As I was focusing on the assignment God had given me, the devil tried to discourage me by overriding what God said to me just like he did Adam and Eve in the Garden of Eden when God told Adam not to eat of the garden. Eve fell for Satan's lies and Adam followed the woman and ate. Satan is relentless. Of course, he wouldn't be doing his job if he hadn't come to discourage me right after God spoke. He's very deceitful. He told me I waited too late to get my business in order because I would soon die. I didn't listen and didn't have dialogue with him. I brought my thoughts into captivity to the obedience of Christ and began concentrating on what God told me to do. That evening I discussed with my husband what the Lord had said, and we obeyed.

I was still in so much pain from the back surgery and now I had to fight for my life. I'm a woman who has fought and won many battles with the Lord on my side. I've faced oppression, depression, anxiety and doubt. I've been overwhelmed, terrified and paralyzed by fear. But through it all, the storms that I've gone through has made me stronger, built my faith, and has drawn me closer to God. This was a devastating setback. This wasn't a battle this time, it was a war I was fighting, but I had faith that I would win this war with God holding my hand and carrying me through the storm.

The oncologist wanted me to begin radiation treatments as soon as possible, so he scheduled me to see a radiology doctor the following morning to set up my appointments. The doctor office was near the hospital where I had the back surgery in Ocoee, Florida, so my husband and I had to travel the long ride once again to see the doctor. The doctor examined me, then explained the procedure of the radiation treatment. He said he would be the one arranging how much radiation to administer. He asked if I wanted to have my treatments at the office in Ocoee, or the location in Orlando. I chose the location in Orlando because it was in the same building as my Oncologist, and nearer to my home.

I had to be at the Cancer Center at eight am to receive treatment for seven days. I would receive radiation treatments on Thursday and Friday, but I would not receive treatment on the weekend. The treatments would continue on Monday for five more days. My husband and I sat in the waiting area until they called my name. My husband pushed me to the back in my wheelchair where my radiation treatment would take place, but he wasn't allowed to stay with me due to the strong radiation. The smell was horrendous. It smelled as though someone had been cremated. Fear tried to overcome me, but I began praying within my heart and I calmed down.

I always heard that radiation treatments were worse than chemo treatments. The two technicians were an older lady and a young man. They were both very nice and professional. The female helped me get into a gown then rolled me to the radiation room. She explained everything that would take place before they began the treatment, and told me the doctor sent orders as to how much radiation to administer. She assured me that the procedure would only take seven minutes and it shouldn't hurt, but let her know if I felt any discomfort.

They both helped me onto the table. It was a nightmare getting upon the step and laying on the hard equipment after having had back surgery just a few weeks prior. I was praying while lying there asking God to keep me safe, and to let the technician give me just the amount of radiation the doctor ordered, no more, or no less. After lying there for what I felt was more than seven minutes and they hadn't started the test yet, I knew something was wrong. Finally the lady came back in the room and said something was wrong with the machine but not to worry.

I laid there for another ten minutes on my back and just as soon as I was about to call someone to let them know I couldn't lay there much longer because of the discomfort, is when both technicians came into the room and apologized saying the machine was new and he had to call the technician who works on the machine for advice. Sounds similar to the story told to my family at the hospital where I had the first back surgery. What a way to start my first treatment. By that time, I was ready to run.

Yes, I still had faith but I had learned to speak up and be aware when it came to my health after experiencing bad doctors with fancy degrees, beautiful offices, who camouflage themselves as good doctors. This lady assured me it would only take seven minutes and my treatment would be over. Now it's been seventeen minutes that I've been laying on a hard surface after having back surgery, and they had not begun the treatment yet. I had to ask the Lord to keep me calm.

All I could think of was this young man who is going to administer the radiation don't know how to work the machine. Something is wrong and I don't want this guy giving me too much radiation. I guess they saw the concern in my eyes because both of them began telling me they had everything under control and not to worry. They said they got it worked out and were ready to start.

I hesitated for a minute, and then said, "Alright, only seven minutes right?" They both said yes. I laid there as still as possible because they told me not to move. They pulled this big machine over my body as I laid on my back, and a light beamed down directly onto the thoracic area where the tumor was. Finally, seven minutes past and it was over. The seven minutes felt like thirty minutes because I had laid there for so long prior to the treatment.

I wasn't sure how the treatment would make me feel afterwards, but it was painless. The female technician helped me to the dressing room. After helping me get dressed she called my husband to bring my wheel chair. She bided us goodbye and said she would see me tomorrow, and told me I would begin to feel better after the third treatment. I went home in pain but told myself, in three days I will feel better.

I repeated the same process on Friday and everything ran smoothly. I was on the machine for seven minutes and out the door in twenty minutes. I had been back and forth to so many doctor appointments since getting out of the hospital, I couldn't wait for the weekend to come so I could rest and spend time with God. I was still a bit stunned about the bad news I had received, so that weekend I had time to really spend time with God. After much prayer, I read Psalms 121:1-2 KJV, "I will lift up mine eyes unto the hills, from whence cometh my help. My help cometh from the Lord, which made heaven and earth." After spending time with God, I felt my help coming. I began quoting Psalms 118:17 KJV again. "I shall not die, but live and declare the works of the Lord." I began to draw strength from the scriptures.

Even Christians have emotional distress after something traumatic happens in their lives at times. This was a hard pill to swallow and fear knocked me down for a minute, but I got back up. I thank God He stirred my confidence and hope while going through emotional and physical struggles to still trust Him like I had so many times before. I've known Christians who have cursed God for allowing them or a love one to go through devastating storms. No matter what I would face during this journey I had to walk by faith and not by sight, and lay my burdens at Jesus feet. Although I had concerns, God gave me peace. I knew God would carry me through this storm just like He had in the past. I believed He was going to perform a miracle in my life, although I couldn't yet see it.

After the third treatment the pain in the thoracic area had almost completely gone. But later that day, when I tried swallowing my medications, I had trouble swallowing. When I swallowed the pill, my stomach hurt so badly it took me to my knees. I called and spoke with the technician and she told me this was temporary and would subside in a few days.

Thank God it was. It lasted for two days and everything was back to normal.

I would have to wait two weeks before starting chemo after the radiation treatments were completed. This time would give my body time to heal. During this time, I drew closer to God than I had ever been before. I began thanking Him for carrying me through the radiation treatments without any harm to my body. James 5:14-16 KJV says: "Is any among you sick? Let him call for the elders of the church, and let them pray over him, anointing him with oil in the name of the Lord." I called on the elders of my church and they didn't hesitate to come.

The Women Missionaries came to my home the following Saturday afternoon. There were at least eight ladies who came and prayed, sang, read scriptures and encouraged me. One precious sister left healing scriptures to encourage me. The following Saturday, my Pastor and nine Deacons came to my home and did the same thing while I lay there on a hospital bed in my den.

My Sunday school class and choir sent beautiful cards and monetary gifts. Some church members sent flowers, fruit, and food. It warmed my heart to feel so much love from my church family. Our church's motto is "The Family That Cares," and they truly proved they cared. This gave me a big boost that I needed to get through the long eight months of chemo treatments. Expressing love to others especially when they are going through a storm means so much. It uplifts and give others hope. I love and appreciate my church family so much.

The time had come for me to begin chemo treatments. Like the radiation treatments, I didn't know what to expect. The radiation and chemo treatments were done in the same building where my oncologist's office was located. It was very convenient for me because the office was only fifteen minutes from my home. My oncologist had explained that in time, he would have to tweak the amount of chemo he prescribes. He said every patient is different so he gives the dosage according to how the body reacts to the medicine. I was scheduled to have chemo three times a week, on Mondays, Wednesday, and Friday. That Monday I began my chemo journey. My first treatment was eight long hours.

I sat in a reclined chair for eight long hours with a PICC line inserted into a large vein in my arm, with a bag hung from a pole filled with chemo medication that dripped slowly through a flex tube into my veins. The medication constantly dripped, so whenever I went to the bathroom I had to roll the pole with me. I prayed that I would be able to endure sitting in one spot for eight hours since I still suffered with nerve pain from the first failed surgery.

Muscle spasms would shock the left side of my body whenever I would sit in one spot too long. God was with me, I made it through without any spasms. The team of nurses seemed nice and knowledgeable all accept one. Out of all the nurses, life would have it that she would be my nurse because she worked the shift that I was scheduled to come in. I thought she would be knowledgeable in every area being that she was the head nurse in charge, but that didn't prove to be true. She found it hard to run a PICC (Peripherally Inserted Central Catheter) in the patients arm or hand. One day after sticking me three times and couldn't find a vein, I asked her if another nurse could try putting the PICC line in.

Before receiving chemo, a catheter (pick line) had to be placed in a vein in the arm or hand which allows the chemo medication to go through the veins. Without the catheter being placed in my vein I wouldn't be able to receive the chemo treatment. After the third try, the nurse called the phlebotomist who worked up front to come insert the PICC line in my arm. He was kind enough to help her out. The next visit was the same thing, she couldn't find a vein. I must admit, after having so much blood extracted from my veins over the years, my veins were hard to find but she didn't even try. She would search for a vein for a second then stick the needle in my arm like she was sticking frozen ice with an ice pick.

I tried my hardest to be still and not say anything because I could hear my mother-in-law who was my mentor, and best mother-in-law ever say, "Whenever you go to the hospital be kind, because if you are rude they have the upper hand and can give you a shot that can put you to sleep and you'll never wake up." But that day when she stuck that needle in my arm the third time, it would be the last time she would ever have the opportunity to stick me again. Although I could hear my sweet mother in laws voice, this nurse hurt me so bad I shouted, "Ouch! You hurt me." I said, "Wait just a minute, I'm not a test dummy." She said, "Your veins are hard to find," then walked away.

She went to the nurses' station and called the phlebotomist again to come do her job. From then on whenever he would see me come into the office he would say, "Don't worry Mrs. Jackson, tell the nurse I'll come back to insert the PICC line." Sometimes I would have to wait an hour before he became available. After having treatment three times a week for five months, I received a phone call from the Oncologist office telling me that I had to go to the hospital from now on to get the PICC line inserted by the PICC team before coming to get chemotherapy. I asked, "Why?" She said she was just relaying the message.

This would be such an inconvenience because the hospital was across the street from where I received chemo treatment. Now my husband had to drop me off at the hospital, and then wait in the parking garage in the cold weather until I called him to pick me up. Then he would have to take me to get my chemo treatment and wait hours until my treatment was over.

After doing this for a few days, I told him to go home until I called him instead of sitting in the waiting room wasting time when he could be doing other things. It was a long day for both of us on the days I had chemo treatments, but we learned to endure and take one day at a time.

One day after leaving the hospital and arriving at the chemo center, I peeped into the room where the nice young phlebotomist worked. When he saw me he looked very upset. I asked him what happened and why did he stop placing my PICC line. He kindly explained that he almost lost his job because someone reported he was working in the chemo area doing PICC lines. He told me he was contracted by a private company who hired him to collect blood only, and not to help nurses in the chemo area run PICC lines. By him helping the nurse do her job he was in violation of his contract with the company he worked for. I felt so bad for him, I had no idea. I apologized and thanked him for all he did to help me. I told him he was the best phlebotomist I had ever had because not once did he miss my vein on the first stick. It was inconvenient having to go to the hospital three days a week before going to get chemo treatment, but I preferred that routine rather than trusting the nurse to stick me.

When the nurse came to administer my chemo treatment, I asked her why the young man couldn't continue inserting my PICC line just to get her response. She said the rules had changed and the young man was no longer permitted to come in the chemo area anymore. Wow! What a big lie she told. She knew that was the rules when she asked him to help her. He also knew the rules, but because of his kindness and big heart, he almost lost his job because of her incompetence. He was such a nice young man who really knew his job. Whenever I had to go to him to get my blood drawn, he always had a smile and expressed his kindness towards me.

Eventually, I heard other patients complaining to the other nurses about the head nurse. One man said she didn't know what she was doing. One day an older lady screamed out telling her she was mean. I figured I better treat her nice although she wasn't fully competent, and wasn't always nice. I remembered what my mother- in law said, "BE NICE BECAUSE THEY HAVE THE UPPER HAND". I began having conversations with her while she was hooking me to the machine for my treatment and she soon warmed up to me.

I found out she was a loner. She told me she had no family except her father and she was his caretaker. She said she felt bad leaving him home alone while she worked. She would stop and call to check on him periodically. I would sometime overhear her asking him if he ate the lunch she fixed for him. As I got to know her better I began to show her compassion. She began sharing personal stories with me. After awhile, the nurse became nicer and more attentive to me. A few times she took off work to take her father to doctor appointment, and I would have another nurse administer my chemo. I had noticed how all of the other nurses would read the names of the medication to their patients before they infused it into their veins. They did the same with me whenever they were my nurses.

When I would come in for treatments the nurse's assistant would weigh me, take my temperature, and check my blood pressure then my nurse would take over from there. She would say good morning then began hooking me up to the machine. Not one time did she read the name of my medication to me before administering it. One day I went to the bathroom while pulling the pole with the IV bag and PICC line in my arm. I purposely took a pen and paper with me so I could write the name of my medication that was on the bag. I wanted to make sure she was giving me the same medication that the other nurses gave me.

CHAPTER SEVENTEEN

Gods Timing

I had compassion for my nurse when I realized the stress she was under at home with her father, but this was my life. We should leave our troubles outside of the work place, especially when others' lives can be jeopardized by our negligence. I felt better knowing it was the same medication that the other nurses had given me. She just didn't take the time to explain to her patients all they needed to know like the other nurses did their patients.

My doctor had ordered a PET scan some time ago but no one ever called me about scheduling the appointment. One day after receiving my treatment, I walked up front and asked one of the receptionists if she would check to see when I was scheduled for the PET scan. She said she didn't see me scheduled for that test, and that someone must have dropped the ball and didn't schedule the test.

This test provides a fully digital array of molecular imaging that detect most cancers, and to see if they have spread. I told her patients were fighting for their lives and how could someone be so negligent that they drop the ball on such an important test. She had the smart mouth and told me I have to be my own advocate. That was the best thing that lady could have ever said to me. She taught me a good lesson that day because now I'm my own advocate. I ask many questions and pay attention to every detail, and I make sure people do their jobs responsible.

I had to learn how to be gentle, but stern in order to make sure people focused on their jobs when it comes to my health. It's really sad when a person has a job that calls for compassion and empathy, and they don't exude those characters. I kept encouraging myself that this too shall pass, and I held on to hope because this cancer journey wasn't easy.

Finally, I was scheduled to take the PET scan but now my insurance refused to pay for two scans in a year unless the doctor sends a letter stating it was deemed necessary. Wow!

These big organizations care more about money rather than the patient's life. I mentioned to my doctor what my insurance said and he said he would do what was necessary for me to have the PET scan. I was feeling great but I had four more months of chemo treatments and I couldn't wait until it ended.

I was given vitamin D injections to keep my bones strong, and once every six weeks I had to get an injection to increase my white blood cells. The effects of the medication for the white blood cells were very painful. It made my bones hurt badly and caused me to have terrible spasms. Day after day I had to encourage myself by saying this too shall pass, and I continue taking one day at a time trusting God to see me through.

I was still going to the hospital to get my pick line before going to receive my chemo treatments. So much blood had been drawn from my veins that they had literally collapsed. I was a hard stick, but the doppler machine was accurate and never missed the vein. By now I had gotten use to the routine. I had learned to relax while getting my four hour treatment. I would sometime watch television or read a book. But most times I would look over the script of the play "The Blind Barber and Five Hairstylists". Although my timing wasn't Gods timing to present the play, I knew it would one day come to fruition because of Philippians 1:6 KJV, "Being confident of this very thing that He which began a good work in you will bring it to completion until the day of Jesus Christ."

One day I was sitting reading over the script while receiving chemo and realized I had made a mess of this play. I began thanking God for not allowing me to present it to the public. It would have brought shame to Him and me. The quality of the script was poor, and the message was not clear because I rushed to write it. I thanked God for covering me. I repented for going ahead of God adding my two cents to the play and not relaying the message he had given me.

One of Satan's greatest weapons he uses is discouragement. At my weakest moment, after having a second back surgery and was still in pain, I was deceived by Satan. I rushed to write the play that God had given me, because he deceived me by telling me I didn't know what my future held. He made me feel as though I would die without completing the assignment God had given me. So I hurriedly and half-heartedly completed the assignment. Every Christian will encounter the devil's lies and tools of discouragement at one time or another because he hates us. We must learn to resist the devil and trust God.

God was faithful and I knew He would never start a good work in me and not see it to completion. Sometimes when something traumatic happens in a person's life they lose focus, and some lose hope. That day as I reclined in the chair while the chemo was going through my veins, God gave me a peace beyond my understanding. I began thanking Him for keeping me through all that I had endured.

I no longer had pain in that area of my back where the tumor was. I could have still been walking around with the tumor eating away at my spine, but God stepped in on time. The doctor said it's a miracle that I'm not paralyzed and in a wheelchair. God with His powerful hand of mercy kept me for a reason. My God is amazing and worthy of all the praises. We should surrender our lives to Him, and trust Him in every aspect of our lives because He knows what's best for us.

I used to hear my grandma say, "Lord! Lead, Guide, Direct and Protect me while I'm on life's journey." Now I find myself praying the same prayer. While sitting long hours with my eyes closed while receiving chemo, I prayed asking God to give me directions about the play he had assigned me to write. My relationship had become more personal since spending tranquil hours with God. I looked forward to our time together. This had become our favorite meeting place although I was reclined in a chair receiving chemo.

There were no distractions. God could talk to me and I could hear His voice clearly. God answered my question about what direction I should go with the play. He simply said write the vision I inspired. He reminded me of the vision, and guided my thoughts into actions of of fulfilling His purpose.

I began making corrections to the script as God guided my thoughts. My mind was focused solely on fulfilling my assignment that He called me to complete. Writing took my mind off of the challenging times I was going through. I would sometime find myself laughing out loud while writing. I would say, God you have such a sense of humor. Some scenes in the play were very funny. My nurse would come over and say you must be still writing that play and I would say yes. It took months, but I finally completed the script "The Blind Barber and Five Hair Stylists." The play finally had come alive in my mind. Whenever I would share the title of the play people would laugh.

They must have thought it was a comedy because of the title of the play. The play depicts a gifted barber who was engaged to be married. One late night, while working in the barber shop he was beaten, robbed, and left for dead. The severe beating caused him to lose his sight. He went into a deep depression after losing his sight, job, home, and fiancée so he moved to Florida for a new start. He met a salon owner while they were both giving free haircuts at a park to children whose parents couldn't afford to pay. The salon owner couldn't believe her eyes when she witnessed a blind man cutting hair better than a barber with sight.

After hearing his story, she offered him the opportunity to work in her salon with herself and four other stylists. This is where he met his future wife. This play spoke volumes about Gods love, forgiveness, compassion, empathy, hope, and brought awareness to the beauty Industry. It also brought laughter to the audience. Proverbs 17:22 KJV tells us, "A merry heart doeth good like a medicine, but a broken spirit drieth the bones."

In Gods timing and guidance, I completed the script. I prayed over it and tucked it away in my files until I heard from God for further instructions. I had learned that obedience is better than sacrifice. I thanked God that all of the pain that I was experiencing from the tumor had gone. The radiation and chemo treatments worked and I was feeling great, except for the pain I was still having from the nerve damage from the failed back surgery. I was told I might have to learn to deal with it for a lifetime. I will never give up hope for my healing because God is the great physician, and I know Him as a healer. But I understand that some of our afflictions won't be healed until we get to heaven. I asked God to heal me from this nerve damage but if I have to wear this thorn, I asked Him to give me the strength to bare it. My Strength and energy level was almost like it was before I received the bad diagnosis of cancer. I felt like I was ready to get back on the battle field for my Lord. It had been only a month since I tucked the play away, when I heard God say it's time for the play to come to fruition. Most of the previous cast I had chosen could no longer be in the play for one reason or another, but God sent the ideal cast who were all mature Christians and dependable. Three of the cast members were ministers of the gospel. There was also a young boy in the play. Each actor fit their character role perfectly. It was as if the script was personally written just for them. They all did an exceptional job portraying the message God intended.

I was ready to get back to work doing what God called me to do, although I didn't have the extra money to fund a play at this time. I had spent so much money on co-payments, medicine, and medical bills. I was reminded of the woman with the issue of blood. She spent all of her money going to doctors while trying to find a remedy for her problem. But I knew that if God told me this was the time to present the play, He would provide the resources. After telling me it was time, God also gave me the venue where to have it.

I heard Him say Olympia High School Performance Arts Center. I said Olympia High Lord! He repeated. Yes, Olympia High School Performing Arts Center. I quickly remembered when I tried doing things my way pertaining to this play before. So, I said yes Lord! I'll do your will. I didn't know where the money was going to come from to have a gospel stage play in a big venue such as that, I had only had plays in churches. Nor did I know the diagnosis of where my health stood at this time, although I was feeling great. The doctor never mentioned anything else about the PET scan. But no matter what, I was going to be obedient to God if I had to die trying. I asked my doctor about the PET scan and he said he didn't order a second one because my blood work looked good and he was satisfied so I left it at that.

I would have to hire a Graphic Designer, Photographer, rent the venue and furniture. Rent a U-Haul, buy props, and hire a videographer, a security guard, Music Director, and so much more. I knew that the expense would be at least ten thousand dollars or more, but I was going to step out in faith and do God's will. I had no doubt that He would provide.

Finally, eight long months had finally passed since I had been receiving chemo treatments three days a week. Today my doctor will let me know if I can stop my chemo treatments, and continue on just the maintenance medication. I had become my advocate and done research on receiving too much radiation and chemo. It can destroy the organs faster than the disease itself. I was hoping and praying that I wouldn't have to continue treatments, plus I was exhausted from having to get treatment three times a week, and sometime had other appointments also. I know my husband was too because he was my chauffeur.

Although my husband was patient and never complained, I knew he was tired because sometimes he would get confused and go the wrong direction to one doctors' office, even though I had reminded him the night before which doctor I had to see. I would say, "Honey, we are going to the neurologist today, not the heart doctor." He would say, "Oh, I thought we were going to the heart doctor." We would laugh and he would turn around and go in the right direction.

Thursday had come. I had an appointment to hear the decision whether I had to continue chemo treatments or not. My husband prayed for good results before going to bed and again that morning before going to see the doctor. As we sat facing the doctor that morning, the memories of the day the day he gave me the bad news of my diagnosis came to mind. The doctor showed me the paper work of my last blood test and told me the levels show that I'm in remission. I said, "Exactly what does that mean?" He explained that the cancer is not cured but the radiation and chemo has the cancer at bay. He said I won't need to have anymore treatments, but I would have to take a maintenance medication to keep me in remission.

My husband and I were so happy. I began to thank God out loud and didn't care who saw or heard me giving God praise. My complete joy came back the minute I heard that good news. The first thing that came to mind, was now I can travel to see my ninety two year old mother again. I couldn't travel before because of the chemo treatments. Now I can travel and do other things I desire.

That mean old devil had told me I would never see my mother again, and that God no longer had use for me. Well! God made the devil out of a liar. God wanted me to write this play so others would be encouraged and He would be glorified through this play. At the time I didn't know how God was going to provided for me to have this play, but I was ready to run through a wall if He asked me to do so. I was overjoyed to hear such great news. In the early stages of me seeing this doctor, he asked me what kind of work I previously did. I told him I had been a cosmetologist for thirty six years and a playwright for seventeen.

I mentioned to him that I had written a stage play but couldn't have it performed because of what I was going through. I asked him if would it be alright health wise to move forward with the play, he said yes because I was doing just fine. I knew it would be, because God had predestined this time to bring the play to fruition. If God brings us to it, He will see us through it. The doctor said he would give the nurse the script to call in to the specialty Pharmacy so I can begin taking the medication to keep the cancer at bay.

The prescription was delivered to my door a few days later. It was a medication named Revlimid. The doctor also gave me prednisone, which was a steroid for inflammation. It caused me to gain weight but it didn't matter, I was just happy to be alive. They continued giving me vitamin D injections every six weeks, and the shot to help keep my bones strong. I took the Revlimid for two days and on the second day when I swallowed the pill, my stomach began to hurt so bad as it was being digested, I had to bend to my knees to get some relief. This was the same reaction I had during the time I received radiation treatments.

I called to speak with the nurse but she was with a patient. The receptionist said she would have the nurse return my call. The nurse called and said the doctor wanted me to stop taking the medication and he would try a different medication. She said as soon as he gets the script ready she would send it to the specialty pharmacy. I would now see the doctor every six weeks. I was grateful that I no longer had to get stuck in the veins, or sit in the chair for four hours during treatments. Sitting in that recliner chair had become my main meeting place to talk to God and I would miss our time there together, but I made sure I had a quiet place in my home where I could continue my quiet time with the Lord daily.

I received my new medication named Polmalyst and had no trouble with it. It seemed to be working just fine. I would have to have it refilled once a month through the specialty pharmacy which I didn't like. I would rather go to a regular pharmacy to pick it up because someone had to be home the day of delivery to sign for it. I had to schedule my doctor appointments around the day of delivery.

I had been taking the pills for two months and felt great. I had four pills left and normally the pharmacy would call me when I had four pills left to schedule a delivery date for the next month but I had not heard from them. I called the pharmacy and they told me they had not received a script from the doctor. I called the nurse and told her the pharmacy was waiting on the doctor to send a script for my medication. She said she would let the doctor know and would make sure the pharmacy receive the script once the doctor signed for it.

CHAPTER EIGHTEEN

A God of Impossibilities

After waiting three days and hadn't heard from the pharmacy, I called the doctor office because I had one pill left. I asked to speak with the nurse and the receptionist said she would relay the message because she was with a patient. The nurse soon called and said she gave the doctor the message about leaving the script for her to send in for a refill, but he must have forgotten. Then she told me he left yesterday for a two month vacation to visit his family in India. She said she checked my records and it wasn't recorded that I was even taking the Pomalyst. She said the doctor didn't mention anything to her after she gave him my message.

She apologized and said there was nothing she could do. I would have to wait until the doctor returned to get the prescription filled. I could not believe what I was hearing. I told her, "I have an appointment to see the doctor in four weeks, and you're telling me he won't be here." She apologized and told me to call and rescheduled because the doctor would be gone during that time. I had to hold my tongue. No one had the courtesy to call me to reschedule my appointment. But mostly, I wondered if the doctor was that tired and anxious to go on vacation that he neglected to make sure everything was in order for his patients before leaving? His assistant was recording the notes while he was explaining everything to me at my last visit. I couldn't understand why the most vital information, which was my medication wasn't in the notations or my records.

I was very upset, but I calmed myself because I remember the doctor saying chronic stress causes cancer to spread faster. I asked the nurse if would I stay in remission for two months without the maintenance medication, and she said I should be just fine until the doctor returned. After hanging up I prayed, thanking God for how far he had brought me. I asked Him to remove all distractions that would prevent me from doing his will. Lastly, I told God I put my total trust in Him and not man.

After praying, God calmed my emotions. I was feeling really good and no matter what, I was going to move forward with the play as the Lord instructed me. This time I wasn't going to let anything distract me. I had listened attentively to Gods instructions when to have the play and I trusted Him to make the provisions. I had given the script to the cast when God instructed me to present the play so they could begin learning it. This would allow the cast to learn the script in advance. Instead of rehearsing four months, we would only need two months of rehearsal before presenting the play.

My youngest sister Cindy had mentioned several times that she desired to be in one of my plays and would fly to Florida to do so. I had the perfect role for her, but I dismissed it from my mind because she had recently had a knee replacement and was still going through therapy. Plus, she was our mother's caretaker and she couldn't leave her to travel to Florida to be in my play. Cindy would also have to be here two months prior to the play for rehearsals even if I mailed her the script in advance.

This would be the first stage play out of the six plays that I had written that my mother wouldn't be able to attend. I talked to my mother about the play, and mentioned that I wish she and Cindy could be here. Right away my ninety two year old mother said we can be there. I told mama it might not be safe for her to travel such a long distance at her age with all of her ailments. I also mentioned that Cindy would be uncomfortable traveling such a long distance after recently having a knee replacement.

As long as I can remember, Mama has been a woman of faith. "No" was not in her vocabulary. Mama said, "I'm coming if I have to come by myself." I laughed and told Mama she was too much. My mother was diagnosed with dementia about eight years ago, but never accepted that diagnosis. Although my sister is her caretaker Mama still lives by herself. The doctor's diagnosis may have been wrong because Mama knew what each pill was for by its color. And she kept track of every penny that she had in the bank. Mama said I'm not claiming no dementia, that doctor must have dementia because he don't know what he's talking about.

I laughed then called Cindy after hanging up with Mama. I told her what Mama had said about coming to Florida for the play. I told her I would love for her to be in my upcoming play but I knew it was impossible. Cindy was surprised to know how well I was doing after being so sick. I had previously mentioned the play to her when I first began writing the story. She wanted so badly to play the character named Mother Johnson but I had to postpone the play due to being sick at that time.

Although Cindy was having medical problems, she surprised me when she said she still wanted to come and be in the play. She expressed that the only thing that would keep her from coming would be her funds. God is the God of impossibilities. He's a God of favor, and He's our provider who gives us our hearts desires. A week before rehearsals began, my husband and I picked my mom and sister up at the Orlando Airport. God made a way for them both to come all the way from Yuma Arizona to Orlando Florida and stay for three months. Nothing is impossible with God! I would soon experience it for myself.

They traveled two thousand, two hundred, and sixty two miles to get here. What a mighty God we serve. The enemy had told me I would never see my mother again because I was too sick, and she was too old to travel. I shall believe the report of the Lord! Well, here she is in the flesh. Look what the Lord has done! Faith is the key that unlock doors. My mother's faith brought her to Florida. In recent years while going through storms I cried many tears, but this time tears of joy fell from my eyes. Every year for the past thirty five years I had gone to Arizona to visit my family, or I sent for Mama to visit us in Florida. I had not seen my mom nor Cindy in almost five years since my first back surgery and it saddened me tremendously.

I was overjoyed as I walked down the airport concourse and saw a lady sitting in a wheelchair with several big hat boxes on her lap. I wasn't able to see her face because the hat boxes were stacked a mile high but I knew that was Mama, because every where she traveled, she carried her church hats with her. As I got closer, I looked down at her feet and saw she had on panty hose and a long dress, with church shoes on. I knew for sure that was Mama. I took a glimpse around the hat boxes and there mama sat with her church hat on her head and her pretty dress. She always travel dressed up as if she's going to church.

Mama has always been a stylish dresser, even now in her nineties. I shouted, "Mama!" Then gave her the biggest hug and didn't want to let her go. We looked at each other with joyful tears in our eyes, and then I told Mama I loved her and was so happy to see her. She gave me the same sentiments as tears filled her eyes. I knew she had been concerned about me. I noticed Cindy from afar limping going to retrieve their luggage so I rushed over to help her. I hugged my baby sister tight. We had a special bond because she lived with our family for three years when she was young. I felt like a mother to her during that time instead of a sister because of our ten year age difference. Over the years our sisterhood grew into a beautiful relationship. It was a blessing to see them both. Before coming to Florida Mama knew I was sick, but not to what extent.

The family hadn't told Mama that I had been diagnosed with cancer and Cindy had been very concerned about me ever since she heard the news. Mama is a praying woman and had the spirit of discernment, especially when it came to her children. Every time I talked to her on the phone she would constantly ask me if I was alright. She knew I was sicker than my siblings let on. I told mama I was having some medical problems but it wasn't anything that God couldn't fix. I told Cindy that Mama needed to be told about my condition before coming to Florida. God forbid if He called home to heaven without Mama knowing how sick I was she would be devastated. She had already lost my older brother Herman, the one who was my hair mentor. Mama was still grieving over him and it had been years since his death.

I felt it would be better to give her the news before coming to Florida so she wouldn't be shocked to know my diagnosis. Cindy and my brother Ricky agreed and sat Mama down before coming to Florida and told her everything, and Mama wasn't shocked at all. She said the Lord had already shown her that I was sicker than she was told, and she was prayer for God to heal me. I knew the primary reason for Mama and Cindy wanting to come to Florida was to check on me.

The plan was for them to stay three months so Cindy could be at rehearsals for the play, and to get some fun time in while visiting. The first two weeks of Mama and Cindy's visit I felt great. We really enjoy each other. We reminisced, laughed, went to church and out to dinner every Sunday. God had provided everything that I needed for the play and I was ready to put this gospel play on the stage. Rehearsals were going along great. Everyone had learned the script, even my sister Cindy. In every production I have someone play the role of mother Johnson in honor of my mom, whose last name is Johnson. Cindy played that role and she played it well. My ninety two year old mom attended every rehearsal, and to our surprise Mama had learned most of Cindy's lines. One day at rehearsal as Cindy began to act out her role as mother Johnson; Mama shouted out and interrupted her saying "That's not how you say it." Then she began reciting Cindy's lines as if she was in the play.

She told me I should have let her be in the play, because she could play the role of Mother Johnson better than Cindy because she's the real Mother Johnson. That was hilarious and the cast fell out laughing. Mama might be up in age but she's still witty and has always been a natural comedian without realizing it. Mama reminds me so much of the actress LaWanda Page, who played Esther on Sanford and Son. If Mama had been given the opportunity to play the role of Esther, I believe she would have made LaWanda Page look like an amateur actress.

Mama wouldn't have needed many rehearsals because her natural God given humor would have fit right in with Red Foxes humor. God gave Mama a gift to make people laugh in an extraordinary way. Cindy has the same gift. The night of the play Cindy was in excruciating pain but she played her role as Mother Johnson. The audience laughed hysterically, and was on their feet clapping and singing along with her as she sang an old gospel song to the blind barber while dancing on her walker in the beauty salon. Proverbs 17:22 says, "Laughter is good medicine."

At the age of ninety two, Mama still loves to be on the move. If she sees keys in your hand she will ask where are we going. I had plans of taking Cindy and Mama to explore the town once the play was over since I was feeling much

Nunn family on front porch

better. The cast and I were excited and looking forward to the upcoming play. Ticket pre-sales were going great and we couldn't wait until the exciting night. My family traveled far as Seattle Washington, Utah, Arizona, and some people traveled from New York to witness the play.

CHAPTER NINETEEN

A Turn For The Worst

Two weeks before the play was to be presented, out of the blue I became very ill. I woke up in the middle of the night soaking wet and trembling like a leaf. I tried to walk to the bathroom but didn't have the strength to make it on my own. I woke my husband so he could help me. We didn't understand why I suddenly became sick, but I refused to allow my mind to think negative thoughts. I began to pray while in the bathroom as my husband changed the linen on the bed. I asked God to help and strengthen my body so I could do what He called me to do. My husband helped me back in the bed and he prayed for me.

I could see the concern in his eyes although he is one who trusts God in every situation. Three hours later the same thing happened again. I began shaking uncontrollable and the sheets were soaking wet. I felt dizzy, and it felt as though shock waves were shooting through my head. My brain and body functions were not working properly. This went on for two days until my husband took me to the hospital on the third day. By then, I didn't want to eat and I could not control the shaking. I now see why God made a way for my mom and Cindy to be here. He knew I would need Cindy's help more than ever.

I was admitted to the hospital on fifth floor in the cancer unit. I was sad when I saw the big sign that said "Cancer Floor." As I laid in bed tears began to fall. I had been through so much and just when I began to feel better, this happens. My mind began to wander. All I could think about while lying there was how was I going to get the money to reimburse the people who had bought tickets to see the play if the play was canceled.

I had already spent thousands of dollars on this play in advance with the money from the ticket sales. The stress only made my health worse; my blood pressure went up and I began to run a temperature. The nurse gave me medication to lower the fever and my blood pressure. I had to encourage myself. I said, "SELF, why are you allowing your carnal mind to speak death over the play God ordained? Believe with your spiritual mind what God told you." As I laid there, the spirit of the Lord began to console me and give me peace. He let me know that, "He will never leave nor forsake me." He let me know that the assignment He had given me would come to fruition, and produce the results He intended.

Although I couldn't see how I was going to get up off of my bed of affliction in time for the play, which was now only two weeks away, I trusted God. Proverbs 3:5-6 KJV gave me strength. "Trust in the Lord with all thine heart and lean not unto thy own understanding. In all thy ways acknowledge him and he shall direct thy path." I rolled all of my burdens over to God and began thanking Him for what He was about to do. All of the worry and stress left my mind and body. I had faith that God was going to do a miracle.

The symptoms continued. Every three hours the nurse would come in to change my linen and gown because of the fluids that continued to pour out of my body. I was extremely cold and couldn't stop shivering. I asked the nurse to turn the heat up to ninety degrees. Numerous tests had been taken. My diagnoses were dehydration and anemia. I was given fluids and was released after the third day. I was told to follow up with my Oncologist. I lost thirty two pounds in five days. I looked sick and malnourished again after gaining a little weight back. My husband brought me home from the hospital and I went straight to bed still feeling just as weak and sick as I did before I went to the hospital.

Mama and Cindy had been very concerned and they were happy to see me return home. Cindy had the house spick and span. She cooked the meals and waited on me as if she was my nurse, although she was in pain herself from her knee replacement she had four months prior to coming to Florida. Cindy had found a therapist here, and had made arrangements before leaving Arizona to have therapy for her knee while her three months stay in Florida.

Cindy woke up at 6:00 am every morning to prepare Mama's coffee so it would be ready when she woke up. She would then go to therapy at 7:00 am and returned home by the time Mama woke up. She would help Mama shower and get dressed, then feed her breakfast. Then she would take care of my needs. Cindy wouldn't allow my husband to lift a hand to do anything. She had worked in the medical field too, and she waited on me with special care. It was only through Gods strength that she was able to do all the things she did while experiencing pain.

It was only a week and a half until the play was to be presented. Rehearsals had been scheduled for every night leading up to the play. I was still too weak to attend the rehearsals, but I was holding on to Gods promise that He would bring the play to fruition. I asked Cindy if she could meet the cast and set up for rehearsal and she said yes. She went above and beyond what I asked her to do. She took the torch and ran with it.

My fifteen year old granddaughter, Xaria, had two years of drama in high school and was interested in helping me with directing the play. I gave her the opportunity to be my assistant director at previous rehearsals and she did a great job. My dear friend Sandra stood in for me and assisted Xaria. Sandra had supported me in many ways, even acting in some of my plays. My oldest granddaughter Lanasia, who was sixteen, has a gift of systematizing. She was my stage manager. She did a great job making sure everything was on point behind the scenes. Without these three, I don't know what I would have done. The last week of rehearsal I made it official that these ladies would take charge.

I'll never forget the night I pressed my way to rehearsal, because I knew what God had said and I wasn't going to throw in the towel. As we stood in our prayer circle before rehearsing, I tried to pray but I began to shiver so bad I couldn't continue praying. My sister Cindy is a prayer warrior. She prayed for me daily and I know her powerful prayers reached heaven. Cindy took over where I left off and continued praying. Mama and the Saints began to pray also. At that point they were not cast members; they were prayer warriors who were sincerely concerned about me.

I know their prayers reached God on my behalf. The Saints could have easily walked away like the first group of cast members did, but they stood beside me believing the play would come to fruition as God had said. Even if I wasn't able to attend the play the cast could have carried on without me being present. I was so sick I felt as though I might not make it through the night, but I was holding on to Gods promise. He said I would see the play come to fruition and I believed Him.

I didn't let anyone know I was in the hospital, because so many people had purchased tickets and I didn't want it rumored that the play might be canceled; that would have been disastrous. It was less than a week until the play and I could see the worry in Cindy's eyes. I had lost so much weight and didn't look like myself. Cindy needed to run some errands and my husband wasn't home. I told her Mama and I would be alright. She said she wouldn't be gone long. Mama was in her room and I wanted to spend time with her. I managed to lean onto the wall and walk down the hall to her room. She was surprised to see me out of bed.

She smiled, then patted the bed and told me to come and sit next to her. I sat next to her on the edge of the bed as she watched television. Mama put her arms around me and drew me into her chest like I was still her little baby. Tears rolled down my eyes as she comforted me. Mama held me tight and prayed like never before, crying out to God to heal her daughter. Afterwards, she told me not to worry everything would be alright. Then she said, "I love you BIG RED," a name I'm effectually called by my siblings. I felt safe in Mama's arms and my spirit was revived.

Mama was a strong woman of faith, but I was concerned about her because she was ninety two years old and was still heartbroken after my oldest brother's passing. I told Mama not to worry about me because God had me in the palm of His hand. She said I'm not worried, I know God is going to heal you. I was so glad that God allowed me to see my mother again. It was almost unbelievable to see her back in the same room where she had slept many times before. I believed the report of the Lord that I would see Mama again.

That evening, Cindy made sure everything was set up for rehearsal but I was still too weak to attend. The team carried on and Cindy said the rehearsal went exceptionally well. That made me excited, and I was even more determined that God was going to raise me up from my bed of affliction in time. No matter how I was feeling, I wasn't giving up.

All of a sudden, I began receiving phone calls from other family members saying they were coming to see the play. My sister Janice, the nurse, called first and said she and her husband Sherry were coming to see the play. She said they would be here two days before the play. Mind you, they live more than two thousand miles away in Arizona. I was so happy and couldn't imagine them coming this far just to witness my play, which they had never done in the past.

The next day I got a call from my brother Ricky who lives in California. He said he and his wife Patrice were also coming to see the play. They would arrive a few hours after Janice and Sherry. I felt exuberated and excited to see my family who I had not seen in quite some time. Our family is a close knit family and we normally meet every year to celebrate Mama's birthday. I had not been able to attend any family events in five years because of all the physical problems.

My family would be here tomorrow and I felt so good just knowing the thought of them coming many miles to support me. I continued praying that God would do a miracle and give me strength to get out of the bed. It was hard enough seeing my mother and Cindy watch how fast I was diminishing, and although I was looking forward to seeing my family, I dreaded them seeing me sick and frail. It's now three days before the play, and I'm still in bed shaking and fluid pouring from my body waiting on God to raise me up from my bed of affliction. Cindy had gone to therapy early that morning, but she always returned home by the time Mama woke up so she could get her bathed, dressed, and fed. Cindy took the same care for

Mama while she was in Florida as she did when she was home in Arizona. Mama was a feisty ninety two year old, and she insisted on living in her own apartment although all of her children welcomed her to move in with them. Janice had recently moved back to Arizona and she helped Cindy take care of Mama. Although neither one of them live with Mama, they took turns coming by early in the morning to prepare her meals, clean, and to fulfill her physical, spiritual, and mental needs. Linda, Ricky, and Eddie lived out of town but they would come to town to relieve my sister's and looked after Mama. My brother Mike lived near Mama, and he was always there to help Mama before Cindy and Janice moved back home. Having eight children paid off for Mama.

I had so many places I had planned to take Mama and Cindy once the play was over; I had no idea I would become sick. Cindy went to therapy early one morning, and by that afternoon she had not returned from therapy which was unusual because she kept Mama on a schedule. I told Mama maybe she stopped by the mall just to get a break, but I couldn't understand why she didn't call to let us know where she was.

Mama had not had her morning medications, and she was hungry so my husband fixed her a bowl of cereal. I tried calling Cindy's phone numerous times but she didn't answer. Mama insisted that she knew how to take her medication but I told her she should wait until Cindy returned. Mama always tell us that she can still cook, get her own self dressed, and take her medicine by herself. She said she was tired of her children treating her like a baby. Mama would speak her mind even at age ninety two. We would explain to her that we were only making sure she was protected and being well taken care of, but she didn't want to hear it. Mama has always been an independent woman, and she didn't mind telling her children that she was the mama not us.

After Mama finished eating, she went to her room and got her medication and brought it to me. She said "I'm not waiting on Cindy, I got to take my medicine on time." Cindy was well organized. She had Mama's medicine prepared in the medicine container with the days of the week, and yes, Mama knew what every pill was for. She pointed out each pill as she explained to me what they were for. She said the pink pill is for high blood pressure, the blue pill is for cholesterol, and so on. Thank God she was able to take her medicine that day. After Mama finished taking her medicine, she made her way down the hall on her walker to the bathroom. I shouted from my room for her not to try and get in the tub by herself. She said she was just going to brush her teeth and wash up. I told her she should wait until Cindy came back, but she insisted on doing it herself.

I felt so bad that I wasn't able to get out of bed to help her, but I did the only thing I could do. I called out to her every few minutes, asking her if she was alright, and she would answer yes. Mama managed to get washed up and sit on the edge of the bed to dress herself. As she stood to sit in the chair across from the bed she fell onto the floor. She was calling for help but I didn't hear her because the televisions were on in our rooms, and she had closed the door while she was getting dressed.

My husband was in his office on the other side of the house, and thank God he heard Mama's faint voice all the way in the back of the house. All of a sudden I heard my husband yell out loud that Mama fell. I jumped up as if nothing was wrong with me. I knew it was God's strength that carried me into Mama's room that day.

One night after I had the first back surgery, I needed to go to the bathroom but I didn't want to wake my husband because he was worn out from taking care of me. So, I got up and tried to go on my own. As I got to the foot of the bed and stood up, I began to fall forward. I screamed and my husband jumped up onto his knees and grabbed me from behind. To this day I call my husband my Superman, because it was God's super powers that caused him to be able to jump up that fast and catch me before I fell to the floor.

It was amazing to see God's strength in my husband, who was much smaller than me at that time. He was able to catch me and sit me on the foot of the bed until I could get my grip. The day my mom fell, no matter how hard my husband tried he couldn't get her up from the floor. I made an attempt to help my husband pick Mama up, but he kept telling me to sit down. I told him I had to help him get Mama up. God gave me that same super natural power that He had given my husband that night. I was able to help my husband pick Mama up and sit her in a chair.

Those who don't believe in God's power have yet to experience Him for themselves. After picking Mama up I asked her if she was hurting anywhere, and she said no. I began examining her from head to toe to make sure I didn't see any injuries. Mama told us that she pressed her medic alert button because we didn't hear her calling for help. I felt so bad, but I thank God she had the mind to press that alert button that was on the string around her neck. I knew all of my siblings would soon be calling out of concern for Mama.

The alarm company was advised to call all seven of Mama's children whenever her alarm signaled for help because mama had several falls in the past. It doesn't matter what state Mama is in while visiting her children the alarm location can be tracked. The EMTs arrived within minutes.

Thank God Mama didn't have any complaints and didn't sustain any injuries. After the fire fighter's left we made Mama comfortable and she watched her soap operas as if nothing happened. I heard about people having super strength when they see someone in danger. Now I know it to be true because I experienced it that day through God's power.

Now I was very concerned about Cindy because I knew she must have gotten the message from the alarm company about Mama, but she still hadn't called or come home yet. It was now four o'clock in the afternoon and she left that morning at seven am. I had to stay positive believing that Cindy was alright. By now Mama was hungry, she had only eaten the cereal that my husband had given her that morning. My husband had to run an errand so it was just Mama and me at home again. I know it was God who gave me strength earlier to help get Mama off of the floor, because now I could barely make it to the bathroom. I asked Mama what she wanted to eat, she said she would wait until Cindy came back because she wanted me to stay in bed.

I told her I would be alright. Mama loved liver and said she would like to have that with the eggplant that she had bought. I was so weak, but I knew Mama was hungry so I literally had to drag myself to the kitchen. Mama walked down the hall on her walker and sat in the dining room to keep an eye on me while I cooked. She sat at the table and cut up the eggplant while I leaned on the kitchen counter and prepared the liver. Finally, I managed to get all of the food on the stove and then sat at the table with Mama as the food was cooking. When I got up to check on the liver I became faint. I could barely make it back to the dining chair. Mama had such fear in her eyes but she couldn't do anything to help me. I put my head on the table and knew I couldn't continue cooking. Mama was so concerned she kept asking if I was alright. I told her no, and at that very moment I heard Cindy putting the key in the door.

Thank God she came back just in time because I couldn't have made it back to the stove.

Cindy apologized for being gone all day. She said she needed some items for the play so she went to several stores, then to the mall. She felt so good being out walking and looking around she lost track of time. She said the medic company had called her phone and left a message about Mama falling, but she forgot to get her phone out of the glove compartment after leaving therapy. She didn't get the message until she was leaving the mall then she rushed home. I told her I understood, because she had not had a minute to herself in almost two months since being in Florida.

She asked Mama if she was alright, Mama said yes. She said she had gotten phone calls from all of our siblings after they got the message about Mama falling. She said she would call them after she got things situated. She put her items in the room, then finished cooking where I left off. Tomorrow would be Thursday and my family would be arriving. I woke up early that Thursday morning and called to see if my doctor had returned from his two month vacation so I could come in as soon as possible to see him. I told the nurse I fell gravely ill and had been in the hospital. Thank God he was back and I was given an early appointment at 8:00 o'clock Friday morning.

I was hoping he could do something to help me feel better because the play was two days away. The cast members were hyped and prepared. The directors and stage managers were on point; the band was ready and I believed I would be there too. Late Thursday morning, I was still in bed very weak with a fever, and was still having the same symptoms I had while in the hospital. I knew my family would arrive soon, so around eleven o'clock that morning I struggled to take a shower. While I was sitting on the edge of the bed getting dressed, Cindy knocked on the door and asked if I needed help. She said my sister Janice and her husband Sherry were here.

I told her I could manage and would be out in a few minutes. I opened the door and began walking down the hall leaning on the wall for support. I looked up and saw my sister-in-law Patrice and a man standing next to her at the end of the hallway. This man resembled and had a deep voice just like my dad. I thought I was hallucinating like I did when I was on all of those narcotic drugs after back surgery.

I had also been experiencing shock waves in my head that caused me to have forgetfulness. I stood there trying to figure things out as I stared at them both. I began to think to myself, "That's Patrice, my Brother Ricky's wife, but where was he? Who is this man standing next to her looking just like Daddy?" The man said, "Hello, Alice," with his deep baritone voice that sounded just like Daddy's voice. He just stood there looking at me. At that moment I no longer saw Patrice. I solely focused on the man. Daddy had been deceased for many years so I didn't understand.

I had spoken to my brother Eddie Lee on the phone a week prior to the play. He said he would have loved to come to support me and to be with the family, but he couldn't afford the trip at that time so I wasn't expecting him to come. Eddie Lee resembled Daddy so much when he was born that Daddy named him Eddie after him. He also has the baritone voice like Daddy. As this man walked towards me I just couldn't put two and two together. He walked up to me and put his arms around my shoulders, then said, "Hello, sister." He looked as though he was in shock too, to see that I had lost so much weight. I realized it was my brother Eddie Lee. I cried and melted in his arms as I shook all over. I was confused, and surprised to see him after he said he wouldn't be able to come. I hugged him so tight, then hugged my sister-in-law Patrice after coming out of the shock.

By then my brother Ricky, sister Janice, and my new brother-in-law Sherry walked in the house after the surprise was over. It was a family reunion! That many family members had never visited us at the same time. I couldn't believe my ninety two year old mom, four siblings, and there mates were here to support me. We were overjoyed to see each other, but I could see the sadness and worry in each of their eyes as they looked at my physical body. It looked as though they were in mourning although I was still alive. I had always been the heaviest in weight of all of my siblings, and the one with the lighter complexion so my sister Linda nicked named me Big Red. Now I could no longer live up to the big part because I had lost so much weight.

My family tried not to show their sad emotions after seeing how sick I was, so they began discussing their flights here, and how beautiful Orlando was. I tried my best to stay up and enjoy my family, but after an hour had passed, we took family photos, then I apologized for having to go lay down. They understood and no one mentioned anything about me needing to cancel the play after seeing how sick I was. Before lying down, we held hands in a circle and my family prayed for me. Afterwards, I thanked them and went to bed. Cindy asked if I wanted something to eat but I still didn't have much of an appetite.

I laid there with tears of joy, and still couldn't believe so many family members had come. I knew they were here because they were concern about me, and the play was a good excuse for them to come check on me. I had presented plays in the past and Mama was the only one who flew in to see them. So, after putting two and two together, it became clear that they were deeply concerned. I would later find out that Cindy was so concerned about me when I was admitted into the hospital for those three days, that she thought it would be best to called each sibling and let them know how sick I was.

Although I was still holding on to the promise God had given me when I was in the hospital, my body felt like it could shut down at any moment. So, I could imagine how Cindy and Mama must have felt watching me deteriorate right before their eyes more and more each day. I appreciate that Cindy contacted my family, because just seeing them gave me the strength to fight. That was pure love expressed from my family to drop everything and come to see about me.

My brother Eddie Lee who lives in Utah called and said as badly as he wanted to come, he just didn't have the funds. But to his surprise! God stepped in right on time. A few days after we spoke, he won a raffle drawing on his job. He won enough money for a ticket to fly to Florida and enough money left over to take in some sights and buy some souvenirs. What a mighty God we serve! John 5:14-15 KJV says, "And this is the confidence we have in him, that, if we ask anything according to his will, he hears us, and if we know that he hears us, whatsoever we ask, we know that we have the petition that we desire of him." God is never late but always on time!

My doctor appointment was early the next morning, the Friday before the play. I had not seen the doctor in more than two months. I felt something was seriously wrong because I had lost so much weight in such short time. I wasn't feeling any pain except from the nerve damage in my leg, but I just felt lifeless. My husband and I sat there waiting until the doctor came in the room. Finally, the doctor walked in the room with a gloomy look on his face. He stood there a minute and stared, seeing how much weight I had lost. He asked me how I was feeling. I told him terrible. He said he had read over my records from the hospital and it wasn't good. He told me that the cancer had come back and he needed to admit me into the hospital immediately. I said they told me I was dehydrated and was an anemic. He said, "Your blood work shows that the cancer is back."

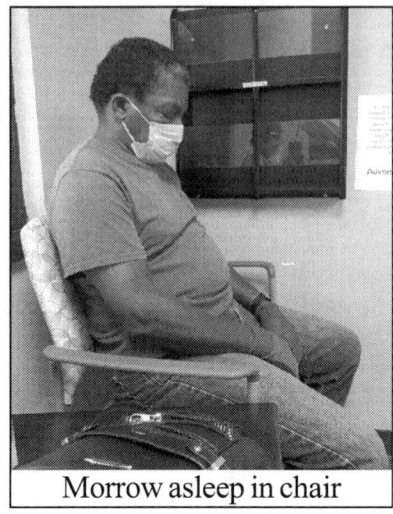

Morrow asleep in chair

I said, "Whose fault is that?" He began to apologize and said he forgot to leave the information with the nurse for my maintenance medication before he went on vacation. I asked the doctor if I had continued taking the Pomalyst medication if I would still be in remission, and he said yes. I wish I had recorded this conversation. My heart plummeted. I had gone through so much to get to the point of feeling better, and because of his negligence I'm back at square one. I was angry. I asked him if it had been his mother or sister, if he would have gone out of the country for two months without making sure they were on the proper medication before leaving.

Tears formed in his eyes and he began apologizing telling me he was sorry. He said he had done everything he could to take care of me in the past the same as he would for a family member, but this was his fault and he was sorry. I was upset even more after hearing him admit it was his fault. I know most doctors, especially those who are specialists, are busy with lots of patients, but once they accept you as a patient it's their responsibility to care for the patient to the best of their ability. There's no room for negligence from a doctor when it comes to a person's life. I remembered what that nurse told me about being my own advocate. That was the best thing anyone in the medical field could have ever told me because it taught me how to speak up when it comes to my health. God had truly delivered me from fear of people.

I sat there this time not with tears in my eyes, but with a fighting spirit. The scripture that I leaned on the most was Psalms 118:17 KJV, "I shall not die, but live, and declare the works of the Lord." I didn't care what the doctor was saying, I was going to trust God to lead and guide me. I told my Oncologist that I thank him for what he had done for me, but I wanted to get a second opinion from a doctor at Moffitt Cancer Center. This hospital is one of the best cancer Hospitals in Florida. The doctor was happy to give me a referral to see another doctor. It's seemed as though he had come to the end of the road and didn't know what else to do to help me. He mentioned that Moffit was a busy hospital and it may be a while before they could schedule me for an appointment. He suggested that in the meantime, he felt it was best for me to start receiving chemotherapy treatments again. He wanted me to check in the hospital that same day to get started with the treatments.

He knew about the Gospel stage play that I was going to present, so I told him that the play was going to be presented tomorrow which was Saturday, September 21, 2019. I told him I had to be there, although I was so weak I could barely stand. He said he would make arrangements for me to check in the hospital the Sunday after the play. I didn't know how long I would be in the hospital, and I needed to make sure all of my business from the play was taken care of before going. I asked the doctor if I could wait until Monday before going to the hospital. He said, regretfully, that I needed to go to the hospital as soon as possible. I told him I would like to go Monday morning, so he said he would have everything in order.

I went home and didn't tell my family, only my husband and I knew of the bad news. Cindy and Mama were anxious to hear what the doctor said. I told them that he was going to admit me in the hospital to see what was going on next week after the play was over. I had decided to go ahead with the play. I didn't believe God would go back on His promise. He told me it was time to present this play and I would see it come to fruition, so I was determined to be there.

We went home, and after I showered then laid down I began to pray. My prayers led me to begin praising God. Praise is one of the most powerful weapons we can use. Things began to happen in the unseen world when we began to praise God.

I was praising God for what was to come. I believed God was going to perform a miracle in my life. I couldn't stop praising my God while lying in bed. I trusted God in the unseen and began calling on the name of Jesus, asking for strength to get up off of this bed of affliction. I didn't want to let God down, nor the waiting people.

People had been waiting and spent money to traveling this far to witness "The Blind Barber And Five Hair Stylists." After praising God, I fell asleep. About four o'clock that Friday evening God heard my prayer. One minute I felt I was near death, and the next minute God raised me up from my sick bed. He performed a miracle! God is real and He is an amazing God. While I slept, God gave me inner strength just like He did when I helped my husband pick Mama up off the floor. As I got up to go to the bathroom I was amazed at the strength I had. I could stand without leaning against the wall and I felt strong.

Cindy and Mama were in the living room watching television when I walked in the room. They looked shocked! They were amazed at what God had done and began thanking Him. That Friday evening would be the last rehearsal for the cast and I was overjoyed that I felt well enough to attend. When I walked in the room the cast were ecstatic. They gave me hugs and were overjoyed to see that I was better. God had given me strength to go forward with the play.

God sent a great cast to perform this play. They saw the vision and took the torch and ran with it. They rehearsed eight long weeks and remained dedicated from beginning to end, to make sure they perfected the script as much as possible. The last rehearsal was phenomenal. Everyone did an awesome job and felt ready for the big stage. I could imagine them probably being on edge wondering if I would still have this strength tomorrow so the play could go forward. I held on to my faith and Gods promise that it would.

CHAPTER TWENTY

The Big Performance

Saturday, September 21, 2019 had finally come. This was the day of the big performance. I woke up still feeling great. My husband had reserved a rental truck and we didn't cancel the reservation because I knew God would keep His promise. Even when we can't see how He is going to work things out, we should keep the faith and trust God. It may be at the twelfth hour, but he will show up. Early Saturday morning, my husband and best friend Eddie Edwards picked up the rental truck to load the furniture and props that was stored in our garage. My brother's Eddie and Ricky joined in to help. I thank God my brothers were here to help out because I was too sick to get a crew together to help with the loading and unloading.

They loaded furniture for an entire beauty salon. Booths, salon chairs, mirrors, couch, table, curtains for the back drop and much more to set up the stage. The entire team who were involved in the play including the musicians, videographers and camera person met at the Performing Arts Center at 2:00 pm that afternoon. Based on my experience, some cast members come to performances hungry and they sometimes rush to get there on time. Because of that reason, I make sure I have a table set up with food for the cast.

I once witnessed a Christian stage play that was held at a huge auditorium where hundreds of people anticipated seeing this great play that had been announced all over the media. The night of the play the audience became frustrated because the play started late. Finally, the starring actor came out with the script in hand reading his lines. There was little acting on his part, because he sat at a desk most of the time with his head down reading the script as if he was reading a book out loud. Immediately I knew he was a last minute fill in.

The playwright came out at the end of the show and apologized to the audience. She said the show didn't go as planned because the guy playing the starring role didn't show up so she had to get a stand in at the last minute. Later I found out they had a disagreement the night before and he decided not to show up for the play at opening night. What a disaster, but my heart went out to the well-known playwright because she didn't have time to cancel the play. Thank God I never encounter that before because it is extremely hard to find extras for stand in roles.

Arriving early on play day also lets the director know that everyone is on time and counted for. It also gives the cast time to pray, get familiar with the stage, and to concentrate on the script. It also gives me time to make last minute decisions if necessary. Doors were to open at 5:30 pm and the play would start at 6:00. The cast were all excited to go on stage as we gathered in the green room in our prayer circle to pray. As we held hands, I suddenly began to shiver. My granddaughter Xaria who had got promoted to the role as director was holding my left hand. She asked if I was alright and I told her yes. By the time the powerful prayer had ended, I felt ice cold.

The cast gathered around me with much concern, but I told them not to worry I would be alright. I smiled and said just go out there and have a great time. It would be time for the curtains to open in twenty minutes and I began to feel worse. I began shaking uncontrollably. My precious fifteen year old granddaughter had the weight of the play on her shoulder as director, but she took me on stage behind the curtain and sat me in a chair where I could see the cast performing. She wrapped me in a blanket, and then kissed me and told me not to worry her and my friend Sandra had everything in control. Then she ran and got in place.

My sixteen year old granddaughter Lanasia was stage manager. She and her crew worked hard to make sure everything was in place for every scene. Sandra and I had worked together in just about all of my plays. She had even directed, as well as acted in several of my plays, but this time I wanted to give my granddaughters an opportunity to be involved. I thank God for my dear friend Sandra Crudup, who made time to take on the responsibility as assistant director to help my granddaughter Xaria. As I sat behind the curtain on stage, I began to thank God as tears filled my eyes for the miracle He had performed. As sick as I was, God kept His promise.

It was only by the grace of God that I was sitting on stage getting ready to witness God bring "The Blind Barber And Five Hair Stylists" to fruition just like He said I would. Two days ago I was walking in the valley. Although I was on stage shivering, and shock waves were going through my head, I was excited and happy. I thank God we all had worked closely together as a team because now it was time for the curtains to open. All I could do was sit in a chair behind the curtain on stage, and rely on everyone to do their part. Every now and then I was able to peek around the curtain and see the audience as the cast performed. They were really enjoying themselves and it was a packed house. I made sure Freddie Maxwell who has been Orlando's longest black female salon owner, who has been in business for more than fifty years was recognized. There were roaring applauses on her behalf as she stood.

Although I was shivering and feeling weak, I laughed and cried right along with the crowd. The cast did an exceptional job, they gave it their all. I was so grateful and proud of each of them. My granddaughter Xaria and friend Sandra had walkie-talkies so they could talk to each other from across the stage as they directed the play. My granddaughter Lanasia and the stage crew made sure the props were on stage in each scene.

The message expressed through this cast of the "Blind Barber and Five Hairstylists" spoke volumes to those who witnessed it. It was a love story about forgiveness, love, charity, and hope. It also spoke to those who work in the Beauty Industry. The play had rave revues from the audience. To this day people are still talking about how the play blessed them. One man thought the man who played the blind barber was really blind. That goes to show how well he played his character role.

After the play ended, it was time for the curtain call. The cast was introduced, and my name was called last as the playwright. I managed to stand behind the curtain while the cast was introduced, but by the time my name was called it took every ounce of strength I had to walk across that stage. I was still shivering as I took each step. The audience stood and applauded as I walked across the stage. My daughter saw how weak I was so she stepped out of the line and met me halfway. She held my hand and walked the remainder of the way with me across the stage. Then she stood next to me so I could have support as I leaned my shoulders against hers. My precious daughter has always been very attentive to me and I knew she was concerned.

We took our final bows, and then the cast greeted the audience in the lobby to sign autographs. I was like a reunion. So many people who had not seen each other in years were reunited that night. What a great night it was! The lobby was crowded and the people didn't want to leave because they were enjoying chatting with family and friends. I felt so weak I told my daughter I wasn't going to go to the lobby to greet people. As I sat backstage waiting for my husband, I received a message that my friend Bettye, who was the box office manager, wanted to see me as soon as possible. I had not seen her in a couple of weeks and she had no idea I had become so ill. If she did, she wouldn't have asked me to walk to the lobby.

There was no one to walk with me because everyone was in the lobby or helping my husband load the U-haul. I had lost so much weight and looked so sickly that I was almost unrecognizable. I didn't want the people to see me in this condition because I knew there would be stares and questions, but I had to go see what Bettye wanted. Yes it's Bettye.

I made my way to the stairs and didn't know how I was going to make my way down the steps. I heard a voice say, "Do you need help?" I looked up and there sat Pastor Sidney Crudup, my friend Sandra's husband sitting on the front row. I said, "Yes." He helped me down the steps and I managed to make my way to the lobby holding on the seats in the auditorium. As soon as I walked through the lobby door, I got lots of stares from people who knew me but didn't know I had been sick. I probably would have stared too out of concern for the person if I had seen them shaking uncontrollable and had lost so much weight. People surrounded me telling me how much they loved the play but I could see the looks on their faces that they were wondering what was wrong with me.

One man told me how much he enjoyed the play and asked me to autograph his program. I tried my best to stop shaking while signing my autograph but couldn't. I managed to sign the best I could and thanked him for coming. The man stared as if he was wondering what in the world was wrong with me. So many friends and church members were waiting to talk to me. I wanted so badly to thank them for coming but I had begun to feel weaker.

After seeing what Bettye wanted and taking a few pictures with my family, my granddaughter helped me return to the auditorium to sit down. Tears filled my eyes again as I looked around the auditorium. I began thanking God again for allowing me to witness what He promised. Although there were many difficulties along the way, I had completed the assignment God had given me. It may seem foolish to others when they see you doing something that seems strange to them, but if God tell you to do it, do it.

I'm a witness that God can use anyone, at any time to accomplish what He assigns. Even those who are on their bed of affliction can do something, even if it's as small as making a phone call to check on someone else who is sick. He used me while being broke and in despair. When God gave me the assignment to write this play I didn't understand how I could do it while being sick, but I stepped out on faith with the little energy I had, and without any money to do God's will. Some may have assumed I was doing this for a profitable gain or recognition.

I even heard later that some people who knew me thought I was delusional and had faulty judgment to perform a play while being that sick. These were some of the same people who told me how much they enjoyed the play. Remember to stay clear of the three kinds of people I mentioned earlier: The Loquacious, the Inquisitive, and the Data Processor. They are dangerous people.

That didn't bother me, because they weren't there when God gave me my assignment. No matter how sick I was, I knew that if God brought me to it, He would see me through it. I've learned that when God speaks, I listen and do my best to do His will no matter what people think or say. Philippians 1:6 KJV lets us know that being confident of this very thing that He which hath begun a good work in you will perform it until the day of Jesus Christ.

Sometimes, family and church members can be our worst Debbie Downers. Some are pessimistic never having anything good to say but they always look for the worst aspect of things. Some may have said it out of concern, but we must be careful what we say and not be so judgmental, especially when we are on the outside looking in and not having all the facts. I didn't ask God for this assignment, especially when I was at my lowest point. But nothing was going to stop me from doing the will of God. When the Lord Jesus calls us, He gives us power and the strength to do the work of the ministry.

The play

God knows best! He inspired me to write this play at the perfect time, because it took my mind off of my problems and allowed me to concentrate on blessing others through ministering through this play. If it had not been for this play I might have died in self-pity. God provided, He blessed it, and brought it to fruition and many were blessed, and I give God all the glory and all the praise.

CHAPTER TWENTY ONE

Waiting in His Presence

Sunday after the play, I managed to complete the business aspect of the play and early that Monday morning I was admitted into the hospital. Most of my siblings and their spouses had returned home after their visit. Cindy and mama were still here and had no plans to leave until they knew I would be alright. Janice and her husband Cherry were getting ready to fly back to Arizona, but not before stopping by the hospital to check on me.

There was a nurse who was assigned to me only during my stay in the hospital. Janice asked her if she knew what actions the doctor had planned that would help me feel better. She said the doctor's plan was to administer chemo and blood transfusions, and said I would feel much better after the treatments. Janice sat in the chair across from me and we talked awhile. It was time for her to go, so she prayed and told me everything was going to be alright, then we hugged and said our goodbyes.

As she walked away, she kept looking back with a smile on her face, and assured me that everything would be alright. Janice had been a nurse for more than thirty years and I'm sure she had seen many people die along her journey. I know my sister was a strong Christian and prayer warrior who trusted God, but I could see through her smile as she walked away the concern she had for me.

Thank God, the play was over and the heavy load was lifted. I was now able to relax and wait in God's presence. I knew God was with me so I focused my attention on Him instead of my problems. Finally, my Oncologist arrived, and at his first glance of me tears swelled in his eyes. He looked extremely worried after seeing how much weight I had lost, and the poor condition I was in since he saw me four days ago. He witnessed the severe trembling, and how my body was soaked as if someone had poured a bucket of water on me. He told me I would have to have chemotherapy and a blood transfusion immediately.

After seeing my failing condition, he was indecisive about what procedures to start first. He couldn't decide whether he wanted me to begin with the chemo treatment first or the blood transfusion. After going back and forth confusing the nurse, he told her to start the chemo treatment first. I was lying there praying asking God to direct the doctor in his decision making because he seemed nervous and indecisive. Once again, he changed his mind and told the nurse to give me the transfusion first. He told me he wanted me to have three pints of blood so I can get my strength back and it would also stop me from shaking.

I can tell the nurse was a bit agitated with the doctor but she was very respectful. As soon as the blood was delivered to my room, she kindly explained the procedure of the blood transfusion to me. While I was being transfused, the doctor left to see patients at his office across the street from the hospital but he called the nurse several times to check on me. Before the transfusion was completed, the doctor returned to make sure everything went well and to make sure the nurse started the chemotherapy treatment as soon as the blood transfusion was completed.

The doctor had already admitted his negligence and said the maintenance medication would have helped keep me in remission longer. So now he was making sure he was on top of things this time. Some of my family members thought I should file a medical malpractice law suit against him. Yes, I was upset and had contemplated hiring a lawyer, especially after thinking about how one doctor had left me with permanent nerve damage. But then I thought, what if God had not extended me compassion? I may not be here today.

God had already blessed me to live through so much, so why couldn't I show compassion to this doctor. The doctor didn't spitefully try to cause harm to me. He was a very compassionate doctor, but he was overworked and extremely tired after caring for so many patients. I understood that his human mind just forgot, although that's not an acceptable excuse when someone's life is on the line.

It's not Christian like for Christians to sue each other. If we have a dispute against another Christian, we should first go to them and try to resolve the matter. But I can't find any scripture that it says I shouldn't be allowed to sue someone who works for a big corporation who brings harm to me. Matthew 5:40 KJV and if any man will sue thee at the Law, and take away thy coat, let him have thy cloak also. But instead of suing my doctor, I chose to forgive him. Colossians 3:13 KJV says, "Forbearing one another, and forgiving one another, if any man have a quarrel against any; even as Christ forgave you, so also do ye."

God always judges our attitude, and just because something is allowable doesn't mean it's the right thing to pursue. I didn't want to look after my own personal interest by seeking revenge, but I thought about how this doctor family and his practice could have suffered if I had sued and won. His name and reputation could have been destroyed forever. Yes, I know doctors have malpractice insurance, but instead of fighting a drawn out lawsuit I concentrated on praying and trusting God for my healing. The doctor stood at my bedside with his head held down sincerely repeating how sorry he was. He called for the nurse and she came immediately. He told her that as soon as the transfusion was completed she needed to start the chemo treatment. He repeated himself, and then told her to have me hooked up to chemo in less than five minutes after the transfusion treatment ended. He assured me that everything would be alright. The poor nurse seemed to be so nervous, having to disconnect the transfusion bag and connect the Chemo bag in less than five minutes. I was praying for her. Thank God she managed to accomplish such a mindboggling task on time. She apologized that I had to wait until my treatments were over before she could change my wet gown and linen.

The treatments didn't work right away. Fluid still poured out of my body and I trembled all night. The nurse changed my linen and gowns three times during the night. The more body fluid I lost, the more weight I lost. After staying in the hospital two days and receiving six pints of blood, and having two rounds of chemo treatments I was released and felt much better. A few days later I saw the doctor and I had lost thirty five pounds in three weeks. Since that first trip to the hospital, I had now lost sixty three pounds.

My Oncologist had made the arrangements for me to go get the second opinion that I had requested at Moffitt Hospital, the top ranked Cancer Hospital in Florida. I was scheduled to go in the next two weeks. A week after being released from the hospital, my strength was restored and the fluid pouring out of my body had finally stopped, but I would have to continue with Chemo treatments.

Mama and Cindy had returned to Arizona after being here for three entire months. I'm forever grateful to my precious sister for taking great care of me and expressing agape love when I was walking through the valley. God sent her at the right time, just like He did my sister Janice when I had back surgery. It was an amazing blessing to see mama. I didn't know if I would ever see any of my family members again, especially mama. But God had given me so many blessings and joy through seeing and spending time with my family, I knew that if I didn't see them down here, I would see them in heaven one day. God gave me enough strength to accomplish what He set before me. God carried me through an overwhelming storm and I knew He was going to do something even greater.

CHAPTER TWENTY TWO

Feeling Great Again

A few days after leaving the hospital, I was feeling great again and wanted to attend church. All of my clothes were too big, but I put on a dress and went anyway. I got stares from some of the members who seemed to be shocked of my sudden weight loss. They probably wondered how I lost so much weight in such a short time. Some member's made positive comments telling me that I looked good with the weight loss, but they didn't know the disease I was battling that caused me to lose the weight so fast. There will always be a Debbie Downer in the crowd no matter where we go. I enjoyed the service, and as I walked out a church a member said, "You need to pull that short dress down." The dress was knee length. I smiled at her and said, "Thank you." I wanted to say "You Pharisee."

Some folks always try to tell others what to do while being hypocrites themselves. We are the same age, and I have witnessed her with dresses on much shorter than the one I had on. I didn't have time to be concerned about the small things, so I let it fly right past me. God had brought me from the valley of the shadow of death. I was a living Miracle and I recognized it was Satan using this church member to discourage me. He was mad because I didn't die. But God! As Christians, we should be quick to listen, and slow to speak as James 1:19 KJV instructs us. The tongue is the smallest member of the body but it's the deadliest. Many people have killed people spirit with their deadly tongues. Some people never return to church because they have been hurt by church folks who call themselves Christians.

I knew I looked sickly after losing so much weight, but after all I had gone through what other's thought about my weight loss was the furthest thing from my mind. I just wanted to make it to the house of God, to participate in corporate worship with other believers. I make it a point on a daily basis to worship and spend time with God, but I felt the need to come together with other believers to pray, sing, learn, and worship together. Proverbs 27:17 KJV says, "Iron sharpens iron so a man sharpened the countenance of his friend."

God created us to be among other people. I felt much better after attending church that Sunday, and I continued to press on and trust God. Every day I quoted Psalms 118:17 KJV: "I shall not die, but live, and declare the works of the Lord."

The day had come for me to go to Moffitt Cancer Center. I was looking forward to hearing another doctor's opinion about my health after my Oncologist gave me such little hope. He had informed me that I would have to go back to having chemo treatments four hours a day, three days a week for the remainder of my life. He even gave me a short time line to live. Thank God I didn't give up after hearing what man had said, because I would have been gone a long time ago by his diagnosis. My faith was in God, not man. I had faith that God was going to heal me.

My husband and I got up at five o'clock the morning of my appointment, so we would have plenty of time to drive the seventy eight miles from Orlando to Tampa, Florida. My appointment wasn't until nine o'clock that morning, but we left at five o'clock not knowing what the traffic would be like. After arriving and checking in, we didn't have to wait long before they called me for blood work and a few other tests. At promptly nine o'clock, the nurse called us back to see the doctor.

We sat only a few minutes before a tall heavy set young black man walked into the room and said good morning. He shook our hands, then introduced himself as Dr. Brown and told us he was a Cancer Research Doctor. He looked too young to be a Cancer Research Doctor. He was a gentle giant who was very nice and seemed very concerned about me, and my health. After getting to know us, he immediately began to discuss what he had previously read in my records from my oncologist. The doctor sat in the chair across from us with my medical records in his hands, and began explaining my condition in a way that was easy for us to comprehend.

The concern this doctor had for me was like a son would have for his mother. He didn't try to sugar coat anything or sooth my emotions, he made it plain as he drew a diagram on a piece of paper that explained my situation intensely.

First he drew a mountain, and next to the mountain he drew a deep valley. He repeated that drawing twice more. When he had finished his drawing, there were three mountains and three valleys joined together.

He then pointed out that when I was first diagnosed with the cancer, I was on top of the first mountain which was very bad. He then explained that after receiving radiation and chemo treatments, it brought me down in the valley which was good. He stressed that I need to stay in the valley. He asked me a few questions, and then explained that if I was in remission, it was only for a short time before the cancer returned because I wasn't on any maintenance medication.

He said I had returned to the mountain top again, which was very bad. But now that I had gone through a second round of chemo treatments when I was in the hospital, I was again in the valley. Doctor Brown told me I needed to have a stem cell transplant immediately if I wanted to live. He explained that I only get two times to be on the mountain top. If I had one more mountain top experience it would be my last. I had no choice but to say I wanted to have the transplant as soon as possible if I wanted to live. The doctor said time is of the essence and I needed to have the transplant while I was in the valley and my body was strong enough to withstand a transplant.

Doctor Brown told us that they could schedule the transplant there at Moffitt Hospital as soon as possible, but said it may entail us moving closer to the hospital for a year for my aftercare appointments. The aftercare treatment would consist of me seeing the doctor on a daily basis for a while. I told Dr. Brown that I wanted to have the transplant as soon as possible. My husband was in agreement, but he told the doctor it would be impossible for us to move to Tampa and rent a place because of the financial responsibilities we have in Orlando.

He said we would love to have the transplant done at Moffitt, but we couldn't afford the operating expenses in two locations. He then asked Doctor Brown if he could recommend a doctor, and a hospital in Orlando that does stem cell transplants. We knew someone who had undergone a stem cell transplant, but we didn't know who her doctor was or the hospital where she had it performed. Shands Hospital in

Gainesville Florida also performed stem cell transplants, but that hospital was much further than Moffitt and we would have the same problems having to move there for a year.

The doctor was hesitant about recommending a doctor, but I could tell he wanted too. I was impressed even more by him because he was following protocol. He followed the correct conduct and procedures. He said he would send his recommendations to my Oncologist as soon as possible, and he should be the doctor to recommend a transplant doctor for me. He did tell us that Advent Health in Orlando had recently merged with Moffitt Cancer Center and were doing stem cell transplants. He said most of the doctors there were trained at Moffit. We were so grateful for that information, especially to know that I could have the transplant done in Orlando.

Now my concern was would my insurance pay for a transplant when they denied me of having a second PET scan when I was so sick. A pet scan is one of the most important tests a person need to have when they have cancer, because it helps identify the location of cancer cells. It's really sad when saving a person's life can depend on what kind of insurance they have. Money becomes more important than a person's life.

Before leaving, Doctor Browns stressed again the importance of me having the transplant as soon as possible. It was October, and he wanted me to have the transplant before Christmas if possible. He had taken time to explain to my husband and me, step by step the long process of all that would need to take place even before the transplant could happen. I was excited about having it done because I wanted to live. I told Dr. Brown I had been praying, asking God to send me the right doctor who had a heart of compassion and knew how to care for me properly. I told him God answered my prayers. He said thank you.

My Oncologist had been treating me for the past two years, and because of his negligence, I almost died. He was a nice doctor and had good bedside manners, but I no longer felt safe with him treating me because he had run out of options and had begun playing the guessing game with my health. I was tired of being his test dummy. Doctor Brown said he would be glad to work with my doctor. We thanked Doctor Brown and returned home with a lot on our minds. The following day

Doctor Brown called to let me know he had talked to my Oncologist. I don't know what was discussed between the doctors, but He said my doctor was in agreement and was willing to work together so they could improve my health.

At my next appointment to see the Oncologist, all of a sudden he wanted to stop the chemo treatments. He said I had been getting chemo for quite some time, and a test that I had previously taken showed that my heart was being damaged by the treatments. He said if I continued the chemo it could destroy my organs.

This doctor had just told me after I got out of the hospital that I would have to continue chemo treatments for the rest of my life. During that time, I asked him would it be safe for me to continue taking chemo and he said yes. Now, suddenly, he's telling me he wanted to stop all treatments. I'm sure my heart didn't suddenly become damaged. I asked him what method of treatment he was going to use once he stopped the chemo treatments. He said he would continue monitoring my blood to see if the cancer returns.

At that point I was fuming. I no longer saw this man as a doctor because it seemed as though he was playing games with my life. He had become so indecisive that I lost all trust in him. He had taken me off all treatments. He just stood there dumbfounded. I reminded him how sick I had gotten without being on maintenance medication when he was on vacation. This doctor was so confused that he asked me what I wanted him to do. He then said he could continue chemo treatments at a lower dose, and try a different maintenance pill if I wanted to go that route. He had stopped all treatment a few minutes ago which I believed was a recipe for disaster. Now he wanted to start treatment again, after telling me the chemo was damaging my heart and could affect my organs.

That broke the camel's back, he just contradicted himself. I became so infuriated that I told him, "I'm not the doctor, you are, and I can't make a medical decision about my health. That's why I come to you." My husband tried to calm me down, but at that moment I wanted to tell him he was incompetent. Thank God I held my tongue and didn't say anything further. Being a Christian doesn't mean you just go through life being passive all the time, while people treat you bad and walk all over you. I tried to be respectful but I had to speak out. Maybe my voice will ring in his ear when it's time to help the next patient.

At that moment I decided I would never step foot back into his office again. This really made me wonder if this doctor knew what he was doing, or just making decisions by playing the guessing game with people lives.

A few weeks later, I was scheduled to see Doctor Brown at Moffitt hospital again. I explained to him what had taken place, and told him my doctor stopped all of my treatment. I could see in his expression that this was the wrong thing to do. Because of the medical code of ethic, doctors can't say anything negative about another doctor, but I could tell Dr. Brown was disappointed and concerned about my health. Then a light came on in my head. This doctor might have felt intimidated by Doctor Brown's suggestions during their phone conversation, and decided he no longer wanted to deal with me as a patient.

Dr. Brown asked if my doctor had found a transplant doctor for me, and I told him no, he never mentioned anything about finding me a doctor. I told him I was searching on my own and hadn't found a doctor yet, but I was trusting God to lead me to the right transplant doctor like he led me to him. Looking back, I wondered if I was ever in remission at all because I remember the oncologist telling me that he had to figure out something to get me off of the chemo after being on it almost two years. The very next week he told me I was in remission and wouldn't need to have chemo treatments anymore. He said I would only need to take a maintenance medication to keep the cancer at bay.

When God entrust us to do a job, we should do our best no matter what job it is. If we have a job that could endanger others' lives, we should be capable of doing the job. I told Doctor Brown that I no longer felt comfortable seeing my Oncologist and was searching for a new doctor. He shook his head as to say yes. After looking over my records and hearing my terrible experiences, he understood that I wanted to search for another doctor, but he advised me to continue going to my doctor because they might be able to help me find a transplant doctor. He said it may also take a while to get established with another doctor and time wasn't on my side.

Doctor Brown didn't agree with my Oncologist taking me off of my treatments, but he told me not to worry because I would have to stop treatments three months prior to having the transplant anyway so I should be alright. He told me that I needed to have the transplant within the next three months while I was in remission because if I fell back into the valley I wouldn't be a candidate for a transplant.

Before leaving, we thanked Doctor Brown for his concern and professional advice. He looked me in the eyes with such compassion and concern. It was a look that I had never seen before from a doctor. It was a look that he knew if I didn't get help soon, I wouldn't be around much longer. As we were leaving, he took my hand and held it tight, then told me he would be praying for me and I could call him any time and he would return my call.

This doctor had integrity and a heart of empathy for people. I hoped I could have had the transplant done at Moffitt hospital, because I knew I would be in good hands, but it wasn't feasible for us at the time. That night after returning home I had a lot to consider. I had to continue being my own advocate, and continue searching for a transplant doctor because I couldn't rely on my Oncologist after he had dropped the ball so many times before.

Doctor Brown said he would send the information of his findings to my Oncologist and inform him that I need to have the stem cell transplant as soon as possible. I wasn't going to wait around on my doctor to find me a transplant doctor, or to call my insurance to see if they would pay for my transplant. I would continue praying and following Gods guidance. That night, my husband and I prayed that God would direct me to the right doctor in Orlando, and give us favor with my insurance company.

It was November, and my insurance was going to end in December. I would have to renew with the same company or choose another insurance company by January first. Doctor Brown told me I should have the transplant before my insurance ends in December. That seemed impossible because he had told me there would be a process that I would have to go through, even before I could receive a transplant. I wasn't giving up; I still had faith that God would make the impossible, possible. I knew that all things are possible to them that believe (Mark 9:23 KJV). I wasn't shaken when it seemed like things wouldn't line up. I believed that all things are possible with God.

A transplant would cost thousands of dollars and I wasn't sure if my insurance would pay for a transplant, but I made up my mind that I wasn't going to stress about anything. I gave my request to God in prayer and waited on him to work it out. I feel like praising him right now as I think about the miracles he suddenly performed. When I stopped stressing and rolled my burdens over to God was when the miracles began to happen. Not just one or two but many. If you are reading this book and never witnessed a miracle or don't believe in them, continue reading my story and see the miracles God performed for me.

A few days after visiting Doctor Brown, I called a dear faithful friend named Bettye Edwards who had been supportive long before my medical issues. She became one of my clients and we've been friends and have supported each other for years. Bettye was there for me through three back surgeries and cancer. Now she's by my side through a transplant. She prayed, visited me in the hospital, cooked for me, offered to take me to my doctor appointments, and even offered to sit with me during chemo treatments to give my husband a break.

Bettye called constantly to check on me and wanted to know what the doctor said. I shared with her everything the doctor told me. It's good to have someone that is a true friend. One way to tell a genuine friend is to be sick a long time. A true friend will stick by you through thick and thin. A person who is just an acquaintance will stay in touch for a little while when you are sick, then will soon fade away into the sunset. I told Bettye the doctor said I needed to have a stem cell transplant as soon as possible. My God, My God! He was going to perform miracles. This is where the miracles began! Bettye told me that a good friend of hers had been a caretaker for a lady who had a stem cell transplant a few years prior, and she was doing great.

CHAPTER TWENTY THREE

God Performed A Miracles

She said the lady was now able to travel and have a good quality of life because she no longer had to be hooked up to a machine for treatments. The lady had also gone back to work part time. Bettye asked me if I wanted her to contact her friend and get the lady's phone number so I could talk to her. I said, by all means. She was sure the lady would be willing to give me the name of her transplant doctor. I was hoping she could refer me to her doctors because the clock was ticking and I could hear Dr. Brown saying you need to have the transplant done before December.

A few days later, Bettye called back and said she spoke to the lady and explained my situation, and asked her if she would be willing to talk to me. She explained how urgent it was for me to have the transplant as soon as possible. The lady said she would be happy to, and gave Bettye her number for me to call her. By now the news had spread throughout my family that I needed to have a Stem Cell Transplant. My granddaughter's had mentioned it to their aunt Teresa who was a nurse who worked at a Blood and Marrow Transplant doctor's office. She was concerned and suggested that I come in and talk to one of the doctors. She said they were excellent doctors.

I was most grateful for Teresa being concerned and wanting to help me, but after talking to Bettye and hearing about someone who had physically gone through a transplant, I decided to continue following the path God had put me on. I saw God working in every direction; He was opening doors that I didn't even realize at the time. I called Cynthia, the lady Bettye had told me about. My first impression just by talking to her on the phone was a positive one. After introducing myself and thanking her for taking time to talk with me, I let her know that I was interested in knowing more about her doctors and her transplant procedure. I told her everything I had gone through, and she had such empathy and concern for me.

Cynthia was soft spoken, mild mannered, and was a great encourager. She began explaining everything that I needed to know from A to Z. After talking to her, my soul was soothed and my mind was at ease. She said it had been two years since her transplant and she was doing well. She took forty five minutes out of her valuable schedule to share her experience of going through a transplant. She elaborated that every individual is different and might experience different reactions and side effects. She even discussed what types of insurance that may be best for me to have that would pay for the transplant, then said the financial counselor would explain in dept but she never told me which insurance to choose.

Cynthia gave me the name of her transplant doctor and oncologist and felt I would be happy with both because they were excellent doctors. She mentioned how hard it was to get an appointment at the Oncology office. She said the doctor had a lot of patients, but he was a compassionate doctor and was very attentive to his patients. She told me to continue calling until someone answers the phone.

She explained that after receiving my transplant, I would continue going to the Transplant doctor for a year, then he would put me in the care of the Oncologist. I would periodically go back to see the transplant doctor until I would be completely released from his care. I asked her where did she have her transplant. When she said Advent Health Hospital in Orlando, chills ran through my entire body because I knew God was at work on my behalf. This was the hospital that Dr. Brown told me about in Orlando, where doctors from Moffitt Hospital worked.

Many people travel to Moffitt Hospital in Tampa or Shands Hospital in Gainesville to receive their transplants, but thank God I can have my transplant right here in Orlando. What a mighty God we serve! If we would step back and allow God to work things out, we would be less stressed and more blessed. I told Cynthia that Advent Health was the hospital the doctor at Moffitt referred me to. She said the entire staff at the hospital was great, and had sincere concerned for the patients. God worked it out that the oncologist and transplant doctor offices were both directly across the street from the hospital where I would have the transplant. I felt God carrying me through storm after storm. I had no doubt He was going to work things out.

I had not met Cynthia in person yet, but after talking to her on the phone, it seemed as though we knew each other for years. Cynthia, a stranger who I never met took at least forty five minutes of her precious time to talk to me. She explained everything in detail that I needed to know. Right away, I knew she was a child of God. God has many ways of showing Himself, letting us know that He is right there with us. He promised to never leave nor forsake us. This is a prime example of how he showed himself through Billie, Bettye, Doctor Brown and Cynthia.

God sent the right people in my path that led me to the right doctors to work on my behalf. Hallelujah! I'm forever grateful. After talking with Cynthia, I told her I needed to see her Oncologist as soon as possible. She was very concerned about my health, and told me I needed to begin calling both doctor offices right away to see if they were accepting new patients.

I would find out later that Cynthia had some influence at both doctor offices. Everyone including the doctors knew her very well and loved her. She was so positive, caring, and easy going. You couldn't help but love her. She told me she had an appointment the following day to see the oncologist, and would make the receptionists aware that she was referring me as a new patient. She said she would tell them how urgent it was and I would need an appointment as soon as possible.

The following day I called the transplant doctor office first. Thank God they were accepting new patients. The receptionist took my information, and the first thing she asked was the name of my insurance. It was as though my heart stopped when she told me they didn't accept my insurance. She then said Cynthia had called and referred me as a patient, and said I was in critical need of having a Stem Cell Transplant as soon as possible. The receptionist had told the doctor who performed Cynthia's transplant about my insurance dilemma, and he told her to get me in as soon as possible and not to worry about paying for the first visit.

She explained that I wouldn't be able to see Cynthia's doctors until the end of January because he was booked out, but I could see another doctor in the office sooner. She said all of the doctors were as equally good and they worked as a team while the patient is in the hospital. She said one of the other doctors can oversee my health until the transplant if I wanted to come in. I said yes, how soon can I come in. She said the first appointment available would be December 15, 2020. I could see God working. I got the "Can't Help It's." I couldn't help but give God praise right there on the phone. I told the receptionist to thank the doctor for me and let him know how grateful I was. I thanked God for His favor.

I was happy that I now have a doctor, but I began to think about what Doctor Brown told me. If I were to go on the mountain top again I wouldn't be a good candidate to receive a transplant. By now I should have already had the transplant, but I had to wait until December before seeing a doctor. Then I said to myself, "Why am I allowing myself to stress when I can see God working?" I said, "Forgive me Lord, I put my total trust in you."

I began thanking God for how He was working on my behalf. I called the Oncologist office at least five times, only to get the answering machine telling me to leave my name and number and someone will return my call within twenty four hours. I left a message then called Moffitt hospital and left a message for Doctor Brown to call me as soon as possible. I was surprised when he called back that same evening. I don't know of many doctors who does that. He was happy to hear from me and asked if my oncologist had found a Transplant doctor for me.

I told him I was assertive about my oncologist referring me to a transplant doctor, but he continued telling me he had not found a doctor yet. I let him know that I received my last chemo treatment two weeks ago and refused to step foot back into his office. I told Dr. Brown I put my total trust in God, and YES, He had blessed me with a transplant doctor who worked at Advent Health Hospital, the same hospital that he had told me about. He became excited. He assured me I would be in good hands. I let him know that I couldn't get an appointment to see the doctor until the middle of December. He asked me numerous questions about my health and how I was feeling.

After letting him know I felt well, he told me the last chemo treatment that I had was working and I would be okay for at least three more months. I felt relieved after talking to him. He's much busier than my oncologist, but he took the time to return my phone call. I had only gone to him for a second opinion, and the concern he had for me made me feel as though I was one of his longtime patients.

Dr. Brown had such a big heart and such empathy for his patients. He showed more concern for me than my doctor who I had gone to for two years. Dr. Brown told my husband and I that we could call him anytime, and he would personally call back. He was a man of his word. Most doctors are so busy they don't have time to call their patients. The only time I got to talk to my oncologist was when I saw him at my appointments. If I had a question between appointments I had to talk to his nurse.

I felt at ease after Dr. Brown told me I would be alright. I was excited that God was working on my behalf. Romans 8:28 says, and we know that in all things work together for good to them that love God, to them who are called according to his purpose. The following day I called the new oncologist office again to try and make an appointment, but once again the recording came on telling me the same thing.

Eventually, someone did return my call, but I was always out during that time and missed the call. It was as though we were playing phone tag. Finally, one day I called, and instead of pressing the number two for new patients, I pressed the number one for established patients because I felt I would soon be a patient. Low and behold, someone answered on the second ring. I took in a breath of relief and was praying that they were accepting new patients. The minute I said my name, the receptionist shouted, "Mrs. Jackson! I've been trying to contact you for two weeks." I said, "Yes, we've been playing phone tag."

Before I could ask her if they were accepting new patients, she began telling me that Cynthia had called the office numerous times to see if they were able to get me in as a new patient right away. They told Cynthia they tried contacting me several times but could never reach me. She let me know that Cynthia is one of their best patients and everyone there loved her, just as the lady said at the transplant doctor's office. Finally, after calling every day for two weeks, I was able to speak with a human and not a machine.

Thank God they took me as a new patient and scheduled me for an appointment for mid-February. I had made up my mind that if I had not connected with the oncologist office by the time of my appointment with the Transplant doctor, I was going to walk across the street to the oncologist's office to see if I could make an appointment in person.

I had come to the conclusion that someone was lazy and not doing their job answering the phone, or the doctor must be an excellent doctor and have a lot of patients. The receptionist apologized for not being able to contact me. I was just grateful they accepted me as a patient. Tears filled my eyes with thanksgiving because God had blessed me with a new oncologist. Cynthia never let up from letting the receptionist and the doctor know that I had been trying to make an appointment. The concern she had for me was like one that you would have for a family member or close friend. She showed agape love for me.

God sent her in my life at the right time. One of my favorite songs is titled "He's An on Time God." He may not come when we want Him, but He's always on time. Cynthia was overjoyed when I told her I finally got an appointment with both doctors, Bettye was excited too. I've heard the phrase "It's not what you know, It's who you know." This proves to be true in my case. I knew God, and everything else fell in order. Things would work out just fine because the transplant doctor would see me without charge in December, and my appointment to see the new oncologist would be in February after my new insurance began.

The new oncologist will accept the same insurance as the transplant doctor. Things were looking up! I couldn't stop thanking God enough because so many people die each day who are in need of a transplant, because their insurance won't pay and they can't afford to pay thousands of dollars out of pocket. Look at God performing one miracle after another.

In the past year, I had watched numerous church members and close friends die from cancer, and the enemy kept telling me I would be next. His intimidation gave me the strength to fight even harder and trust God even more. I began to quote scriptures and speak life over myself. The scripture that I held close to my heart that inspired me the most was KJV Psalms 118:17 I shall not die, but live, and declare the works of the Lord. I still quote that scripture often because I know God still has work for me to do. A week later, Bettye scheduled a lunch date for Cynthia and me to meet.

Bettye, Cynthia, Billie and I met at Olive Garden Restaurant. Billie was Cynthia's caregiver when she had her transplant. She was the one who connected Betty with Cynthia. It was like a chain effect because everything was working out for my good.

Cynthia and Me

I had met Billie once, but hadn't seen her in a long time. The ladies were waiting when I arrived at the restaurant. When I walked in, the ladies stood and greeted me with a hug. When I first laid eyes on Cynthia it was surreal. It was as though I was looking at my Angel that God sent from heaven just to help me. During the lunch, we got acquainted. Cynthia was soft spoken, polite, and was a beautiful lady with long hair which had grown back after her transplant.

Just by looking at her, you would never know she had cancer before. She looked like a picture of perfect health. The ladies and I talked awhile, and then Cynthia gave me loads of pamphlets that would inform me about what I would face before, during, and after the transplant. After talking to Cynthia that day and reading all of the information she shared with me was empowering. I didn't know what was ahead of me, but after talking to Cynthia I felt calm and optimistic. I felt ready to conquer any storm that I would have to face. I knew there would be many, but God would carry me through every storm.

I haven't seen Cynthia since that day at the restaurant, we've only talked on the phone, but I know God sent her to be a part of my journey. It's a blessing to have good people in your life. It was incredibly thoughtful for all of the ladies to offer to be my caregivers after my transplant. I thanked them and told them we had already made arrangements that my husband and daughter would take care of me. My husband had done an exceptional job caring for me in the past after having three back surgeries, so I knew he would do the same this time. I thanked the ladies for meeting with me, and told them I would keep them informed.

My daughter Suhdeena has always been there for me, along with my granddaughters Lanasia and Xaria. I'll never forget three months after my second back surgery I wanted my hair colored, and a manicured and pedicure. My granddaughters at that time were eleven and twelve years old. Lanasia, the oldest had an interest in nails, and Xaria's interest was in hair. I still had my salon in my home at that time so I asked them if they could oblige my request. They said yes, and I became their client. I gave Xaria instructions how to apply the hair color, while Lanasia became my nail and pedicure technician. Xaria colored my hair while Lansaia did my nails and feet at the shampoo bowl. They both did an exceptional job and I was pleased with the outcome. I felt like a new woman.

The two youngers grands, Jaylan and Samiah, are my two little prayer warriors. Jaylan is ten now, but he has been praying like a little old Baptist deacon ever since he was six years old. Samiah is seven, and she's been praying like the mother of the church since she was four. God answered those innocent prayers every time they prayed for me. I have three other grandsons, Tyrone Jr. and Taze live in a different county, and Nathaniel (Dino) is our youngest. My grands bring so much joy to me whenever they visit.

It was now the middle of December, and today will be the first step of my transplant journey. I'm scheduled to see the transplant doctor. I have courage, and I'm ready to take the path I need to take to live. I had been advised when I made my appointments that neither doctor accepted my Obama Care Insurance, but because of Cynthia being such a good patient and speaking on my behalf letting them know the concerned she had for my health, both doctors gave me a complimentary first visit. This was nothing but unmerited favor from God. I could never thank, or give Him praise enough for the blessings He bestowed upon me.

God was working things out for my good. I knew then, that both doctors were compassionate and not just concerned about money. I don't know of any doctor who would have accepted a new patient having insurance coverage that they don't accept. Most don't give you an appointment until they have your insurance information. Before my first appointment, I had already been informed by the transplant coordinator over the phone what all would take place on my first visit. She told me the visit would be about two hours long. It might sound strange, but I was looking forward to having the transplant as soon as possible. Cynthia had informed me of some of the things I would have to face, but it would be so much more. It would truly be a journey. My husband and daughter had to be with me at the initial appointment to receive information if the doctor decided I was a good candidate for the transplant because they would be my caregivers.

At that visit I would see a nurse, a social worker, and a Financial Supervisor before seeing the doctor and PA. The nurse was extremely nice, she took my vitals and did my blood work. I'm a hard stick, but she was able to get the vein on the first try. Next the Social worker came in. She was pleasant and just as nice as the nurse. She expressed great concern for my health,and made me feel as though I was the only patient she worked with.

She told me she would be the person to talk to if I needed emotional support, transportation, or a caregiver. She also said she would help me file for disability if needed, and much more. In just a short time of being in this doctor's office, I felt like I had finally found people who really cared about my health. After the social worker left the room, the Financial Supervisor came in. She was all about business of making sure I had the right insurance that would pay for my transplant, as well as the doctor visits.

She had already been advised of my insurance, so she wanted to make sure I chose an insurance company before the end of the year that pays for transplants. She also told me that there were foundations such as the Leukemia Foundation who would help with co-payments, my medications and some of the remainder of my hospital bills after the transplant.

After explaining everything that I needed to know, she gave me a booklet with a list of insurances to choose from who would approve paying for my transplant. She highly recommended one insurance company in the booklet, but left it up to me to check them all out and choose one. Before leaving, she reminded me of the importance of calling the insurance companies right away to see which one fits my needs.

I had to choose fast because my insurance would end in two weeks. A few minutes after she left the room, the doctor and his PA came in. They both greeted us with a smile and a handshake. From the beginning, I felt comfortable with them both. He took time to get to know my family by asking us questions, and he was very professional but down to earth. What impressed me most, was he had studied my medical chart as if he had prepared for a college exam. He was familiar with everything that I had gone through. He noticed that the EKG test my Primary doctor ordered a month ago came back saying I had an enlarged heart. He told me to make an appointment with my cardiologist to take a second EKG.

Although that wasn't good news to hear, I wasn't worried because I had put it all in Gods hand and had faith He had a divine intervention waiting for me like he did Mosses and the Israelites trapped at the Red Sea. Pharaoh was on their tracks and it seemed as though it was no way out, but God stepped in on time. I knew God was going to be on time for me too, because I know Him as the Great Physician, and a miracle worker because He had performed miracles in my life before. I knew he didn't open this many doors for everything to come to a halt because of my heart. I knew that if my heart was enlarged, God would shrink it to its normal size before the transplant took place.

He is the God who made the heart. He's a heart fixer, and a heart regulator. I told the doctor I would make the appointment to see my cardiologist today. The doctor said everything else looked good, and he agreed with Doctor Brown that I needed to have the transplant as soon as soon as possible while I was still doing well. He told me that patients over the age of sixty five are not good candidates for a transplant unless they are in good health other than the cancer. I just barely met the age criteria. I would be turning sixty five in two months. He said if I had been as sick as I was when I was on top of the mountain as Dr. Brown called it, I wouldn't have been a good candidate.

I can see God working. He let me get off of the mountain, and go to the safe place in the valley where He covered me with his peace and protection until I received the transplant. My husband and daughter, along with myself had many questions to ask the doctor. He patiently took time to listen and answered all of our questions. He was forthcoming about everything. He said he was required to provide adequate information to the patient informing them of the risk of a transplant.

He said there may be a chance that the transplant may not be successful, or I could even die during the procedure. He told me all of this in a professional way. I was willing to take my chances. He explained that before he could even consider me having a transplant, I would have to first go through a series of test to see if I would be a good candidate for a transplant. I was willing to go through any test that was needed. He told me the testing would take at least two months, and if all goes well he would schedule the transplant for early March. I told him my concerns of waiting that long after the episode I had gone through when I was off chemo before. I let him know that if I had to wait until March to get the transplant, it would be three months since I had chemo last.

The doctor said although I needed to have the transplant as soon as possible, I had to first go through the test to make sure I was a good candidate. He said my blood test looked good, and said I would be alright until I go through the series of test since I had my last chemo treatment in December. He said he would monitor my lab blood test, and if for any reason that I might need chemo, they would administer it at the Cancer Center across the street from his office where my new oncologist office was.

I explained to the doctor about my insurance, and he said if I'm a good candidate, the transplant would be done in March so that would give me time to choose an insurance company who pays for transplants. I asked him, "How much will a Stem Cell Transplant cost?" He told me not to worry about any doctor or hospital bills, just concentrate on getting well. I wasn't worried about the bill because I knew from the start I couldn't afford to pay for it even with insurance, but I knew God would supply my every need. I was just curious about the price of a transplant.

It really touched my heart to know that this doctor was more concerned about my health rather than money. My previous oncologist mentioned several times before I left his practice that he would only be taking private insurance the following year. He was warning me in advance that he would no longer be accepting Obama Care Insurance. In other words, if I didn't have private insurance, I would have to find another doctor. What he didn't know was God had already reserved a space for me at another location with another doctor. God doesn't want us to lose sleep worrying trying to figure out how things will work out.

God wants us to trust Him. Philippians 4:6-8 KJV tells us, "To be careful for nothing, but in everything by prayer and supplication, with thanksgiving, let your request be made known unto God." I had already done that. I was waiting in expectancy that God was going to perform miracles and heal me. Too often we take matters in our own hands because we don't have the faith to wait on God.

His timing is not our timing. God had already orchestrated doors to be opened long before I even knew I would need a transplant. He gave me a new oncologist and a transplant doctor. After the doctor patiently answered all of our questions, I thanked him for accepting me as his patient, and I let him know how grateful I was for the special exception they made for me. After the doctor left the room, the physician's assistant took over.

She gave me a thick booklet that had all the information that I needed about having a transplant, and she took her time and explained each page. The information was very informative and would later come in handy when I needed to refer back to it. The booklet also had business cards of all the people who I met on my initial appointment, including the doctors in case I needed to contact them. Most importantly, it had the schedule of all the test and procedures that I would need to take. It was a long visit but I would have stayed all day if needed.

I thank God for my husband, he has truly been my help meet. He has never been one to make hospital visits, nor does he like seeing people sick, but God gave him the strength to endure every surgery that I have gone through. He's been right by my side for every doctor appointment, hospital stays, test procedures and now this. Seems as though the past two years we have spent most of our time at doctor appointments. I sometimes tease him when we are going to a doctor's appointment by telling him we are going on a date. We laugh and make fun of it. Laughter is like a medicine to the heart. After looking at the testing schedule in the booklet, I knew it was going to be a journey but I had no idea it would be such an extensive process but I never complained. I was willing to go through whatever I needed to no matter how long it took. I just prayed that I would stay healthy and pass the test so I could receive the transplant.

I thanked the physician's assistant for her patience and being so thorough. As we were leaving, I heard someone call my name. As I looked around, there stood my granddaughter's aunt, Teresa. Teresa was the lady who had encouraged me to see the doctors where she worked. She was just as surprised to see me, as I was her. We hugged and talked a few minutes, and then I asked her did she work there and she said yes. I felt like crying as I witnessed Gods amazing grace upon my life. I knew God had orchestrated His divine plan for me to come to the same doctor's office that both Cynthia and Teresa referred me to. I was flabbergasted!

God is working even if we don't see or feel Him. Romans 8:28 KJV says, "And we know that all things work together for good to them that love God, to them who are called according to his purpose." What a blessing this was. God promised us many blessing if we obey. He promised to supply all of our needs according to His riches and glory.

Before leaving, Teresa encouraged me to have the transplant as soon as possible. It would turn out that Teresa would become my nurse at every appointment, because I was a hard stick and she was the only nurse who could draw my blood without sticking me numerous times. If the other nurses would try once and couldn't succeed, they would call my special nurse Teresa. God was performing miracles for me.

I went home that day thanking God of his miraculous goodness. I sat at my desk and prayed asking God to direct me to the right insurance company that would fit all of my medical needs. There were five insurance companies to choose from in the booklet that the financial supervisor gave me. She told me that all of them would pay for my transplant, but she couldn't tell me which one to choose.

I was lead to call the second insurance company in the booklet. The voice of the male representative on the phone was calming, and he was very helpful in helping me choose the right insurance. I could feel God directing me. The Financial Supervisor said all the insurances in the booklet were PPO Insurances and they all had transplant coverage. HMO insurance was much cheaper, but with a PPO insurance I wouldn't need referrals from my primary doctor for test, or for the doctors I chose. Last year when I was very sick I was denied a second PET scan with my HMO insurance. This test is a lifesaving test that detects cancer to see if it has metastasized to other organs.

I chose PPO insurance because I didn't want anything preventing me from having test when needed. After the representative finished asking questions, I explained that I had signed up for Medicare which wouldn't start until I turned sixty five in February. I let him know that my HMO insurance with the other company would end at the end of the year and I would be left without insurance from January 1, 2020 until February 14, 2020 until my Medicare starts.

He suggested that I continue with the HMO insurance because I would have a thirty day grace period after my insurance ends. In other words, I would still have my HMO insurance and won't be without insurance not one day. Look at God! My Medicare would begin on February 14, 2020 but I would still need a secondary insurance that would help pay for my transplant. After the representative finished telling me all of the good benefits the PPO insurance offered, I knew it was going to be expensive and prayed that I could afford it.

I asked him how much all of this was going to cost. When the man said nothing, I said excuse me. He repeated nothing then explained I wouldn't have a monthly premium because Medicare would deduct the insurance from my social security check each month which will pay for part D prescription drug benefits and part B would take care of the doctor, hospital, and test. I would only pay a $20.00 co-payment for each doctor visit.

I didn't understand all of the part D and B at the time, but I didn't ask any more questions concerning the cost, I just began giving God praise out loud telling Him thank you. The man sat on the line quietly while I gave God praise. I get the "Can't Help It's" sometimes, because when I think of God's goodness and what he's done for me, my soul cries out "Hallelujah," letting God know how grateful I am.

I told the nice man to sign me up. He took my information over the phone and told me I would receive my cards and booklet by February tenth. I called my current insurance and explained that I would be sixty five and would go on Medicare insurance in February. The representative expressed that the company could continue my insurance until Medicare take over.

God was blowing my mind with the miracles He was performing. I was under the impression that I would be left without insurance for two weeks until the primary insurance and Medicare would start in February. God said, "No, I will make it so you won't be without insurance one day." Won't He do it! He continued carrying me over ever storm that I faced. Even when I couldn't trace Him, he was working things out for my good.

Two weeks later, I went to my appointment to get established with my new Oncologist. He would take over my care after the transplant. This doctor was amazing as Cynthia said. He began asking me numerous questions about everything as far back as when I was first diagnosed with cancer. I asked him did he receive my records from my oncologist, and he said yes but there was not much information to go by. The previous oncologist office dropped the ball once again, and failed to send all of my records that the doctor requested. They only sent minimum information that wouldn't tell my new oncologist very much. I explained to him some of what I had encountered, and at that point he took matters into his own hands.

He told me not to worry because he and the transplant doctor would work closely together and would order all of the test they would need. I really did like this doctor, he seemed very knowledgeable. I was impressed when he took a marker and drew on the chalk board that explained everything I had gone through similar to what Doctor Brown did at Mofitt Hospital.

After examining me, the doctor said I wouldn't need to see him again until four months after my transplant. I told him if all of my tests are cleared, the doctor plan was to schedule me to have the transplant in March. Although I had not taken one test yet, the oncologist told the nurse to schedule my next appointment for July. That was confirmation to me that I would be a good candidate for the transplant.

On February 14, 2020, I celebrated my sixty fifth birthday with three of my good friends Bettye Edwards, Patricia Moore, and Sandra Crudup along with our husbands. These couples have been our friends for many years and have supported me through my back surgeries and cancer journey. We had a delicious dinner at Long Horn Steak House, and they showered me with gifts along with two scrumptious cakes.

I thanked God that I lived to see another birthday after all I had been through in 2019. That Valentine's Day birthday was one of the most grateful one's I've ever had. We laughed and had such a fun time. Bettye and Pat added my name to their women's prayer list at their church. What a blessing it is to have friends that will pray for you. Those are the kind of friends that I want to keep in my life.

Now my new insurance was in affect, and I was calm as could be. I could literally see God answering my prayers, and those effectual, fervent prayers of the righteous who were praying for me. God was carrying me through every storm big and small, and He knew everything I was about to face, so he kept me calm.

I would have to take numerous test four days a week. All of the tests accept the bone marrow biopsy test, and blood work would be taken at the Cancer Center Building where my oncologist office is located. The bone marrow biopsy and blood work would be taken at the transplant doctor's office. On Monday February 24, 2020 I would begin taking the first three tests which were all done in one day. The first two tests I took that morning were a CXR and EKG.

The CXR is a chest x-ray that evaluates the lungs, heart, and chest. The second test was an EKG which records the electrical signal from the heart and detects cardiac problems. After taking those two tests at 1:00 pm, I took a PFT test which evaluates the lung function. I didn't have any test done on Tuesday, but early Wednesday morning at 8:30 AM I had a bone marrow biopsy and blood work done.

The bone marrow test is one test that really hurts even after using local anesthetic. The long needle was inserted through the skin in my upper hip and into the Periosteum. Tissue from the bone is aspirated into a big needle to be examined and determine whether cancer or another disease has affected the bone marrow.

On Thursday February 27, 2019 at 7:45 am I took a PET scan. The PET scan scans the entire body and pinpoints both a primary tumor and areas that may have metastasis. At 9:30 AM February 28, 2020 would be the last test I would take that week. These tests would determine if I was a good candidate for the transplant.

On Friday February 28, 2020 at 9:30 am I had to go to the hospital which was across the street from the Cancer Center to take an echocardiogram (Echo). This test shows a graphic outline of the heart movement. This was a long week; it took an hour to drive to the hospital because the morning traffic was so congested.

God had prepared my mind as well as my husbands to take one day at a time. Each day was a new day and I was walking in Gods healing promises. God had already opened so many doors for me so I knew everything was going to work out on my behalf. I was grateful and would not complain about anything because some people traveled hundreds of miles out of state to receive a transplant. We lived only fifteen miles from one of the best transplant hospitals in Florida where I could receive my transplant, so all I could do was give God thanks.

On March 3, 2020 at 2:00 PM I had my second appointment to see the transplant doctor. This would be the big day that I would find out whether or not I would be a good candidate for a transplant. If so, I would sign the consent papers that they had already given me to look over. It was just my husband and I in the room that day to receive the news. We had been praying and believing that God had paved the way for me to have the transplant.

I'm a believer and I know God has our days numbered, but I just knew God was going to perform a miracle. He still had work for me to do in the earthly realm. God gives doctors knowledge and medicines that works together with His divine will, but my total trust was in God. I continued to think positive and allowed my spirit to rest in God.

The doctor and nurse came in the room with smiles on their faces that told the story. The doctor didn't waste any time. He said, "Mrs. Jackson, all of your tests came back, and as you know we previously had some concerns about your heart after seeing your EKG. Well, I'm glad to tell you that you have been cleared to have the transplant. All of your tests came back normal, even, your second EKG." I had passed each test with flying colors. I threw my hands up in the air and said, "Hallelujah!" My soul got happy and I couldn't hold my peace. I got the "Can't Help It's" and began giving God praise with tears flowing down my face.

Just a month earlier, the EKG had shown I had an enlarged heart. God is a miracle worker! If it was large, He shrunk it just so I could have the transplant. I never looked so forward to checking in a hospital before, but I couldn't wait to have the transplant, although I had been told there was a chance the transplant may not work, or I could even die. I knew I wouldn't have a chance of living if I didn't have the transplant. The doctor would use my own cells instead of a donor because I would have better success with my own cells because my body can't reject itself, and it will be much safer.

Although my second EKG test was normal, my heart doctor had to approve the transplant. My transplant doctor showed me the clearance letter that he had received from my heart doctor, clearing me to have my upcoming stem cell transplant procedure. I hugged the doctor and PA as we all expressed our joy. The joy they had for me was the same as you would have for a family member.

The doctor didn't want to prolong the time, so he schedule me to have my transplant as soon as possible while I was still in remission. I was scheduled to have the transplant on March 17, 2020, but I would have to go through more extensive tests to prepare me for the stem cell transplant. I didn't know what all to expect, although everything was explained to me in details. I had made up my mind that I was going to take one day and one procedure at a time. The Lord was holding my hand and carrying me through each storm. I wasn't worried or afraid because I kept my mind focused on Him. My husband's grandmother Laura Revels use to say "Just keep on living" and life journey will bring testing times to all of us. The hard tests were ahead of me.

CHAPTER TWENTY FOUR

Testing Times Begins

We may have different test that we must face in life, but it's up to each individual whether or not we pass our test. I was determined to pass whatever physical tests I had to endure. I had an appointment at the hospital admissions office to fill out papers before checking in the hospital. I was also scheduled to take a few more test in the same building. We got lost in the big building as we were trying to find out if we were on the right floor. We ran into a couple who was also lost. We laughed and said are you lost too. They said yes, and we ended up at the same place.

As we sat waiting to be called in for our appointments, we introduced ourselves to the couple and began talking. They were such kind people. After talking for a short time, Julia and I found out that we both needed to have a stem cell transplant. We had already been told we would need to walk after having the transplant, so Julia volunteered to be my walking partner since our transplants were schedule a day apart.

Julia was a knitter, and while we sat and talked, she gave the prettiest pink and blue knitted caps that she had knitted and had in her bag. Right then, I knew she was a sweet lady with a caring heart. After that day, I was looking forward to seeing Julia and walking with her while our stay in the hospital. We said our goodbyes and looked forward to seeing each other soon. The very next day on March 4, 2020 I would begin preparing for my transplant journey.

The hardest test was about to begin. The first thing the doctor did was increased my calcium, and I had to take one Claritin a day. Thursday March 5, 2020 I was administered a Neupogen injection. This injection is a bone marrow stimulant. It can help the body make white blood cells after receiving cancer medication. It can also improve survival in people who have been exposed to radiation. Neupogen is the same injection I had to take during my chemo treatments. It caused me to have aching pain in the bones and muscles. It also caused tiredness, but thank God I didn't experience any of the other side effects such as diarrhea, constipation, hair loss, skin rash or nosebleeds.

On March 6, 2020 at 7:30 am I had to check in the hospital to receive a Central Venous Catheter which would be my life line. A central line is a type of catheter that is placed in a large vein that allows multiple IV fluids to be given and blood to be drawn. A central line can also be used to measure fluids volumes status, and to determine if a patient is dehydrated or has received adequate amount of fluid to support bodily function.

I was anesthetized, and when I woke up a central venous catheter was inserted in my neck and threaded into a large vein. Once in the vein, the catheter is tunneled under the skin to the lower chest where it exits. The three prong connections allow access to administer medications, chemo treatment, and the transplant is done through the central venous catheter. After recovering for two hours, I was sent home with the three prongs catheter extruding through my blouse. Although a small incision was made in my neck and chest to insert the three prong catheter I didn't experience any pain. The only discomfort I felt was when I took a shower, and at night when I had to sleep with the prongs hanging out of my chest.

That same evening after I received the catheter, I had to return to the Cancer Center for another Neupogen injection to stimulate the white blood cells. The following morning March 7, 2020 I returned to the Infusion Center at the Cancer Institute to receive another Neupogen injection. On March 8, 2020 I returned again for another Neupogen injection and also a Plerixfor injection which is an Immunostimulant used to mobilize Hematopoietic Stem cells into the bloodstream. My labs were also taken.

The following day March 9, 2020 would be the most important day. I would arrive at the Cancer Institute at 7:00 am. This would be Apheresis Day #1. On this day I would have to lay on a bed for six to eight hours connected to a Apheresis machine, that was connected to the central venous catheter while the Apheresis machine harvest my bone marrow. This machine separates the bad cells from the good cells. The good cells are then removed and frozen until the day of the transplant procedure.

The nurse watched the machine carefully as it collected my good white blood cells as I laid in bed. I could only use a bed pan whenever I needed to go to the bathroom because the machine had to continuously run. A certain amount of white blood cells would be frozen and stored so I could have my own cells instead of a donor. If enough cells weren't collected after the first day, I was scheduled to return the following morning for another collection. After six hours, the collection was completed and someone from the lab came to retrieve the cells to count the number of cells collected.

I waited another two hours while the cells were counted and the doctor reviewed my numbers. Thank God I had enough stem cells in the one collection to have the transplant, and additional cells to be stored in case I would ever need a second transplant in the future. Thank God I didn't have to return the following day. But if I had too, I wouldn't have complained because I was at peace, and knew God would carry me through that storm too.

The next six days I prepared myself for my three week hospital stay by praying, meditating on the word of God, packing, and sending love to all of my family. On March 16, 2020 at 9:30 am I was scheduled to be admitted in the hospital for my transplant procedure. As my husband drove, I sang. Then I gazed at him as I thanked God for such a wonderful husband.

Through my two year process of going back and forth to so many appointments he has never complained. He has been right by my side for every appointment. Yes, every married couple should be a helpmate for each other if they are able. Some will be there during the healthy times, but desert their spouse during times of sickness. I give thanks and appreciation to my superman of a husband.

CHAPTER TWENTY FIVE

Peace During The Storms

For two long years I had walked through the valley of death, but I knew God was going to heal me through a stem cell transplant. This would be the biggest storm of my life, but I had such peace. I knew by tomorrow afternoon my life would change forever. The day I checked into the hospital, we entered at the cancer unit. The place was so beautiful. All of the other hospitals I had been, in the cancer units were full of doom. Most cancer units are located in the back of the hospital which made the patients feel thrown away and defeated, but not this place. Advent Hospital was a Christian hospital and the employees in every department displayed a Christian attitude.

As we arrived on the seventh floor, a lady on the health care team took us to an area to wash our hands and arms. They were extremely careful about sanitation because the Corona Virus had just arrived in the United States and people were dying by the thousands. By the time we finished washing our hands, a friendly nurse with a big personality named Fran took us to my room.

As I entered, I looked around at the plush and beautiful room. My room was on the seventh floor and although I don't like being up high, I looked out the window and could see a panoramic view of the city beautiful "Orlando." I felt as though I was in an upscale New York penthouse. Fran explained how everything in the room worked and she made me feel right at home. Before she left the room, she told me I would be receiving chemo later that afternoon. The first impression I had of Fran was she was such a bubbly and friendly nurse.

That afternoon, several nurses came in my room to prepare me for the chemo treatment. I especially remember Gabbie because she was very nice and did her job very professionally explaining the chemo process that would take place. The nurse at my doctor office had previously given me a schedule sheet, but Gabbie explained everything in detail and told me my transplant would take place the following morning.

It was amazing to see how nice everyone there was. They had a way of making their patients feel comfortable and right at home. It was important that the patient feel relaxed and made to feel like someone really cared while going through a life saving procedure. This was a Christian hospital, and everyone from the doctors, check in office, testing units, the transplant team, the housekeepers, food service people, and even the wheel chair attendees were very nice and showed themselves to be Christ like. I had not been treated so kind and cared for in any other hospital.

Later that afternoon, I was given the powerful high dose chemo treatment. The purpose of this chemo was to destroy any bad white blood cells that were left in my body after having the Apheresis (collection) so there would only be good cells when my stored cells were returned to my body. After the remainder of the bad cells is destroyed, my immune system will totally be compromised. I will be susceptible to the slightest infections so I have to be extremely careful about brushing my teeth, bathing, and the foods I eat. As I laid in bed, my husband sat in the recliner while we talked, and then he prayed. I had a peace that surpasses all understanding although I was about to experience one of the worst things a person could experience. After all that I had gone through, I finally could lie down and rest.

Later that day, the nurse came to administer the powerful chemo. I thought she was going to take me to the Infusion Center, but she told me she was going to give me the treatment through the central venous lines right there in my bed. I had been warned that this dose of chemotherapy used in a transplant regimen was the highest dose.

To eliminate cancer cells in my bone marrow as well as my body, it was necessary to use the highest dose possible. Because of the high dose, there was a possibility I would experience more severe and different side effects than the chemo treatments I had in the past. I had already read in my patient booklet about the dangerous side effects that the chemo may cause. It could kill good cells along with the bad cells. It could damage normal fast growing cells such as those in the mouth or throat, bowels, skin, hair and bone marrow.

That wasn't all. I read that I could experience mouth or throat sores, nausea, vomiting, diarrhea, a rash, loss of hair, or it could change my skin color. It could also cause my blood count to become very low. This powerful chemo could also affect other organs of the body.

Although severe side effects are infrequent, they can progress and cause complications such as veno- occlusive disease of the liver, kidney failure, heart palpitations, and stiffening of the lungs. After knowing all of this, I was still willing to go forward with the transplant because I felt the presence of God with me from the beginning of this journey until now. I didn't come this far to turn back now.

God had carried me this far and I knew He wouldn't leave me. I had no fear because my trust was in God. Every day I quoted Psalms 118:17 KJV, "I shall not die but live and declare the works of the Lord." As I laid there in the bed, the nurse inserted a needle filled with the chemo medication into the central venous line that was connected through my neck and chest.

My husband sat in the recliner and watched as the chemo flowed through my entire body. I was amazed at how every treatment that I needed had been done right there in bed through the Central Venous Line. After the treatment was over, I didn't feel any pain or symptoms. My husband left to go home about 2:00 pm that afternoon and I finally fell asleep later that evening. About 3:00 am that morning, March 17, 2020. I was awakened by a visitation from

The Holy Spirit. I was a bit dazed, but I heard God speak through the Holy Spirit with a soft voice saying to Write 'How I Carried You Through The Storms." Then I saw a vision of many things that I had gone through from my childhood into my adulthood.

It was as though I was watching a long movie, then the vision suddenly vanished. I laid there for awhile to make sure I wasn't dreaming before I got up and sat on the edge of the bed. I thought to myself, that maybe God wanted me to write a play once the miracle transplant was over to encourage and give hope to others. Many times before God had spoke to me at peculiar times giving me assignments or confirmation, but this time I couldn't understand why He would come when I was about to go through the biggest storm of my life and ask me to write about storms.

Some things we won't understand because the bible says in Isaiah 55: 8 KJV, "For my thoughts are not your thoughts, neither are your ways my ways, saith the Lord." God already know the beginning and ending of our lives. Although I didn't understand at that time, I told God I would be obedient and do His will. Perhaps, Gods timing may seem strange at times, but His timing is always the right time. In my younger years when I worked long hours, there were times that God would wake me up early in the morning with an assignment.

I would say, "Lord, will you please come back about 7:00 am.?" I guess God laughed instead of rebuking me. I remember when I was eighteen years old when God called me to my first assignment at my church to direct the youth choir. I offered many excuses like Moses did in Exodus 3:11 KJV. I basically told God the same thing. I had no experience, the people won't accept me, and I'm not good enough because of fear.

When I finally obeyed and became youth choir director, the choir grew from ten girls, to sixty five children with both boys and girls. I've learned that when God gives an assignment, He will equip me for the job. I've written many plays, but what God asked me to do would be much more than writing a play. God chooses the most unlikely people to fulfill His purpose. Philippians 4:13 KJV tells me that "I can do all things through Christ who strengthens me." After this mind blowing experience, I laid back down but couldn't go to sleep.

As I laid in the stillness of the night staring at the ceiling, I asked God what storms did He want me to write about, and when should I began writing but I didn't hear a word. I knew it would be sometime later after I recuperated from the transplant that God would have me to do the assignment, because He's not that kind of God who would burden me while going through a storm. He was preparing me for my assignment. Awhile later, the Lord calmed my spirit and I fell asleep.

I was scheduled to have my transplant at 2:00 pm that afternoon. My husband arrived at 11:00 am. After he settled in with his back pack filled with goodies and his laptop, he prayed thanking God in advance for my healing. That prayer touched the core of my soul because we were praying the same prayer without knowing it. Instead of asking God to heal me, I had begun thanking God in advance for my healing.

We believed that He was going to heal me. We were standing on His healing promises. Psalms 30:2 KJV promised that I could call on God for help and He would heal me. On March 17, 2022 at exactly 2:00 o'clock in the afternoon, two nurses entered my room and introduced themselves. The one named Vania said she was going to administer my transplant. These ladies were both very young.

Although everything was explained to me in detail, I don't remember anyone telling me the transplant would be done right there in my room. I thought I was going to be taken into a surgery room where my doctor and a transplant team would be waiting to do the transplant. I totally didn't understand, I had gone through so much; I must have misunderstood the process of how the transplant would be done. Vania explained very plainly that because I wasn't receiving an organ transplant, I would not have to have surgery. There was no need for a doctor to be present, only the transplant nurse because I would be receiving my thawed out cells through the central venous catheter. She said she would be the nurse who would administer my transplant.

Vania explained that the good cells that were previously collected and frozen, had been thawed out and someone from the transplant team would bring them one bag at a time to my room within a twenty minute sequence of each other. Then she explained exactly how the transplant would take place, and said it would be done right there while I laid in bed.

Vania said the good cells that had been thawed would be put back into my body through one of the central venous lines. I was amazed at this modern technology. I thanked her for explaining everything so plainly. Vania and the other nurse worked together to set everything up. By the time everything was in order, a woman that worked with the transplant team entered the room with my thawed out cells in a bag that looked like an IV bag. It was imperative that she arrived every twenty minutes to my room with the bags of cells during the transplant procedure.

My cells looked like tiny eggs. They were yellowish and red in color. The two nurses worked together to get the first bag of cells hooked up to the central venous line. After everything was going well, the nurse who was helping Vania left and now Vania was solely my transplant nurse. She would oversee the entire transplant alone. I still couldn't believe it would be that simple. Vania had such a sweet spirit and I felt the presence of the Lord surrounding and directing her, but I felt she was a bit nervous.

As she sat at the foot of my bed while the cells were entering my body, she explained everything that I might experience as the cells re-entered my body. I didn't feel any pain, but I began to have palpitation and my heart rate went up. I felt as if I was walking on a treadmill while having a stress test. She told me this would happen every time the cells entered my body, but would subside between the twenty minute cycles of receiving the cells.

Once the bag was emptied, my breathing would go back to normal. Every bag of cells had to enter my body in a timely manner once it was thawed. Between each empty bag Vania would monitor my blood pressure. Twenty minutes after each bag was emptied, the lady would arrive with another bag of my cells. I would get out of breath and have heart palpitations as each bag of cells entered my body. It would take four bags of my thawed out cells to complete the transplant. It felt like I had walked on a treadmill for more than an hour. One hour and thirty five minutes later, it was all over. God had performed a miracle. Praise God! I would live and not die and declare the works of the Lord.

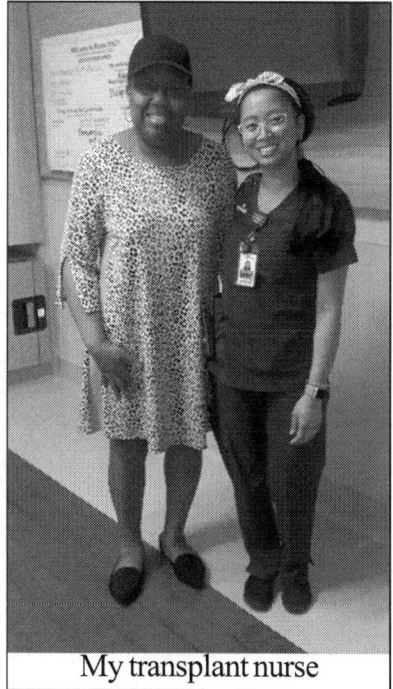

My transplant nurse

I had etched that scripture in my heart believing that God would see me through, although the doctor had given me all the risk. After the transplant was completed I felt happy, grateful, and excited. I thanked God over and over again for a second chance. God gave me peace and carried me through the biggest storm of my life. I thanked my transplant nurse Vania for being such a great and caring nurse. She would forever be a part of my new life. It could have been another nurse but God assigned her to me.

Before Vania left the room, we began to share Christ goodness with each other. I knew she was a Christian because I saw her light shining when she first walked into my room. She told me that she had recently gotten married and moved to Orlando, and God blessed her with the job at Advent Health Hospital. She seemed a bit hesitant but she told me that she had only administered one transplant at the hospital where she worked before moving to Orlando, and I would be her second transplant patient.

She must have felt connected and comfortable talking to me by sharing that kind of Information. Most patients wouldn't want to know information like that. They would want someone more experienced, but I felt God assigned her to me. If I had gotten a nurse that had more experience, they might not have taken the time to do everything precisely like Vania did. She took her time and did everything accurate like it should be done. God steadied her hands and mind, and took away whatever fears she might have had. I felt her kindred spirit and she felt mine.

Hallelujah! It was over. God had brought me through the worst storm I had ever faced in my life, and it wasn't as bad as I thought it would be. Plus, I didn't feel any pain. The back surgeries were more painful. When it was all over, my nurse Vania and I were overjoyed. We both had mask on, so we couldn't help but hug each other although the Corona virus was circulating. God used this young lady to be a part of my life saving transplant journey. I will never forget her; she will forever be a part of my life. That day was one of the most exciting and grateful days I've ever experienced. I had made it through the transplant and had no fear of the side effects that I might experience.

After everything was over, my husband came over and hugged me, and told me he loved me. We were happy that God had answered our prayers. He sat in the recliner and it wasn't long before he fell asleep. I looked at my husband as he slept with his headphones on. He looked as if he could finally get some rest. He had gone through so much with me. Everything that I had gone through for years he was right by my side. After he slept for two hours, I woke him up and told him to go home and get some rest. I assured him that I would be just fine.

I could see the look of relief on his face knowing that I had come through the transplant alright. I knew he was tired, and I was glad he agreed to go home and get some rest. After my husband left, I couldn't sleep because I was so grateful and excited, I couldn't stop the praise on the inside. God had walked with me, and talked with me along the long journey. He encouraged me when I thought I might not make it. He never once left my side so I couldn't help but praise Him!

CHAPTER TWENTY SIX

A Renewed Spirit

I was still amazed at how God had re-energized and brought me back from the brink of death in just one hour and thirty five minutes through a Stem Cell Transplant while using my own cells. Wow! Around seven o'clock that evening, I finally began to doze off. I was awakened by the entire transplant team as they entered my room singing Happy Birthday. They could be heard throughout the seventh floor. I woke up with a big smile on my face, but I was in shock and shaking like a leaf because I was still trying to wake up fully. After realizing what was going on, I tried to get my phone so I could record all of the nurses singing Happy Birthday on my "Transplant Birthday."

They presented me with beautiful and delicious cupcakes, then expressed how happy they were for my new life. I believe it was my transplant nurse Vania who wrote Happy Birthday on the board in my room and drew balloons all around it while I was asleep. Although I was born on Valentine's Day February 14th, they were celebrating the day the Lord turned back the hands of time like He did Hezekiah. March 17, 2020 would be a day to remember because it was the day God restores my life.

My spirit was renewed and I was moved, but all I could do was shed tears of joy, and blow all the nurses kisses letting them know how grateful I was. Of course, I know one day when I reach heaven there will be no need to celebrate birthdays because we will live for an eternity with God, but I was thankful for my life celebration while I'm still here on earth. I was extremely happy and felt so

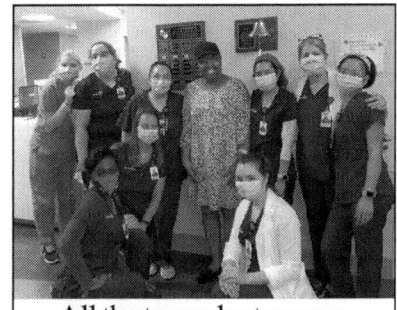

All the transplant nurses

much love from the team of nurses that day.

I was half asleep and totally in shock when they first came into my room singing Happy Birthday, so I couldn't get to my phone in time to record them. I asked them if they would do a reenactment of the song so I could record them and they happily did. When they finished singing a second time, they left my room laughing at the way the other one sang. I will never forget that joyous day. I had never experienced so much love and compassion in any other hospital.

That night, I didn't get much sleep. I had already prepared myself for the nurses coming in and out of my room all night. Throughout the night they checked my blood pressure, temperature, gave me medications, and even woke me up to take my weight. It took me awhile to go back to sleep after they left my room, but that was a small thing compared to what I had gone through. My transplant nurse Vania checked on me every day.

I had been warned of all the side effects that I might experience after the transplant, but I asked God to help me endure whatever I had to go through. One thing I was advised of, was my hair would all fall out after having that strong round of chemo. My husband was standing on his faith that my hair wasn't going to fall out. I'm glad his faith is strong, but there are just some things in life that we will have to go through no matter how much we pray, or how strong our faith is. We can use hair growth cream, or anoint our head with oil, but it won't stop the hair from falling out after being infused with the strongest chemo there is.

I wasn't concerned about my hair falling out, I just wanted to live. If I went bald, I had no problem with wearing a wig. Needless to say, I did lose my hair but it began to grow back in three months like the doctor said. I was told that the hair usually grows back a different texture, usually fine like baby hair. Well, my hair grew back kinkier than it originally was, and before long the gray strands began to overtake the brown strands.

I told my daughter who is a professional hair braider, it was time for me to call on Ms. Clairol to wash that grey right out of my hair. We had a good laugh. It's amazing how vain we women are at times. I've seen Christian women who were so sick, but was concerned about making sure they had their false teeth in their mouths, their wigs on, and some had to have their faces made up before visitors came into their hospital rooms.

I'll never forget one of clients saying if she dies before me, she's requesting that I make sure her hair is nicely done, and to make sure she has on her red lipstick. I said, "Don't worry, if I'm still around I will have your hair fried, died, and laid to the side, and your red lipstick on your two lips." She fell out laughing. We used to have so much fun in the salon, and I kept the ladies in stitches with my humor that I too inherited from my funny parents.

Two days after my transplant I felt fine, almost like nothing had taken place. The only thing I had a complaint about was the food. Oh my goodness, I had never tasted food that made me sick just from the smell. After having a transplant patients are put on a special diet called a Neutropenic Diet. The diet is for people with weakened immune systems. This diet helps protect them from bacteria and other harmful organisms found in some foods and drinks. I know the food was for my good, but several times I regurgitated just from the smell. Although that diet was awful, I kept thanking God that I had come this far. I reminded myself that I wasn't there for the food or to get much sleep. I kept saying "This Too Shall Pass."

By now the Corona Virus was on the rampage. People were dying by the thousands each day, especially in New York. The news became very depressing after seeing so many people dying daily, and being put in body bags and stored in air conditioned semi trucks because the funeral homes were all full. Although the cancer unit was on the opposite side of the hospital nowhere near other patients, it was still a scary time to be in the hospital.

The workers on the cancer floor had to go home to their families and could have easily contracted the disease and spread it on the transplant floor. The cleaning lady told me she was uncomfortable riding the city bus to work, but it was her only transportation. Her, as well as anyone else who worked on the transplant floor, could have contracted the virus without knowing it and spread it to the transplant patients. The only thing I could do was pray asking God for protection for everyone in the cancer unit.

I was so grateful that my transplant was over, but I was concerned about Julia the nice lady who I had met in the registration office. We had exchanged phone numbers when we first met, and we called to check on each other daily but we never got a chance to walk together due to our daily schedule. Julia would stop by my room on her daily walks for a few minutes to see how I was doing. I hadn't heard from her in a few days, and it concerned me so I gave her a call. She had her transplant the day after I had mine, and thank God she came through her transplant just fine but she needed rest.

I walked to her room and peaked in to check on her, and we were happy to see each other. We thanked God that He carried us through the storms that had threatened our lives. Julia and I formed a sisterhood while at the lowest point of our lives. It has been over two years since our transplants, and we still keep in touch by phone and letters to encourage and check on each other. If the world didn't see color, we would get alone better and have a better world to live in. I'm an African American and Julia is Caucasian, but that didn't matter. We saw each other's heart and spirit when we first met, not color. I love my sister in Christ, and I'm always excited whenever we talk, or I receive a card from her.

Later that evening, my doctor came by to check on me. He was happy to see how well I was doing so soon after receiving my transplant. He told me how blessed I was to receive my transplant on schedule, because due to the Corona Virus they had to shut down the entire transplant unit. I was his last patient to have my procedure done. They weren't sure when they would be able to do anymore transplants.

Julia and I had different doctors, but I was so grateful that we both were able to receive our transplants. I began praying for all the other patients on the floor who would now have to wait. Time was one thing that was fighting against most of the patients on that 7th floor. I began giving God praise and tears began to stream down my face because I knew how important it was for me to have the transplant as soon as possible. If I had to wait after my immune system had been wiped out from the powerful chemo, I probably wouldn't have made it. BUT GOD!

I thank Him every day for His grace, mercy, and favor that He extended me. Later that day, a nurse came into my room and told me that visitations may have to stop due to the Corona Virus. It was only the second day after my transplant and my husband had been by my side each day for support. It would be awful if he wouldn't be able to visit anymore during my three or four weeks stay in the hospital. It's comforting having family support after going through something of this magnitude, especially while going through an epidemic that was killing people all over the world.

The next morning, I woke up praying that I would be able to see my daughter in case they stopped the visitation. My husband and daughter were the only two people who could visit me because they would be my caregivers once I went home. I could only have one visitor a day, so my husband visited me the first two days because my daughter worked during the week, but she had plans to visit on Saturday.

The hospital kept changing the visitation rules daily because the virus was getting worse. Thank God, by Saturday we were still allowed one visitor. My daughter got the opportunity to visit me on Saturday, and we were so excited to see each other. She was all masked up and I wanted to give her a big hug so bad, but we had to stay six feet apart because of the Corona virus. What joy it was to see my daughter.

Although we weren't able to physically hug each other, we had our way of hugging without touching. We would extend our hands towards each other and open and shut our hands from afar and we could feel the love from across the room. What a blessing it was to see my only daughter. She has always been there for me. We talked for a while, and I told her how much I missed my grandchildren. She called them on the phone, and I was able to see and talked to them via zoom.

They were all concerned about me. But after seeing how well I was doing, they cheer up and I saw a big relief on their faces. It was as though they were holding their breath but now they could finally exhale. After talking to my grand's, my daughter and I talked for hours until I was ready to take a nap. What a blessing it was to see her. She left thinking we would see each other again the following weekend. That evening, a nurse told me that the visitation rules had changed once again.

She said we could no longer have visitors because the virus had gotten much worse, and the hospital was filled with patients who had the virus. They didn't want the cancer unit patients to be exposed to the virus through visitors who may be a carrier without knowing it. After having a transplant, the immune system is totally wiped out and can no longer fight off diseases. I understood, and was glad they were taking all precautions they could to keep the patients safe. But I was sad that I wouldn't be able to see my husband or daughter the remainder of time that I would be in the hospital.

I thought about my new friend Julia. She would no longer be allowed to see her husband after they had traveled to Orlando from out of town to have her transplant. I called to check on her after hearing the new visitation rules. She was sad too that her husband could no longer visit. I tried to encourage her by letting her know that this too shall pass, and before we know it we will be home with our families again eating some tasty food. We talked and lifted each other's spirits. We didn't know when we would be allowed to see our husbands again, but we knew this wouldn't last forever.

I wasn't anxious about anything. God had given me His peace which surpasses all understanding and it guarded my heart and mind in Christ Jesus (Philippians 4:7 KJV). I was happy and my spirit was renewed although I didn't know the final outcome. The doctor said the worst was yet to come from all of the side effects I would experience, but I had peace because I knew God would be with me through whatever I would endure.

We were experiencing a dreadful virus that brought gloom and death over the entire world, but I held on to Psalms 91:7 KJV, "A thousand shall fall at thy side, and ten thousand at thy right hand; but it shall come nigh thee." Also Psalms 4:8 KJV: "For I will both lay me down in peace, and sleep; for thou, Lord, only makest me dwell in safety." I had concerns about my family, but I refused to worry and fall into depression over something I had no control of. Instead, I rolled my burdens over to God and began thanking Him for bringing me through the transplant safely, and for keeping my family and me safe.

God constantly reminded me of Isaiah 41:13 KJV, "For I, the Lord thy God, will hold your right hand, saying Fear not, I will help thee." God reminded me that He was holding my right hand and promised to never leave nor forsake me. I held on to His promises, especially Isaiah 41:10 KJV, "Fear thou not, for I am with you; be not dismayed, for I am your God: I will strengthen thee; yea, I will help; yes, I will uphold thee with the right hand." The scriptures were reassurance and strength for me.

Every day, one of the transplant doctors would come in to check on me. Finally I met Cynthia's doctor, he was kind and caring. God would have it that my doctor came in to check on me one time before he went on vacation. Cynthia's doctor would end up checking on me daily the remainder of my stay in the hospital. Look at God work. Although all of the transplant team were good doctors, I ended up in the hands of the doctor Cynthia referred me too from the beginning.

The doctor said I was recuperating very well, except my blood platelets were low. He made arrangements for me to have blood cell platelets. It was important to have enough platelets in case I was faced with the problem of my blood not being able to clot. If I were to have a bleeding problem, it would be hard to control the bleeding with the amount of cell platelets I had.

I was made aware of the many side effects that I might have, such as bleeding, bruising, anemia, anorexia from loss of appetite, diarrhea, hair loss, and I was told my nails would fall off. Thank God I only experienced a few of the side effects. My nails didn't fall off, but they did turn dark. As the old nails grew out, the darkness grew out with them. The new nails grew stronger than ever.

I did experience severe diarrhea, and it was the worst ever, and it lasted even after I went home. Finally, on day twenty the diarrhea finally came to a halt. I had been made aware of my hair falling out after having the powerful chemo treatment. Sure enough, on the seventh day after the transplant as I shampooed my hair in the shower, I felt a blob of hair fall on my feet. When I opened my eyes, there was hair on the floor and a handful in my hands. I thought I had prepared myself for this, but it was shocking to see my hair falling out of my head by the strands.

I knew my life was more important than my hair, but I learned firsthand that a woman's hair is her crown glory. I didn't have much hair because I cut it before I went to the hospital. But when I looked in the mirror and saw bald spot throughout my scalp I almost screamed. Every morning I would find more hair on my pillow. I wore a scarf on my head during the day when I walked the hospital halls, and at night I wore a silk cap. I would wake up most mornings to find the silk cap on the floor. I even slept in the knitted caps that my new friend Julia gave me. My hair came out in patches. There was hair in some places, and bald spots in others. When I looked in the mirror I didn't look like myself.

Hair is an important part of a woman's life. I know because I was a cosmetologist for thirty six years. I would watch ladies leave the salon after getting their hair done with smiles on their faces, and a boost in their confidence. Hair is an integral part of our identity, and it's a woman's crown and glory. A women's hair enhances her personality, and it's an important part of her appearance. When I was a cosmetologist, several of my elderly clients would tell me to make sure their hair looked good when they are laid out in the casket. Women of all ages are particular about their hair looking good, even if it's the wig they are wearing.

After being in the hospital two weeks and looking at myself in the mirror, I almost fell into a pity party. I had lost so much weight and now I was almost completely bald. I began to feel sad every time I looked at the stranger in the mirror. I felt as though I didn't know who I was; I had lost my outer identity. Quickly, I began to encourage myself in the Lord. God had brought me too far for me to allow the enemy to discourage me. I remembered the old folks use to say, "Don't give foothold to the devil." When I read Ephesians 4:27 KJV, it said, "Neither give place to the devil," which meant the same thing. We are not to give the devil any opportunity to influence our lives, no matter what storms we face in life. He's our enemy and wants to destroy Gods people. I know firsthand how hard it is to stay encouraged when you are going through atrocious storms. Although we may fall at times, we should quickly get back up again. Although I had a moment of sadness, I never lost my faith, neither my hope.

I began reading the word of God and a praise of thankfulness came over me when I read Psalms 139:14 KJV: "I will praise thee, for I am fearfully and wonderfully made. Your works are wonderful, I know that full well." That scripture took away all sadness and self-pity, and sparked joy and gratefulness down deep in my soul. I then turned to Luke 12:7 KJV, "But even the very hairs on your head are all numbered. Fear not therefore: ye are of more value than many sparrows." Although I was almost completely bald, and didn't resemble myself in the mirror I knew who I was in God, and that He valued my life so much that He knew the numbers of hairs on my head. So I began thanking God for my life instead of being concerned about my outer appearance.

I learned in beauty school in 1984, that hair is the appendage to the skin and it has no feelings, and it grows one half inch a month. It didn't hurt when my hair fell out because hair has no feelings, and I knew in six months I would have at least three inches of hair to cover my head. Hair dressers can take care of all of your hair needs, but they can't make the hair grow, only God can. I fell down but I got back up! I knew God would restore everything that I had lost, so I didn't worry about my weight or my hair one second more. Losing my hair was just a small thing compared to all that I had endured.

This hair loss experience impelled me to pray for women with Trichotillomania and Alopecia Areata. Trichotillomania is an anxiety disorder which gives one the compulsive desire to pull out their hair. Alopecia Areata happens when the immune system attacks the hair follicles and the hair falls out from the root. This may be brought on by severe stress. When we think we have it bad, there's always someone worse off than we are.

I missed seeing my husband so much, but through this process God taught me to depend totally on him and not people. The Corona Virus wouldn't allow us to see any visitors, but no one, or nothing could keep my God from visiting me. I made good use of my time and never had a dull moment because I occupied my time studying my bible, reading, writing, walking through the halls, and talking to my family on zoom.

Although I don't care for being in high rise buildings, I enjoyed watching the cars from my seventh floor window as they drove on Interstate-4. I also enjoyed watching people as they walked from one building to another. I watched my favorite television shows: HGTV and the cooking shows. At the end of the day I enjoyed watching the sunset. The sun would turn bright yellow and red, and I would watch until it disappeared behind the buildings. Although the world seemed to be turned upside down God gave me peace.

I had not forgotten about what God asked me to do. As I sat on the couch one day, I began thinking about all the storms God had shown me in the vision. I wondered am I to write a play, or was it a book He wanted me to write. Every day after my morning worship I would jot down every detail of what I was experiencing while in the hospital. I didn't want to forget anything when it came time to write what God inspired.

We were required to walk twice a day, once in the morning and again in the evening. Before the transplant, my husband would walk with me. I could walk around the entire floor really fast. But after the transplant, some days I didn't feel up to walking at all but I pressed my way. It was necessary for me to walk so I wouldn't get blood clots. The pandemic had gotten worse overnight. Before we entered the hall to walk, we had to put on a mask then wash our hands before re-entering the room. The cleaning lady did an awesome job making sure the patient's rooms were thoroughly sanitized, and the staff used every precaution they could to make sure the patients were safe.

This was the early stages of the Corona virus and people were in fear. The cleaning lady would constantly share with me her concern of contracting the virus because she rode the city bus to work. She began to think that if she were to contract the disease she could easily spread it to the patients. I told her to keep her mask on and stay as safe as possible. I prayed for her each day asking God to keep her safe. I realized everyone doesn't have a car and people have to do what they need to do to survive. Thank God no one on the cancer floor contracted the disease that I know of.

As I watched the news, people were dying in New York by the thousands each day because doctors and scientist didn't know much about this horrific disease. It was hard to believe

I had just had a great time laughing and celebrating my sixty fifth birthday with friends three weeks prior to the virus, and now it seemed as though the world had turned upside down with fear and doom because of the unknown. Doctors and nurses were even dying. Exodus 9: 14–16 describes when God brought plagues upon Pharaoh, his servants, and his people to let Pharaoh know that there was none like Him on earth. God showed him His power. God is the same now, as He was back then, and He has all power in His hand.

Two weeks after my transplant, my doctor was amazed at how well I was recovering and told me that if I continue doing well he was going to let me go home the following week due to the virus. He said it would be safer for me to be at home than in the hospital. Instead of me staying in the hospital three to four weeks, I was released to go home on March 29, 2020 at 2:10 pm, thirteen days after my transplant.

CHAPTER TWENTY SEVEN

God Carried Me Through The Storms

Before leaving the hospital, I called Julia to let her know I was released to go home. She was happy for me. We encouraged each other and said we would have lunch after the pandemic was over. We said our goodbyes, and shortly afterwards one of the nurses who had taken care of me came in with my discharge papers.

After the nurse unhooked my IV she called for a wheelchair attendee to take me down stairs to my car where my husband was waiting. The nurse helped me carry my bags. One bag was filled with yogurt and Ensure drinks that I just didn't have an appetite for. I wanted to leave it all in the fridge, but she said I should take it because I paid for it. The young man arrived with the wheel chair and as the nurse walked alongside the wheel chair. I expressed my appreciation to them both. By this time, we came to the end of the hallway where I saw just about every nurse on the transplant floor gathered near the big gold bell that hung on the wall.

Whenever I would take my walks up and down the halls each day, I would pass by that bell and speak life to myself by saying one day I will ring that bell. Ringing the bell signifies joy and a great accomplishment. Cancer patients often ring ceremonial bells to celebrate the end of their radiation or chemotherapy treatments. The staff began clapping as I came near. I had prayed asking God to give me more time with my family, and to continue using me to spread the gospel of Christ. He honored my request.

When I approached that bell, I knew God had turned back the hands of time for me. King Hezekiah asked God to let him live longer and He added fifteen more years to Hezekiah's life. God is sovereign and He can do whatever he wants to do to fulfill His promise and purpose. God healed me through a transplant from an aggressive cancer. This procedure doesn't work for everyone but I thank God it did for me. I was happy and grateful that God spared my life. As I approached the nurses, they took my bags and helped me out of the wheel chair so I could ring the bell. I stood there in front of that gold bell and extended my hands towards heaven with tears streaming down my face.

I began to cry out, telling God, "Thank you." Then I grabbed hold of the cord and pulled it as hard as I could. You could hear the sound of the bell ringing throughout the seventh floor. That sound to me meant I had graduated from near death to new life. God heard my prayers, seen my tears, and He answered. After ringing the bell I asked the nurses if they would take pictures with me, they were happy to do so. We then said our goodbyes and blew kisses to each other. It was a bitter sweet moment, I felt as though I was leaving my family behind.

I would love to see them again but not under those circumstances, maybe at the mall or elsewhere. If I ever had to go to a hospital for anything I would choose Advent Health Hospital. This is the best hospital ever, and the staff was the best. As the wheel chair attendee pushed me out the front door to the patient pickup area, there stood my husband standing outside the car waiting for me. He rushed over with open arms and gave me the best hug ever. As he put my belongings in the car, the wheel chair attendee and nurse began helping me in the car.

As I stood up from the wheel chair "The Can't Help It's" came over me. I couldn't help but to once again extend my hands towards heaven and began telling God thank you. I didn't care who saw or heard me. I shouted loud, "Thank You Lord" through the mask that covered my mouth. I was so grateful of how He had renewed my life and I was now going home. I couldn't help but to give Him praise. I then took a moment to look around and appreciate the bright sunshiny sky after being in a room for thirteen days.

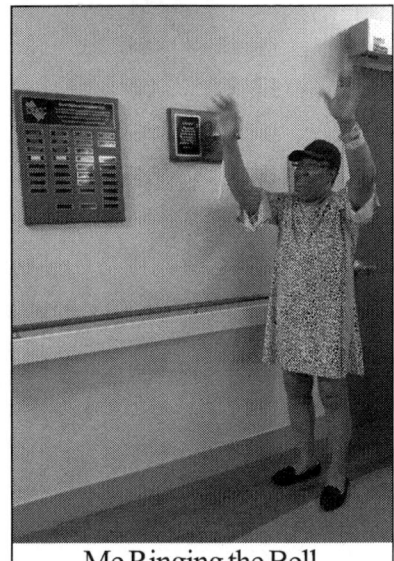

Me Ringing the Bell

The attendee and nurse had tears in their eyes as they looked on. When I finished praising God, they helped me into the car. I said wait! I would like to take a picture with my nurse. I felt safe hugging her because I knew the nurses were being tested daily. This would be the last nurse I would see before leaving the hospital and it would be a memorable picture. The nurse and attendee were both so patient, although I knew they needed to get back to work to attend to other patients. The young man took the pictures of my nurse and I with my phone camera.

The nurse had been so kind, and had taken such good care of me. I looked forward to seeing her whenever she came into my room. I had gotten familiar with the wheel chair attendee because he took me down stairs to have the central venous line taken out earlier that morning. I teased him by saying. "Wow! I can tell you didn't purchase your driver's license at Wal-Mart because you're such a good driver," and he laughed. It was good to have him wheel me to my car as I left the hospital.

All of the people who I had encountered at Advent Heath Hospital had such warm hearts. They were truly concerned about the patient and weren't there just for a paycheck.The nurse and wheel chair attendee both wished me well as we drove off.

Now my husband and I were on our way home. What joy it was seeing him after being apart for almost two weeks. I gazed at him as he drove off, and thanked him for all he had done for me while walking alongside me on this tedious journey. He had truly lived out our vows when it comes to "Through Sickness and Health" my husband is a man of faith. He always thinks positive, and he's a man of peace. His faith and encouragement helped me when I didn't know if I would see tomorrow. Too often we fail to say thank you and express our appreciation to those who are closest to us. Those who have helped us and sacrificed their time, and changed their lifestyle to help us when we needed them the most.

On the ride home from the hospital I was shocked to see most businesses closed. It looked like the world was at a standstill. I didn't see anyone on the streets walking, and there were just a few cars on the road, it was an eerie feeling. The entire world had shut down because of the Corona Virus.

As we arrived home and the garage door opened, I felt like Dorothy in the Wizard of Oz. I said to my husband, "There Is No Where Like Home."

When I walked in the door I had a renewed spirit. I stopped and looked around, and once again began thanking God for His miracle and for bringing me back home. When I left to go to the hospital I wasn't sure if I would return home, but I held to Gods promise that He would bring me through the biggest storm of my life. I walked around and looked in every room and it was just like I had left it.

I had a beautiful room at the hospital, and the bathroom was luxurious, but it didn't matter if it was a five star hotel with breathtaking ocean views, or a luxurious penthouse, it could not compare to my bed and bathroom I was accustomed to at home. My husband and daughter had signed up to be my caretakers once I came home. My daughter worked two jobs. She and my husband worked a part time job at night together. She was going to take a leave of absence from the night job to care for me while my husband went to work. I felt so good when I came home from the hospital. I told my husband I didn't need a caretaker so there wouldn't be a need for my daughter to lose time at her job.

My husband only worked four hours in the evening a few blocks from our home. I told him if I needed him, I would call and he could be home in five minute. He said he didn't think that would be a wise decision. My husband decided to take a week off work to take care of me. He did all of the cooking and house work the first three days I was home, but on the fourth day I felt strong enough to cook our meals and do light work like folding cloths after he washed them.

Five days after returning home from the hospital, my husband went to pick up a prescription for me. While he was gone, I prepared breakfast for myself. As I was going in the family room to sit on the couch to eat, I dropped a portion of the egg on the new carpet we had recently had installed. I didn't want to take a chance on stooping down to pick the egg up, so I got the vacuum to do the job. While vacuuming, I felt my heart palpitating. I felt as though I was having a heart attack. I managed to walk to our bedroom and lie down.

I laid there for five minutes hoping the palpitation would stop but it didn't, so I called my husband. He said he was on his way home and would be there in about ten minutes. I then called my daughter at work and explained what had happened. I asked her to call my transplant doctor's office and ask the nurse what I should do. My daughter thought it would be best if I went back to the hospital since it had been a short time since I had the transplant. I told her I didn't want to go because Covid 19 was really bad in hospitals, and that was the purpose for the doctor sending me home in thirteen days rather than three weeks.

My daughter called the doctor office and explained what was going on and was told someone would call me. In a few minutes the Physician's Assistant who had been so attentive to my health called me right away and asked what was going on. I explained what happened, and she asked me to take my blood pressure while she was on the phone. I kept my blood pressure cuff next to my bed so it was conveniently at arm's reach. My pressure was 186 over 91. She told me to lie down for ten minutes and relax while she stayed on the phone with me.

After ten minutes had passed, the nurse asked me to take my pressure again. Thank God it had dropped much lower and my heart rate had lowered too. She laughed and told me that my heart was not ready for me to do any vacuuming yet. She suggested that I do light duties and leave the big stuff to my husband for a while.

A few minutes after talking to the nurse, my husband ran in the room to see if I was alright. He asked me if I wanted to go back to the hospital and I told him no. I explained that I had spoken to the PA and her instructions help me to feel better. I was much better and he made sure I rested, and told me he was taking two months off of his night job to take care of me. I didn't want him to do that but he said there was no question about it. Thank God I was alright after resting.

Our daughter had committed to being my caretaker, and was willing to take off work to care for me, but we knew she had responsibilities with her family. Since I was doing fine, my husband told her I only needed one caretaker so he would take off. What a blessing it is to have such a dedicated daughter and husband.

After that day I left all vacuuming to my husband. I should have left the egg on the rug until my husband came back.

But no, me being the tidy person that I am just couldn't leave it there. God spoke to me that day through that incident. I saw myself as Martha in the Biblical story in Luke: 38-42. Martha had been distracted by all the work she had to do before Jesus arrived. I was distracted by a little piece of egg on the floor which could have landed me back in the hospital. I just had to get it up before it ruined my carpet.

My parents instilled good work ethic in their children. Saturday's were like spring cleaning in our home. We had to clean the base boards, blinds, wash windows and much more. So it was hard for me to walk away when I see something that needed to be done. Since that time, God has taught me not to sweat the small things. He has also taught me that I'm not the Savior of the world. There's only one Savior and that's HIM!

All of my adult life I had been busy working hard taking care of my family, and reaching out to help other's. I remember some years ago waking up one morning at 2:00 am while my husband slept, to go help a homeless lady I had met. I couldn't sleep knowing it was a terrible storm that night, and she was sleeping on the ground in the cold rainy weather. I felt the need to take her a blanket and umbrella. Before leaving, I prayed asking God to protect me while going out that time of the night, but I never acknowledged Him on whether I should go or not. I just saw a need and ran out the house to help this lady. I had helped her in numerous ways before but she would always end up back on the streets.

When I arrived, the homeless lady was lying on the ground on a pasteboard box with an umbrella over her head. She was just as content as she could be with a smile on her face. She thanked me and we talked a few minutes, then I asked her how she got in this predicament. She told me her story, then said many people have offered to help get her off the streets, but said she didn't want the help because she was happy where she was. I was stunned when she told me her family came all the way from Virginia, forced her in the car and took her back to her home town to get her off the streets.

She said, one day when she was home alone, she walked to the greyhound station and came back to Orlando. At that moment the wool was no longer pulled over my eyes. This lady didn't have a care in the world. I'll never forget these words she told me that night. She said, "The ground is my bed, and the sky is my roof and I'm happy." I knew then my mission was over trying to help this lady. At least ten years had passed, and one day as I approached the door at Wal-Mart, someone said, "Hello Mrs. Jackson." It was the homeless woman. She had a big smile on her face and said I'll never forget what you did for me, thank you.

I thank God that my works were not in vain, but to everything there is a season. When my season was up with this lady I moved on. Sometimes we stay too long when God has told us to move on. This lady was now old, in a wheel chair, and still homeless. As the old proverb goes, "You can lead a horse to the water but you can't make him drink." Since that time I have learned that although I have a big heart for mankind, there are times when I have to step back from those who load me down with burdens, but do nothing to help themselves.

I could have been harmed that night or had an accident in that torrential rain. I have learned to acknowledge God in all things and wait on his guidance. Sometimes people will drain you. I heard a famous preacher say, "What's hurting them, is killing you." He also said there's only one Savior of the world, and it's not you. Those few words have stuck with me and changed my life forever. As some old folks say " I know when to hold, and when to fold."

Sometimes when we rushed to help, we are getting in the way of Gods plan for that person. It could also cause people to depend on us instead of God. Sometimes God will allow a person to hit rock bottom just so they can turn to Him, like the parable of the prodigal son who returned home to his father, and we shouldn't get in the way of that. There were many nights I stayed up late nights praying for those who were living a sinful life, and was happy being as far from God as they could be. God has taught me many valuable lessons since helping the homeless lady.

I've learned to pray for people, then roll those burdens over to God because He never slumbers nor sleep. It doesn't matter if we pray for a person night and day ,they won't change until they're ready. That day after dropping that small piece of egg on the floor, the lesson God gave me will help me throughout the rest of my life. He taught me not to sweat the small things in life. I knew it wasn't important for me to vacuum the egg off the floor that day, but like Martha, I just had to get it up being the busy clean person that I am.

My oncologist informed me that stress causes cancer cells to rage and I needed to live as stress-free as possible. God has "Carried Me Through The Storms" and it would be ungrateful to God if I allowed stress, people, or anything to burden me after He has healed me. I've learned how to say "NO" and not feel bad about it without explanation. I've learned to leave things undone and not feel anxious. I've liberated myself from people who bring stress to my life, and now I sit at Jesus feet like Mary did and wait to hear from the Lord before I make a move. Proverbs 3:6 (KJV) says, "In all thy ways acknowledge him, and He shall direct thy path."

Spending valuable time with God allows us to differentiate what's important, and what's not. Who should be in our lives, and who shouldn't. I thank God for helping me make changes in my life. Now in all of my ways I mostly resemble Mary instead of Martha, the person I used to resemble the most. I've learned not to sweat the small stuff. I've learned how to rest and take care of myself. Without good health I cannot do Gods work, nor could I be a help to my family, church or others. God left me here for a reason, so I must treat His temple with care so I can continue my purpose here on earth.

I thank God that I'm home recuperating well. I miss seeing my family especially my grand children in person because they bring so much laughter and joy to my heart. The last time I saw them was on My birthday February 14, 2020. I wasn't able to see anyone a week prior to my transplant because I had to isolate myself. If I had come down with something as minuscule as a cold, my transplant would have been canceled. The first time I saw my children, and grand's after the transplant I could barely control myself. All I could do was cry and thank God.

It was Sunday, May 10, 2020 and it was a special day because it was Mother's Day. My children and grandchildren always call to say Happy Mother's Day early in the morning, then later come over to bring me gifts. It was now afternoon and I had not heard from anyone. I was a bit sad, especially after God had spared my life. I felt they should be grateful to still have their mother around on this special day.

Our adult children on front porch

A few hours later, my husband told me someone was at the window and wanted to see me. I wondered who it could be at the height of the Corona virus. I went to the window and lifted the blinds and there stood my children and grandchildren. What a surprise! My son Steven had one of my favorite Christian songs filling the atmosphere as they all stood on the front porch at the window.

My family began waving at me through the window with excitement. They were overjoyed to see me. I became overwhelmed with joy! I left the window and sat on the couch and began to cry joyful tears telling God thank you. He knew I needed to see my family at that moment. The enemy wanted me to believe I would never see my family again but God said differently. A few minutes later, I went back to the window to find all of my family crying tears of joy too. All accept my comedian older son Tyrone who was trying to make everyone laugh instead of cry. It touched my heart when I saw all of them crying, especially my sweet grandchildren. We were all so happy to see each other.

My daughter-in-law Teresa is so special to me. She was the first one to arrive at our home when I was given the bad diagnosis. She prayed for me then walked up and down the hall crying. That Mother's Day she stood at the window crying waterfall tears of joy. She put her hand on the window and I put my hand in hers. She said I love you mom, I told her I loved her back. What a blessing it is to have such a sweet and caring daughter in law. I had never seen my adult son Steven cry before. When I looked over and saw him wiping tears from his eyes my heart melted.

Then I looked at my only daughter Suhdeena crying. I thank God for blessing me with a little girl. She was our little princess but now she's our queen. She has always been there for her dad and me in the good times and bad. I looked into her eyes and could see the sigh of relief that mama was back home. My grandchildren were all crying but was so happy to see me. What joy I felt, even though I couldn't hug my children and grandchildren that Mother's Day. It was a blessing just

Our family in yellow at Lake Eola

to see them through the window. They also came bearing Mother's Day gifts that they placed in the chair on the porch before leaving. What a blessed day that was.

March 17, 2021 will be one year since I had the transplant. I thought I would have completed this book by now but Gods timing is not my timing. His will, will be done whenever this book is completed and published. I'm never bored while being in the house because I spend most days writing. My husband did the grocery shopping for three months until my doctor told me I could go to essential places only. After being in the house for four months, I was ready to get out and feel the sunshine. The two places I go now are the grocery store and to my doctor's appointments. I did go to a department store a couple of times, but I mostly remain home due to Covid 19. Believe me, when I go out I'm covered in prayer, I have on two mask, a face shield, goggles, and gloves. The year 2020 is a year I will always remember. It would be the year God healed me from the worst raging storm I had ever faced. I will never forget the sadness the year 2020 brought the world. It was a terrible sad year for so many who lost loved ones to the Corona Virus. It saddened me as I laid there in my hospital bed watching the news seeing so many people being taken out of the hospital in body bags. What bothered me most was seeing human bodies being stored in semi-trucks because mortuaries were filled to capacity.

The virus is still running rampant almost a year later because some people refuse to obey the governments mandate order to wear a mask. Scientist worked hard to come up with a vaccine to help combat the spread of the virus. December 14, 2020 an injection became available and was given first to the frontline workers and people in nursing homes. It was then given to people sixty five years and older and I fell in that category. Some people chose not to get the vaccines, which was there right. My doctor advised all of his patients to get vaccinated because we had no immune system to help fight if we were to contract the smallest thing as a cold. I was hesitant at first, but I prayed and asked God to protect my husband and me from all hurt, harm, and danger that these vaccines might have and decided to get vaccinated. I received the Pfizer vaccine on March 1, 2021. I was told I would need two injections of the vaccine to prevent me from getting the virus. This was not true because December 15, 2022 my husband and I ended up contracting the virus. Thank God my immune system had built up some. I was told that if I had not taken the vaccines I would have been much sicker or could have died.

I received my second Injection two weeks later and didn't have any side effects. Before I received the vaccines I had been receiving my childhood immunizations. I had been informed prior to receiving my transplant that it was imperative that I received my childhood immunizations all over again, because after receiving that powerful chemo it destroyed all of the childhood vaccination shots that I was given as a child. I had received my first childhood immunization December 2, 2020. I was given a flu, pneumonia and diphtheria vaccine all in one day. Those same vaccines were repeated again on January 5, 2021. Once I began receiving the Covid vaccines, my childhood vaccines were put on hold until two weeks after taking the last Covid vaccine which was March 23, 2021. It will take two years before all of my immunization shots are completed.

Today Is March 11, 2021. I went to see my transplant doctor for the last time and I was happy and excited to see him. I had been seeing him or the PA every six weeks for almost a year. When the doctor and the PA walked in the room, they were happy to see me as well. The doctor talked awhile letting me know how well I had done along my transplant journey. Then he told me my blood work looked great and this would be my last visit with him.

He told me I could come back anytime if I had a need. The PA Nichole was awesome! After my transplant, I saw her more than I did my doctor. She really took good care of me when my doctor wasn't there and made sure the staff did the same. She was the one who called and stayed on the phone with me during the episode after vacuuming the egg off the floor. All of the receptionists were very professional. They were caring, efficient, and always had a smile on their faces when I arrived for my appointment. Whenever I called the office with a question or needed information, they made sure I was connected to the person who could help me. All of the nurses were kind and I'm not being partial, but my favorite nurse was Teresa. As I mentioned earlier she is the aunt to my two oldest granddaughters.

The entire staff was great! My doctors, The transplant coordinator, social worker and Financial Supervisor were all awesome. They made sure everything was in order so I could have the transplant that I so much needed. I'm going to miss everyone like I did the nice people at Advent Hospital. It was another bittersweet moment at my last visit, but I'm ready to continue my life doing the things God has predestined me to do. I thank Him for sending such great people in my life.

That last day at the Transplant doctor's office, once again I got the "Can't Help It's." I began giving God praise and thanks for all He had done for me. My doctor and PA joined in, thanking God. They were both happy that I made it through the journey. That wasn't unusual at Advent Health Hospital because it was a Christian Hospital. From the admissions desk on down, the employees would say "God Bless You." Everywhere you went in that hospital there were inspiring words in picture frames on the walls. I am forever grateful to every person who God chose to be a part of my transplant journey.

I no longer have to go to my transplant doctor, but I will be seeing my new Oncologist on a regular basis. God has carried me through many storms, this one being the biggest. I will continue standing on the word of God. Isaiah 53:5 KJV says, "But he was wounded for our transgressions, he was bruised for our iniquities, the chastisement of our peace was upon him; and with his stripes we are healed." HALLELUJAH I'M HEALED!

To the readers, I pray that reading about some of the most horrific stories in my life will strengthen, encourage, and give you hope. I encourage you to "NEVER GIVE UP"no matter what problem you face in life. Some have asked! Why does God allow bad things to happen to good people? Mark 10:18 KJV says, "and Jesus said unto him, Why callest thou me good? There is none good but one, that is, God."

God made a perfect world and sin was not a part of it until it entered the world through Adam and Eve. Because we are carnal,we are subject to sin and sickness. Do not lose heart that one day all of our troubles will be over. No more worry, stress, heartbreaks, pain and sickness, and no more bills. I know you shouted on that one! But mostly, no more death. Yes, bad things do happen to those who we call good people, but God uses those bad things for an ultimate lasting good. Christians have an eternal perspective and we do not lose sight that we will have our everlasting reward one day in heaven. And we know that in all things God works for the good of those who love him, who have been called according to his purpose in Romans 8:28 KJV. "Trust in the Lord with all thine heart; and lean not unto thine own understanding; in all thy ways acknowledge Him, and He shall direct thy paths." (Proverbs 3:5-6 KJV).

Morrow and Me

As I get to the end of this book, I want to encourage you who have not given your life to Jesus not to waste anymore of your valuable time living a life of sin. You can give your life to God right now. Don't wait until something devastating happen in your life, or until you are on your bed of affliction, or even on your death bed before you decide to give your life to God. Romans 10:9-10 KJV tells us, "That if thou shalt confess with thy mouth the Lord Jesus, and shall believe in thine heart that God raised him from the dead, thou shalt be saved. For with the heart man believeth unto righteousness; and with the mouth confessing is made unto salvation." It's that easy! You are saved if you have done this. Get into a Christian bible teaching church so you will grow in Christ. I encourage you to take time each day spending time with God. When we belong to God and spend time with Him, we can hear his voice.

I'm not happy that I had to go through all of these terrible storms in my life, but I never asked God, why me? I know now that every storm had a purpose and they drew me closer to God. As I laid in my bed while still recuperating but feeling great after my transplant. On May 4, 2020 God gave me clarity about what he spoke early that morning March 17, 2020 when he told me to write about "How I Carried You through the Storms." He let me know that it was time to begin my next assignment which blew my mind when He told me my assignment was to write a book titled "God Carried Me through the Storms."

I said Lord I've never written a book before; how do I begin? He said write the vision I showed you. If I had not gone through storms I wouldn't have been able to write this book because I wouldn't have testimonies to share with you. I have some storms that God wouldn't allow me to write about, these were the ones He inspired.

You may have gone through worst storms in life than I have, but I thank God if you are reading this book, God has already, or is carrying you through your storms because you are still here. Continue trusting God and don't try to handle your storms on your own. Psalms 50:15 KJV says, "Call upon me in the day of trouble; I will deliver thee and thou shalt glorify me." Allow God to hold your hand. His strong grip will never let you go. When you are facing dark times in your life and feel like giving up, cry out to the Lord and He will answer.

It has now been three years since I began writing this book and a lot has happened. There were times I had to stop writing. One was when my precious mother went home to be with the Lord. My husband and I traveled back and forth to be with her. Another time was when my loving husband had a massive heart attack and I had to become his caretaker. Storms come and storms go, but we never know when and what storm will come our way. We can only trust God to see us through them.

Gods timing is not our timing, but finally I completed the book! I feel great! My spirit is renewed, and I'm excited to see what God has in store for my future. Already, my husband and I are back on his motorcycle enjoying our hobby riding. Last weekend March 11, 2023 we enjoyed going to Bike Week's 88th Anniversary in Daytona Beach Florida. God has already given me some assignments and I'm already at work. I'm back singing in the choir, and I'm back at my assignment calling to check on our Senior citizens who are sick and homebound. I'm enjoying my family and friends once again. I check on Cynthia and my friend Julia periodically. I will continue doing whatever God inspires me to do, and I will forever give Him praise for carrying me through my storms!

Let me close by saying life is precious! Love, Forgive, Live, Laugh, and Trust God.

Father God I thank you for the guidance of your Holy Spirit, and for entrusting me to minister through writing this book. Although many of the stories that I've shared in this book might seem heartrending, I pray that the reader who is trapped in a cave will be freed, and those who have lost all hope is encouraged to never give up. I pray that they will trust you in good times, as well as their darkest hours. In Jesus Name! Amen.

To God Be the Glory for the Great Things He Has Done!!

About the Author

Alice Jackson was born in a quaint town named Yuma, Arizona. She married and moved to Orlando, Florida in 1972. She's a wife and mother of three adults. She retired after working thirty six years as entrepreneur, and hair stylist in the beauty industry. Working from behind the salon chair was a job she dearly loved. Alice is also an accomplished published playwright and CEO of Kingdom Builder Productions. A company where she writes, directs, and produces gospel stage plays. She has written seven heartfelt Gospel stage plays since 2005.

-A Mother's Prayer 2005
-Deception 2005
-Forgiveness 2008
-Deception Revised 2010
-Order In The House 2012
-Don't Wait Too Late 2016
-The Blind Barber and Five Hair Stylists 2019

The Orlando Times newspaper gave great reviews on her plays "A Mother's Prayer and Deception," and called her the next "Tyler Perry". Her natural ability for writing is a gift from God. She sharpened her skills by attending playwright's conferences, attending classes and workshops. She values the lessons learned in Theatre 101, Entertainment Law, Marketing, Casting, Promotion, Technology and Innovation, Lighting & Stage. Her purpose for writing is to encourage, give hope, motivate, and bring laughter to the audience. *God Carried Me Through The Storms* is Alice's first book written. Her prayer is that this book will bless the readers and encourage them to "Never Give Up" no matter what storms they might face in life.

Made in the USA
Columbia, SC
14 March 2024

32748430R00128